T0192278

Lecture Notes in Computer Science 11934

More information about this series at http://www.springer.com/series/7407

Carlos Martín-Vide · Geoffrey Pond ·
Miguel A. Vega-Rodríguez (Eds.)

Theory and Practice of Natural Computing

8th International Conference, TPNC 2019
Kingston, ON, Canada, December 9–11, 2019
Proceedings

Springer

Editors
Carlos Martín-Vide ⓘ
Rovira i Virgili University
Tarragona, Spain

Geoffrey Pond ⓘ
Royal Military College of Canada
Kingston, ON, Canada

Miguel A. Vega-Rodríguez ⓘ
University of Extremadura
Cáceres, Spain

ISSN 0302-9743   ISSN 1611-3349 (electronic)
Lecture Notes in Computer Science
ISBN 978-3-030-34499-3   ISBN 978-3-030-34500-6 (eBook)
https://doi.org/10.1007/978-3-030-34500-6

LNCS Sublibrary: SL1 – Theoretical Computer Science and General Issues

This Springer imprint is published by the registered company Springer Nature Switzerland AG
The registered company address is: Gewerbestrasse 11, 6330 Cham, Switzerland

Preface

These proceedings contain the papers that were presented at the 8th International Conference on the Theory and Practice of Natural Computing (TPNC 2019), held in Kingston, Canada, during December 9–11, 2019.

The scope of TPNC is rather broad, including:

- Theoretical contributions to: ant colony optimization, artificial immune systems, artificial life, cellular automata, cognitive computing, collective behavior, collective intelligence, computational intelligence, computing with words, developmental systems, DNA computing, DNA nanotechnology, evolutionary algorithms, evolutionary computing, fuzzy logic, fuzzy sets, fuzzy systems, genetic algorithms, genetic programming, granular computing, heuristics, intelligent agents, intelligent systems, machine intelligence, metaheuristics, molecular programming, multiobjective optimization, neural networks, quantum communication, quantum computing, quantum information, rough sets, self-organization, soft computing, swarm intelligence, unconventional computing.
- Applications of natural computing to: algorithmics, bioinformatics, control, cryptography, design, economics, graphics, hardware, human-computer interaction, knowledge discovery, learning, logistics, medicine, natural language processing, optimization, pattern recognition, planning and scheduling, programming, robotics, telecommunications, web intelligence.

TPNC 2019 received 38 submissions, and the papers were reviewed by three Program Committee members. There were also a few external reviewers consulted. After a thorough and vivid discussion phase, the committee decided to accept 15 papers (which represents an acceptance rate of about 39%). The conference program also included three invited talks as well as some presentations of work in progress.

The excellent facilities provided by the EasyChair conference management system allowed us to deal with the submissions successfully and handle the preparation of these proceedings in time.

We would like to thank all invited speakers and authors for their contributions, the Program Committee and the external reviewers for their cooperation, and Springer for its very professional publishing work.

October 2019

Carlos Martín-Vide
Geoffrey Pond
Miguel A. Vega-Rodríguez

Organization

TPNC 2019 was organized by the Royal Military College of Canada, from Kingston, Canada, and the Institute for Research Development, Training and Advice (IRDTA), from Brussels/London, Belgium/UK.

Program Committee

Mohammad Amin	D-Wave Systems, Canada
Plamen P. Angelov	Lancaster University, UK
Thomas Bäck	Leiden University, The Netherlands
Peter Bentley	University College London, UK
Mauro Birattari	Université Libre de Bruxelles, Belgium
Christian Blum	Higher Scientific Research Council, Spain
Shyi-Ming Chen	National Taiwan University of Science and Technology, Taiwan
Carlos A. Coello Coello	CINVESTAV – National Polytechnic Institute, Mexico
Claude Crépeau	McGill University, Canada
Marco Dorigo	Université Libre de Bruxelles, Belgium
Matthias Ehrgott	Lancaster University, UK
Andries Engelbrecht	Stellenbosch University, South Africa
Juan José García-Ripoll	Higher Scientific Research Council, Spain
Deborah M. Gordon	Stanford University, USA
Jin-Kao Hao	University of Angers, France
Wei-Chiang Samuelson Hong	Jiangsu Normal University, China
Thomas R. Ioerger	Texas A&M University, USA
Etienne E. Kerre	Ghent University, Belgium
Chung-Sheng Li	Accenture, Ireland
Gui Lu Long	Tsinghua University, China
Chao-Yang Lu	University of Science and Technology of China, China
Pabitra Kumar Maji	Bidhan Chandra College, India
Vittorio Maniezzo	University of Bologna, Italy
Carlos Martín-Vide (Chair)	Rovira i Virgili University, Spain
Luis Martínez López	University of Jaén, Spain
Serge Massar	Université Libre de Bruxelles, Belgium
Marjan Mernik	University of Maribor, Slovenia
Hossein Nezamabadi-Pour	Shahid Bahonar University of Kerman, Iran
Norman Packard	Daptics, USA
Sidhartha Panda	Veer Surendra Sai University of Technology, India
Elpiniki Papageorgiou	University of Applied Sciences of Thessaly, Greece
Geoffrey Pond	Royal Military College of Canada, Canada

Kai (Alex) Qin	Swinburne University of Technology, Australia
Celso C. Ribeiro	Fluminense Federal University, Brazil
José Santos-Victor	Instituto Superior Técnico, Portugal
Shahab Shamshirband	Norwegian University of Science and Technology, Norway
Narasimhan Sundararajan	Nanyang Technological University, Singapore
José Luis Verdegay	University of Granada, Spain
Fernando J. Von Zuben	University of Campinas, Brazil
Xin-She Yang	Middlesex University, UK
Bo Yuan	Rochester Institute of Technology, USA
Yi Zhang	Sichuan University, China
Xudong Zhao	Bohai University, China

Additional Reviewers

Mohammad Bagher Dowlatshahi
Mahdi Eftekhari
Massimo Esposito
Xiumei Han
Wei-Chiang Hong
Maciej Huk

Lijuan Liu
Xiaofeng Qi
Esmat Rashedi
Han Wang
Yao Zhou

Organizing Committee

Sara Morales	IRDTA, Belgium
Manuel Parra-Royón	University of Granada, Spain
Geoffrey Pond (Co-chair)	Royal Military College of Canada, Canada
David Silva (Co-chair)	IRDTA, UK
Miguel A. Vega-Rodríguez	University of Extremadura, Spain

Abstracts of Invited Talks

Analysing Emergent Dynamics of Evolving Computation in 2D Cellular Automata

John S. McCaskill[1] and Norman H. Packard[1,2]

[1] European Centre for Living Technology, Venice, Italy
johnsmccaskill@gmail.com
[2] Daptics Inc., San Francisco, CA, USA

Abstract. Conway's Game of Life (GoL), a famous 2D cellular automaton (CA), is extended to allow evolution by associating genetic information with individual live cells, that specifies variant local CA rules. Genomes are formed by copying (potentially with mutation) or movement from one of the live neighbour cells and are destroyed at death. Just as biological evolution discovers innovations in the space of chemical and physical functionalities, we explore how the addition of genetic information enables an evolutionary process that can coordinate robust complex dynamics by exploring spatially inhomogeneous local modifications to the non-robust GoL rules.

We discovered a large family of deterministic rules which avoid stochastic choices of ancestor for genetic inheritance. Systematic genetic variations near to the game of life rule are investigated and found to produce signs of computational complexity with an abundance of spaceship and glider gun structures. We investigated evolution for four successively more differentiated symmetry cases in the nearest neighbour rules: semi-totalistic, corner-edge totalistic, 8-rotation symmetric, and physical 2D symmetric (4-rotations and 4-reflections).

The genetic evolution is analysed by fast ongoing genealogy construction and population weighted activity statistics. The spatial structure is captured using hash encoded quadtrees of the connected components, which are also mapped through time for novelty and with activity statistics. This together with a novel genetic tracking of the dynamical displacement ancestry of live genes allows an efficient recognition of regular dynamical structures such as spaceships which transport information while changing shape, solving an open problem in finding efficient alternatives to ε-machines for 2D automata.

Keywords: Evolution · Cellular automata · Artificial life · Genealogies · Self-organization · Game of life · Activity statistics

Optimisation Trajectories Illuminated

Gabriela Ochoa

Computing Science and Mathematics, University of Stirling,
Stirling FK9 4LA, Scotland, UK
gabriela.ochoa@stir.ac.uk

Abstract. This talk will present our findings and visual (static and animated) maps characterising computational search spaces. Either by exhaustive enumeration of the search space, or sampling representative solutions, our work provides new insights into the trajectories of optimisation algorithms and the structure of fitness landscapes. A multitude of heuristic and bio-inspired search algorithms has been proposed, each trying to be more powerful and innovative. However, little attention has been devoted to understanding the structure of problems and what makes them hard to solve for a given algorithm. Formal theoretical results are difficult to obtain, and they may only apply to problem classes and algorithms chosen more for their amenability to analysis than for their relevance and difficulty. Heuristic methods operate by searching a large space of candidate solutions. The search space can be regarded as a spatial structure where each point (candidate solution) has a height (objective or fitness function value) forming a fitness landscape surface. The performance of optimisation algorithms crucially depends on the fitness landscape structure, and the study of landscapes offers an alternative to problem understanding where realistic formulations and algorithms can be analysed. Most fitness landscape analysis techniques study the local structure of search spaces. There is currently a lack of tools to study instead their global structure, which is known to impact algorithm performance. Our recently proposed model, *Local Optima Networks (LONs)*, fills this gap by bringing tools from complex networks to study optimisation. This model provides fundamental new insight into the structural organisation and the connectivity pattern of a search space with given move operators. Most importantly, it allows us to visualise realistic search spaces in ways not previously possible and brings a whole new set of quantitative network metrics for characterising them.

Keywords: Local optima networks • Fitness landscape analysis • Visualisation • Optimisation • Evolutionary algorithms • Heuristic search

Human-Inspired Socially-Aware Interfaces

Dominik Schiller⊙, Katharina Weitz⊙, Kathrin Janowski⊙,
and Elisabeth André⊙

Human Centered Multimedia, Augsburg University, Augsburg, Germany
{schiller,weitz,janowski,andre}@hcm-lab.de

Abstract. Social interactions shape our human life and are inherently emotional. Human conversational partners usually try to interpret – consciously or unconsciously – the speaker's or listener's affective cues and respond to them accordingly. With the objective to contribute to more natural and intuitive ways of communicating with machines, an increasing number of research projects has started to investigate how to simulate similar affective behaviors in socially-interactive agents. In this paper we present an overview of the state of the art in social-interactive agents that expose a socially-aware interface including mechanisms to recognize a user's emotional state, to respond to it appropriately and to continuously learn how to adapt to the needs and preferences of a human user. To this end, we focus on three essential properties of socially-aware interfaces: Social Perception, Socially-Aware Behavior Synthesis, and Learning Socially-Aware Behaviors. We also analyze the limitations of current approaches and discuss directions for future development.

Keywords: Socially-interactive agents · Social signal processing · Affective computing

Contents

Genetic Algorithms, Swarm Intelligence, and Heuristics

Quantum Computing and Information

Invited Talks

Analysing Emergent Dynamics of Evolving Computation in 2D Cellular Automata

John S. McCaskill[1]([✉]) [iD] and Norman H. Packard[1,2] [iD]

[1] European Centre for Living Technology (ECLT), Ca' Bottacin, Dorsoduro
3911, Calle Crosera, 30123 Venice, Italy
johnsmccaskill@gmail.com
[2] Daptics Inc., San Francisco, CA, USA

Abstract. Conway's Game of Life (GoL), a famous 2D cellular automaton (CA), is extended to allow evolution by associating genetic information with individual live cells, that specifies variant local CA rules. Genomes are formed by copying (potentially with mutation) or movement from one of the live neighbour cells and are destroyed at death. Just as biological evolution discovers innovations in the space of chemical and physical functionalities, we explore how the addition of genetic information enables an evolutionary process that can coordinate robust complex dynamics by exploring spatially inhomogeneous local modifications to the non-robust GoL rules.

We discovered a large family of deterministic rules which avoid stochastic choices of ancestor for genetic inheritance. Systematic genetic variations near to the game of life rule are investigated and found to produce signs of computational complexity with an abundance of spaceship and glider gun structures. We investigated evolution for four successively more differentiated symmetry cases in the nearest neighbour rules: semi-totalistic, corner-edge totalistic, 8-rotation symmetric, and physical 2D symmetric (4-rotations and 4-reflections).

The genetic evolution is analysed by fast ongoing genealogy construction and population weighted activity statistics. The spatial structure is captured using hash encoded quadtrees of the connected components, which are also mapped through time for novelty and with activity statistics. This together with a novel genetic tracking of the dynamical displacement ancestry of live genes allows an efficient recognition of regular dynamical structures such as spaceships which transport information while changing shape, solving an open problem in finding efficient alternatives to ε-machines for 2D automata.

Keywords: Evolution · Cellular automata · Artificial life · Genealogies · Self-organization · Game of Life · Activity statistics

1 Introduction

Interest in cellular automata (CAs), as models of emergent complexity, began with von Neumann's 29-state CA, designed for universal construction [1], and became widespread with Conway's discovery of a simple 2D Game of Life (GoL) [2] and

Electronic supplementary material The online version of this chapter (https://doi.org/10.1007/978-3-030-34500-6_1) contains supplementary material, which is available to authorized users.

C. Martín-Vide et al. (Eds.): TPNC 2019, LNCS 11934, pp. 3–40, 2019.
https://doi.org/10.1007/978-3-030-34500-6_1

Wolfram's analysis of computational complexity classes in 1D CAs [3], also extended to 2D [4]. Conway's and Von Neumann's life-like CAs are defined with strong relaxation to the ground state in order to facilitate computation by rational design, and universal computation has been proven by construction in both cases [5, 6]. Both however involve fundamentally unprotected computations, in which perturbations, in the form of even the simplest travelling patterns, will almost certainly destroy not only the computed result but the carefully crafted computing architecture as well. Because of this, and despite the widespread continuing interest in novel computational structures in the GoL and related CAs, there is a major jump to evolving systems in which computation needs to survive robustly in the presence of potential interactions with many competitors. This paper is concerned with bridging this gap, maintaining deterministic computation as far as possible, apart from random and rare mutational changes, while supporting locally determined genetically encoded rule changes that enable evolution.

The GoL [2, 7] is a deterministic dynamical system that takes 2D spatial patterns of binary states (1 'live' or 0 'not-alive') on a square lattice to new patterns as time progresses discretely, through the action of a local rule (CA), each site's state at time $t + 1$ being dependent on its state and the states of its eight nearest neighbours at time t. The game of life is a semi-totalistic cellular automaton (CA) rule, the influence of neighbours on the next state being determined by the sum s of their state values only. A live cell survives only if $s = 2$ or 3, otherwise dying (changing to state 0), and a non-live cell undergoes birth (transitions to 1) only if there are exactly 3 live neighbours at time t. The GoL has become a canonical example of a complex system, with simple local rules that produce complex dynamics. It has a rich phenomenology of dynamics from special initial conditions, documented in massive catalogue projects and other articles [8]. Specially engineered initial states can have extremely long transients, occupying large regions of space, and indeed the Gol has been shown to support universal computation [5, 9, 10] via a set of motifs including so-called *spaceships*, *glider guns* and *still-lifes*.

Notwithstanding these properties, the GoL has not been a good model for studying the emergence of complexity, for two main reasons. The first is that starting from random initial state patterns on a finite compact domain, it is well known that the GoL almost always settles down to a combination of isolated static and simply periodic structures which are individually of limited spatial extent. Although specially engineered initial states can have extremely long transients, occupying large regions of space, the absence of complex interconnected pattern persistence starting from random initial conditions means that it is not a good candidate for the emergence of complexity. In fact, this behaviour is so robust that, as in a sand-pile, random isolated birth events cause the relaxed state to self-organize to a critical state where there is a power-law of frequencies for cascade magnitudes [11, 12]. Secondly, the complexity generated by GoL is not robust, in the sense that perturbations destroy functionally complex structures. Even when a complex dynamical structure happens to be produced by a random initial condition, it is typically destroyed by any *glider* or *spaceship* that perturbs it.

In biology, genetics is coupled to real-world physics and chemistry, enabling evolution to produce a complex biosphere. In the present work, we use nearest neighbour CAs to provide homogeneous models of rich but simple physical chemistry.

We then enhance these CAs by including genetic information, with the aim of understanding how complex information may emerge from this simple spatial version of evolution. The coupling of GoL to genetic information has already been attempted in various ways (precursors: *immigration*, *quadlife*; with genetics: *Sprout Life* [13], *HetCA* [14, 15], *evolife* [16–19]), but a systematic investigation of evolving dynamics is still outstanding. We add genetics to GoL-like binary CAs by associating a genome with each live cell. The genome of a live cell encodes local departures from the GoL rule, making the system a spatially inhomogeneous cellular automaton. Genetic inheritance is ensured by a newly born live cell's genome being moved from one or copied (potentially with mutation and recombination) from one or more of the live neighbour cells (there are three in the GoL) and being deleted when the cell dies. In this article we focus on the simplest case of mutation and asexual reproduction without recombination. We specify (i) how departures from the GoL are determined by genes; and (ii) how genes are propagated from one time-step to the next, deriving deterministic inheritance rules that may be genetically neutral or sequence dependent. The addition of genetics to the GoL alters long term dynamics; the long-term dynamics of the GoL is a field of static patterns or patterns with low periodicity (blinkers). Figure 1 illustrates such a state, compared with an example of an evolving *genelife* population with interacting spaceships.

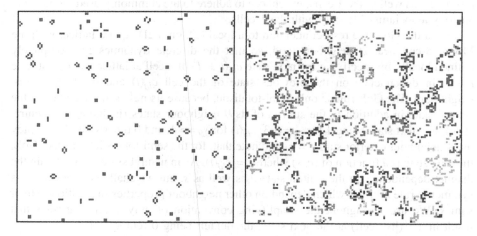

Fig. 1. A comparison of the classic Game of Life's long-time dynamical state after 2000 time-steps (on the left; fixed patterns and simple local periodicity) with an example of an evolving genelife population after the same time (on the right; ongoing generation of novel patterns). For the genelife population, different genomes are shown with different shades of grey (different colours online).

This investigation is motivated by a fundamentally interest in the interaction between computational complexity and evolution. Computational complexity in CAs has addressed the relationship with universal computation, universal construction [3, 4, 20] and the edge of chaos [11, 12], also for the evolution of CAs [21]. Information transfer measures of complexity have been applied [22–24] and, most notably, statistical complex dynamics captured with the ε-machine formalism of Crutchfield [25–29]. Complex dynamics have also been addressed in combinatorial game theory [7], with complex spatial pattern formation emerging also in evolving systems [30, 31] including evolutionary games [32, 33].

2 The Genelife Model

A genome is associated with each live cell and contains inherited information, copied from its ancestors at birth, which may be used to track the flow of information in both the GoL and the wider family of CA models investigated here. The genome of a live cell encodes the local CA rule governing that cell, and this rule may deviate from the GoL local rule, making the system a spatially inhomogeneous cellular automaton. The local state of a cell is described completely by the presence or absence of a genome (the live/empty (1/0) state in the GoL) and for the case of a live cell, the 64-bit sequence comprising its genome. The restriction to 64-bit binary sequences is not fundamental but enables fast computation using machine integers. Note that it makes more sense to refer to 0 cells as empty (or inanimate) than dead: they contain no bioinformation. Our model could easily be extended to include information strings for the 0 cells (complex resources) as well as the 1 cells; we choose to adhere to the commonly used biomorphic analogy associating life only with the 1 cells.

As in the GoL, we restrict attention to a local CA on a 2D square lattice, with the Moore 8-cell nearest neighbourhood, so that the discrete dynamics are completely defined locally by specifying the next state $c_{i,j}(t + 1)$ of a cell at lattice site (i,j) at time $t + 1$, in dependence on the previous state of the cell $c_{i,j}(t)$ and of its 8 nearest neighbours. The GoL rule is only semi-totalistic, because its next state depends on the central state in addition to the sum s_9 of its 9 neighbour states (including the central state), the next state being 1 for $s_9 == 3$, $c_{i,j}(t)$ for $s_9 == 4$, and 0 otherwise. We employ the 8-neighbour exterior sum $s = s_8$ and note that, for the semi-totalistic rules like GoL, the next state is a function of (c, s) where $c = c_{i,j}(t)$. As in natural systems, we retain the distinct dependence on the central state c as well as s, but we shall also consider less symmetric rule families which depend on other neighbour properties in addition to their sum s. We use throughout the simplifying convention of only specifying rules that result in a 1 (live cell) at the next state, the default being 0 (empty cell).

To complete the specification of the Genetic GoL system dynamics, we need to specify (i) how live/empty next states are determined by the configuration of live neighbours and their genomes (departure from GoL rules are possible), and (ii) how the information in the genomes attached to live states is propagated when the next state is live.

Local Genetically Determined Rules. We use the term genome to refer to the full genetic sequence, reserving the term gene to refer to a specifier of part of the rule-table. How such LUTs are encoded in the genome must be decided by the model. Rather than always to allow all possible rules in a given symmetry model, which may result in ubiquitous proliferation, it is also of interest to consider restricted models in which a global constraint is introduced so that only a subset of the possible local states can be specified for active rules, i.e. for gene-dependent modification of the default GoL local rule. For example, in the semi-totalistic case, a birth-survival mask is introduced which would have 1-bits signifying permission for a subset of positions corresponding to particular s values for either survival or birth. While the genes may contain other entries, the model would not allow these genes to enable birth (survival) for local state configurations that correspond to s values for which there is a 0-bit in the birth (survival) mask. For example, with the 16-bit birth-survival mask 0x0406, in the semi-totalistic case 2, only at most GoL rules are allowed, and with the mask 0x0606 the genetically encoded extension of the s = 2, 3 case 1 model family is specified. For the lower symmetry models, the birth-survival mask will contain up to 64 bits. Thus, the mask bits corresponding to birth and survival bits of the genome determine whether the local rule can be affected, according to the local configuration. The globally specified birth and survival masks determine the universe of local rules that will be explored by evolution. Zeros in these masks reduce the size of the universe, ones in the masks enlarge the universe. Exactly how many bits are in the birth and survival masks depend on the degree of symmetry breaking employed in rule construction, as described below. More complex symmetry breaking results in more bits in the mask, generally giving finer grain control of the evolutionary process.

In this work, we consider two types of genetic encodings of rules:

1. a direct position-dependent encoding assigning specific genome bits (or possibly contiguous sets of bits for redundant encodings) at certain positions to specific LUT entries.
2. a modular variable-length position-independent encoding in which the genome encodes (at any block-aligned position) the local states which result in a next state of "1".

With s live neighbours and a centre cell state c (0 or 1), there are $s + c$ genomes in the neighbourhood, $s + 1$ for survival (and birth with overwrite) transitions and s for pure birth transitions (0 $\rightarrow$ 1). We chose to treat pure birth and overwrite transitions in the same way, and hence in the standard models neglected the central cell's genome influence on overwrite processes, and to keep things uniform also for survival. For survival we did compare this with the natural alternative of only the central genome determining rule departures (1 of the option bits in the replication scheme control word). It remained to decide how the s genomes in the neighbourhood should determine the rule departures. Seeking compelling constructions which apply to all possible non-zero s values, we identified three ways of combining the information in the individual genomes for particular LUT entries that should result in a central live cell state at the next time step: (i) And (ii) Or (iii) Majority. "And" means that all, "Or" at least one, of the genomes must contain the LUT transition for it to be effective locally. "Majority" means either $\geq 1/2$ and $> 1/2$ of the genomes must encode a LUT transition for it to be effective. While we have encoded each of these variants in *genelife*, we concentrate on the case (i) in this paper. We return to the different symmetries of CA rule generalizations, beyond the semi-totalistic rules of the GoL, after explaining the choice of ancestor.

Choice of Ancestor. Here we address the choice of ancestor genome to copy when a live cell is created or overwritten. In evolution models, the usual procedure to choose an ancestor for offspring is to use either random (neutral) selection, a weighted probabilistic sampling or tournament selection based on the sequence-dependent fitness properties of the genomes. In the context of extending the GoL however, introducing random choices of ancestor introduces a possibly unnecessary lack of determinism into the model. If we consider firstly the neutral case, then it is important to observe that, in the GoL, birth occurs only for 3 live neighbours, and we observe that for all possible 3-live-neighbour configurations there is a deterministically unique most different neighbour as seen in Supplementary Fig. 2. The same is true for all odd s values, $\{1, 3, 5, 7\}$. Only for the four non-zero even values $\{2, 4, 6, 8\}$ of s are there ambiguous configurations in which it is not possible to distinguish positionally between ancestors. In these cases, there are a number of options still to deterministically resolve matters: (i) not allow birth in these ambiguous cases, (ii) use the neighbourhoods of the neighbours to complete the choice of ancestor, (iii) complete birth with another $e.g.$ GoL rule encoding sequence, (iv) perform recombination between the unresolved sequences, (v) distinguish sequences by fitness if different, or instead (vi) use random choice if other distinctions fail. Our implementation allows any of these options to be employed. The important point is that only a subset of configurations need resolution and even a deterministic algorithm which disallows transitions (as in (i)) in these cases is viable. Note that one version of (ii) of significance is to prefer ancestors which will not survive in the next time step, which brings us to the next point.

Movement vs. Copying. Whereas the indistinguishability of 1-states in binary CAs means that it is not possible to distinguish movement from death and rebirth, in this paper with genetic information attached to the live states, this is possible. We found that in the GoL and many related CA rules, in almost all cases in which a gene is chosen as an ancestor of a new live state, the gene does not survive at its previous location. This is significant because it means that two or more birth events are usually required for proliferation, and that single birth events can usually be interpreted as motion. We implemented an option for genelife in which we enforce death for parent genome cell states (in the cases that they are not anyway overwritten or not marked for survival by the CA rule table). This had little impact on the dynamics in the case examined. With this modification, the distinction between birth and movement is clear: movement occurs if an ancestor gives rise to one live cell at a neighbouring position and birth occurs if more than one live cell (and their copied genomes) arise from that ancestor. It would make a difference if mutation were deemed not to occur for transitions involving movement. Also, it might be appropriate to make the choice of an ancestor sensitive to the interpretation of movement vs birth: e.g. to minimize the number of births needed to maintain the dynamics. For example, an isolated rod of three live states is a GoL oscillator between vertical and horizontal configurations. In the deterministic most different ancestor canonical assignment of ancestors from three live neighbours, the central gene is copied to two new sites so that (without mutation) the rod becomes genetically homogeneous in one step. This process is clearly a copy mechanism. On the other hand, in the 0-bit canonical assignment of ancestors, the two peripheral genes circulate anti-clockwise and this is more naturally understood as a process of motion and as such should be carried out without mutation. We postpone further investigation of the ramifications of distinctions between movement and copying for later work.

Additional Selection Mechanisms. Fundamentally, models of selection distinguish three modes of selection:

1. The neutral model, for which the deterministic position-dependent choice of ancestor outlined above, see also Electronic Supplementary Material, is an alternative to random choice.
2. Selection based on comparing fitness as a property of a single individual, independent of the presence of other individuals in the neighbourhood. This has the property of well-ordering all the genetic sequences (by fitness), with transitivity in comparisons ensured: *i.e.* A > B and B > C implies A > C. The focus is here on selection mechanisms that attribute an increasing cost to more prolific (less GoL-like) and more specific rule specification, fostering complex dynamics close to GoL. We do investigate the impact, for comparison, of a number of simple sequence-level selection pressures like selection favouring genetic sequences with more or less ones.
3. Selection based on a contest or tournament between individuals in which fitness depends on the other individual involved, there is no transitive ordering of genomes, and in population terms the fitness of a genome is population density dependent. Perhaps the best-known example of strongly not well-ordered fitness is in the scissors-paper-stone game A > B > C > A. We chose instead the four sequence classes (A, B, C, D) with selection A > D > C > A as well as D > B and C > B. This scheme is interesting in specifically supporting a multi-sequence coexistence making use of multiple spaceships.

Note that independently of these optional additional selection mechanisms on the choice of ancestor, the cooperative genetic coding of rules for LUT transitions means that there is also an underlying selection for sequences which can induce proliferation in their locality effectively through supporting birth or survival rules.

Rule Symmetries. For genetically dependent rules, a natural first family is the extended GoL symmetry class of 2^{18} semi-totalistic rules, distinguishing 18 states (2 central states times 9: the sum s of live neighbours ranging from 0 to 8). The sparsity of such rules with properties near to the GoL led us to also consider the broader families of rules with lower symmetries, distinguishing up to 64 local neighbourhood states (the maximum for which a 64-bit genome can encode the rule). The full set of $512 = 2^{8+1}$ distinguished, local states (9 cells), giving rise to 2^{512} possible rules, is too large to explore initially, especially with our restricted length genomes, and is physically less appealing because it does not take spatial symmetry into account. Between semi-totalism and full asymmetry we identify three intermediate symmetries (cases 3–5 below). This leads to the following six cases, of which we implement and study the first five:

1. Semi-totalistic rules with $s = 2, 3$ (gene dynamics with fixed homogeneous rules) (4/4)
2. Semi-totalistic rules $s = 1$–8 with LUTs for 1-states determined by genes (16/18)

3. Quarter-totalistic rules $s = 1–7$, $se = 0–4$ with distinct corner and edge counts (46/50)
4. Octavian-rotation symmetric rules for $s = 2–6$, $crot = 0–9$ (64/68)
5. Isotropic rules in 2D (4-rot'n, 4-refl'n) for $s = 0–4$, $crot = 0–12$ (64/102)
6. Full set of rules without symmetry reductions (512).

The numbers in parentheses are the number of distinguished local configurations in the specified family of local CA rules: i.e. the number of bits required to specify the rules, for (chosen s/all s). These configurations divide into the two equal-sized subsets, birth/movement and survival: The birth/movement rules involve copying/moving a genome from one of the neighbours. The survival rules for current state "1" define the other exceptions to the default rule which is next state "0". For each value of s, we also introduce a control bit "overwrite" which determines whether birth/movement rules can overwrite an existing live cell or not. These are collected into a mask *overwrite* for the eight s values 1–8, with semi-totalistic control of this property (no $s = 0$ overwrite).

We found that the semi-totalistic case is too coarse an encoding of CA rules, to allow significant genetic evolution of complex structures beyond the classic game of life. We investigate the more differentiated rules and find that they produce a range of interesting dynamics. When coupled to a genetic population, these differentiated rules rapidly evolve to proliferate unless very strongly constrained (by the birth-survival mask introduced above).

We preface this study in Sect. 2.1 with rules which, like the GoL rule, can only yield live cells for $s = 2, 3$ and for fixed rule departures without genetic determination. As we shall see, some of the interesting evolutionary phenomena revealed by Genelife are already captured by this simplest case. Naively, one would expect $2 \times 2 = 4$ distinguished states $(c, s) = (0$ or $1, 2$ or $3)$ that can possibly lead to live states and hence $2^4 = 16$ different genetic extensions. We perform a survey of the additional choices available for coupling genetics with the dynamics in this first case and implement these in a unified computer program to explore the model properties.

2.1 Semi-totalistic Rules Involving Only s = 2, 3

Since the GoL starting from random compact patterns of live states almost certainly relaxes to a set of unconnected simple patterns or periodic structures, with new live states only being produced in a small number of contexts, it is not as it stands a good substrate for evolution. In contrast, the conventional approach generalizing the GoL [20], requires that the birth and survival rules form a single interval of neighbourhood sum values, with lower and upper limits in the sum variable s, restricting the possible rule-tables to a family with members specified by four integers $S_l S_u B_l B_u$. Most of these rules lead to strong proliferation of live states or their extinction, and in order to allow genetic encoding to deliver novel dynamics of interest it turns out to be important to further dissect the rule-tables in the vicinity of the GoL rule 2333.

Genetic modifications that reduce the number of configurations resulting in live states will further restrict the potential for ongoing evolution, which requires more active rules (more neighbourhood state configurations leading to live cells) than the GoL. The most parsimonious first choice is, as for the GoL, to continue to consider only rules with next live states for $s = 2$ or 3 live nearest neighbours, *i.e.* distinguishing 4 neighbourhood states as candidates for a live next central state c: $(c, s) \in \{(0, 2), (0, 3), (1, 2), (1, 3)\}$. Since there are 4 starting states and 2 predicted outcomes (live or not) for the next central cell state, there are 2^4 such rules, corresponding to the subsets of the starting states that give rise to a live next state. The GoL rule has survival for $s = 2$, 3 and birth for $s = 3$, corresponding to the subset $R_{GoL} = \{(0, 3), (1, 2), (1, 3)\}$. Since we need more active rules, it is logical to begin with letting the genes control the missing birth rule $(0, 2) \rightarrow 1$ for $s = 2$. If the proliferation induced by this extra birth process should prove too strong, then one could counter this by removing one or more of the elements of R_{GoL}. This compensation could either be fixed or dependent on the genes. Since there are a number of intermediate and hybrid cases, we summarize the various options that we have investigated in Table 1.

In order to distinguish the genetic dependency from uniform changes in the rules, we split the survival and birth processes into two optionally executed stages, the first depending on the selective genetics (S_g and B_g) and the second genetically independent (*i.e.* enforced, S_f and B_f), as shown in Table 1. The first 8 binary options in Table 1 give rise to 144 different cases. For birth, all of the $2^4 = 16$ cases are different, in contrast with the case in survival, where there are only $3 \times 3 = 9$ cases. Even if birth is enforced, the genomes of the live neighbours may still have a vital impact on the future dynamics by determining which of them becomes the ancestor of the newly born genome. In addition to the distinction of birth and survival depending on the state of the central cell, there is another possibility opened up by the genetics which is not distinguished in the binary GoL: Instead of simply remaining alive, the genome of the next state may be overwritten by one of the neighbouring genomes according to a birth process. We label this binary option $O_{2/3}$ as it may be allowed independently for $s = 2$, 3. This corresponds to the well-studied Moran model of population genetics [34]. There are thus 576 different genetic extension models, even before one considers details of the genetic dependency.

In the interests of further limiting and analysing the extent of rule departures from the GoL, we also record here for completeness two further binary options N_r and N_s, which enforce GoL rules if respectively the previous transition rule was a non GoL rule or the current state was last produced by a non GoL transition. In near GoL simulations colouring cells by departures from the GoL rules in these two ways allows an assessment of both the potential and effective impact of the modified rules on the dynamics.

The first column of the table records the transition processes extending the GoL rules. Of the 4096 options opened up by this table, only 9/16 i.e. 2304 of them are distinct because only 3/4 of the selective/enforced survival options are distinct. The remaining columns consist of an index number nr, the central cell state c to which the transition applies, the sum s of live neighbours, the transition notation where S and B stand for survival and birth and the subscripts g and f for genetic and enforced. All twelve options except for 4 and 5 have been realized in the genelife software.

Table 1. Binary options for the control of *genelife* restricted to 2 or 3 live neighbours.

Transition	Nr	c	s	$S/B_{g/f}$
Selective genetic birth for 3 live neighbours	0	0	3	B_{g3}
Selective genetic birth for 2 live neighbours	1	0	2	B_{g2}
Enforce birth for 3 live neighbours	2	0	3	B_{f3}
Enforce birth for 2 live neighbours	3	0	2	B_{f2}
Selective survival for 3 live neighbours	4	1	3	S_{g3}
Selective survival for 2 live neighbours	5	1	2	S_{g2}
Enforce survival for 3 live neighbours	6	1	3	S_{f3}
Enforce survival for 2 live neighbours	7	1	2	S_{f2}
Birth overwrite for 3 live neighbours	8	1	3	O_3
Birth overwrite for 2 live neighbours	9	1	2	O_2
Enforce GoL rule if last rule non GoL	10	0/1	2/3	N_r
Enforce GoL if last state change non GoL	11	0/1	2/3	N_s

There are still several decisions to be made associated with the choice of ancestor, even after the choices in Table 1 have been made. For example, even for neutral models one can support birth only if two genomes are the same or different making a neutral choice of which will be the ancestor for offspring between them if this criterion is fulfilled.

2.2   Genetically Encoded Semi-totalistic Rules for s = 1–8

For the semi-totalistic case, if we exclude the special cases of spontaneous birth (B_0 *i.e.* birth for $s = 0$) and lone survival (S_0) then there are $8 + 8 = 16$ distinguished states that may be independently part of an active next state ruleset. In this case, genomes may specify any look up table (LUT) depending only on the central state c and neighbour sum s via two separate subsets of s-1 values for survival ($1 \to 1$) and birth ($0 \to 1$). The omission of $s = 0$ birth is equivalent to there being no spontaneous generation of life without neighbouring information (as in the Pasteur experiment) but [20] uncovers interesting cases with $s = 0$ survival allowed. For $s = 1..8$, there are 2^{16} CA rulesets, and these may be encoded by a binary genome of length 16 with one bit per LUT entry. In this paper, we restrict our attention to genomes of maximal length 64, and often use the term genome to refer to this full sequence, reserving the term gene to refer to a specifier of part of the rule-table. We may also employ multiple bits (n_c) to encode each LUT entry for an active rule, for example with only one of the possible n_c gene patterns being active, then genomes of length $16 \times n_c$ are required. In this paper, we only consider this option for the semi-totalistic case, where there is sufficient length in the genome to allow the range of values $n_c = 1, 2,$ or 4.

An alternative modular encoding employs 4 bits per entry: 3 bits to encode the values of s for which the next state is live, plus 1 bit for survival or birth. The standard GoL would require at least $3 \times 4 = 12$ bits to be specified, 0xb23 in hexadecimal notation, so that 64-bit genomes such as 0xaaaaaaaaa22221111 or any other combination of only the three digits 1, 2, a would encode the GoL. Longer genomes may contain the same entry repeatedly allowing for mutational error resistance, especially when the birth-survival mask makes a significant number of entries ineffective. For example, the sequence 0x0000000000000a21, encodes the GoL local rule if the birth-survival mask is 0 for s = 1.

2.3   Quarter-Totalistic Rules $s = 1–8$, $se = 0–4$, Counting Corners/Edges (46)

It is clear from geometry that of the 8 neighbour sites, the four corner sites are further away (distance $\sqrt{2}$) from the centre site than the edge centred sites (distance 1) on a unit square lattice. We count the number of live edge centred sites as se, then if distance is taken into account and neighbouring groupings otherwise ignored the state transitions of a quarter totalistic CA depend on the tuple (s, se) with the possible values of se ranging from max(0, s − 4) to min(s, 4) with numbers of different configurations for s = 0–8 of {1, 2, 3, 4, 5, 4, 3, 2, 1}, in total 25. If we exclude the configurations s = 0, 8, for which this distinction plays no role compared with the semi-totalistic case, then there are 23 different neighbour configurations distinguished by this symmetry and a total of 46 different LUT entries for survival and birth. Only 1-bit direct encodings of LUT transitions are possible in a 64-bit genome, but modular encoding of individual rules is also allowed: using 6-bits per rule as a combination of (i) 4 bits to specify B/S and $s − 1$ (ii) 2 bits to specify se in the range 0..3. The value $(s, se) = (4, 4)$ is placed (and decoded) as an exception in one of the unreached bit combinations. At most ten such modules can be encoded on a single genome, sufficient to specify the GoL rules and many others.

Actually if we count the sum of the weighted distances, each s, se configuration is different, and so that this quarter-totalistic symmetry actually warrants consideration as a variant in the semi-totalistic family of rules which only depend on the sum of the live neighbours (in this case weighted sum).

2.4   Octavian Symmetry Genetically Encoded Rules for $s = 2–6$ (64)

An alternative symmetry breaking of the semi-totalistic case involves 8-fold rotation symmetry in which distinctions between corner and edge states are ignored (the 8 neighbouring lattice positions being regarded as lying equally spaced on a ring). While it is not possible to do this simultaneously in 2D for all sites, one could consider this symmetry as being physical when the potential of direct contact to a neighbour is more important than the distance. In contrast with the semi-totalistic case we then distinguish the groupings of live cells around this ring, regarding all 8 rotations of the ring as symmetric. This simple octavian symmetry results in the following numbers of different patterns for each value of s from 0–8 {1, 1, 4, 7, 10, 7, 4, 1, 1}. Since we are most interested in cases generalizing the $s = 2, 3$ GoL rules, and the cases $s = 0, 1, 7, 8$ can be deemed fundamentally of less interest, we concentrate on the central values of $s = 2–6$ for which the 32 different configurations (up to octavian symmetry) allow possible 32 survival and 32 birth rules. This choice is expedient, allowing a direct one-bit genetic encoding of each transition rule for a 1 at the next time step to fit in a 64-bit genome. An alternative hybrid modular encoding of rules uses a combination of (i) 5 bits to specify B/S, $s - 1$ and which of two sets of 5 distinguished configurations is addressed and (ii) 5 bits as a mask specifying which of these 5 configurations is active. At most six such modules can be encoded on a single genome, sufficient to specify the GoL rules for example.

The symmetry class and hence LUT entry for any specific configuration of live neighbours can be found efficiently by defining a canonical minimum value over the eight possible rotations of an eight bit pattern, regarded as an eight bit integer, and mapping any configuration to its canonical minimum value to find its index in the LUT.

2.5 Isotropic Genetically Encoded Rules for $s = 0$–4 (64)

With full 2D spatial symmetry (4 rotations and 4 reflections), the numbers of distinguished configurations for $s = 0..8$ are $\{1, 2, 6, 10, 13, 10, 6, 2, 1\}$ with sum 51, still many fewer than the full asymmetric distinguished numbers C_s^8, $\{1, 8, 28, 56, 70, 56, 28, 8, 1\}$, with sum 256. In this study, with our 64-bit genomes, we will only fully investigate the evolution of differentiated rules for the lower range $s = 0..4$, with 32 distinguished configurations, using 1 bit each in the genome to specify survival and birth rules in the direct encoding. As in Sect. 2.4, an alternative hybrid modular encoding of rules uses this time a combination of (i) 6 bits to specify B/S, s and which of two sets of 6 distinguished configurations is addressed and (ii) 6 bits as a mask specifying which of these 6 configurations is active. At most five such modules can be encoded on a single genome, sufficient to specify the GoL rules for example.

3   Analytical Tools for Spatial Genetic Computation

We focus in this section on a defining a set of analysis tools that can be applied to analyse both the spatio-temporal and genetic evolution in genetic cellular automata models as well as the extent of natural computation taking place. Not only can the system be analysed at the current time in terms of spatial patterns for both the binary live/dead cell states and for genetically resolved patterns, but the spatio-temporal dynamics can also be studied in terms of the time-evolution of spatial patterns or of genes, the latter involving potentially both genealogies and spatial patterns. We commence with simple local classification tools and then extend them to more global ones.

3.1   Spatial Visualization of Cell Array

The first and most immediate set of tools for analysis involve classifications of local information on the cell array, using specifically graded or discrete colour combinations.

Genomes. The black and white representation of empty and live cells in the array for binary cellular automata can be further differentiated by using a variety of colour schemes for genetic information: genotypic, phenotypic or ancestral, all pertaining to the genomes present locally, either at the current time or in relation to previous times.

Genotypic Hash Colouring. The genetic sequence space (currently binary of length 64) can be mapped to 24-bit colour on 3 8-bit channels (red, green, blue) by a pseudo-random hash function. This will ascribe a particular colour to any live cell based on the gene value at the cell, with empty cells being displayed as black. This colouring does not preserve the topology of Hamming distance in the sequence space, but typically separates nearest neighbours strongly, so that even single point mutations can be readily detected.

Phenotypic Colouring. A phenotype in evolutionary biology is the set of observable traits or properties of an individual (which may be determined in complex ways from a genetic sequence or genotype) that contributes to its fitness (survival of its inheritable information to the next generation). For example, if the choice of ancestor in a proliferation rule is based on the number of 1s in its binary genetic sequence, then a graded colour scale which changes from blue to red as the number of 1s increases from 0 to v is an example of a phenotypic colouring. For genes encoding local LUTs, the number of coded entries or the number of rules for survival or birth may be regarded as phenotypic indicators and coloured accordingly.

Ancestral Colouring. Since the topology of the hypercube is high-dimensional, it is not possible to embed this smoothly in colour space, to allow neighbouring sequences to have neighbouring colours, although a self-organizing feature map could in principle be employed to approximate this. Instead, we may group related sequences by common ancestor, choosing the hash colour (see above) of the ancestor to label cells. Two types of ancestor are employed in this work, both at a selectable number of genetic changes back in the past, producing two families of colourings. The novel ancestry approach steps directly from a gene to the first entry of the gene's ancestor in the population history. In contrast, the clonal ancestor steps to the immediate clonal ancestor of a clone. A clone is a set of identical sequences produced by a connected sequence of birth events. These spatial analysers of genetic relations are complemented below by the corresponding structural and temporal genealogies in the set of tools with temporal axes.

Dynamical Patterns. The genelife model exhibits spatiotemporal pattern formation, both in the sequence of spatial arrangements of live cells and in their genetic differences. The temporal sequence of these patterns can be analysed locally or globally in time and space. In order to support global temporal analysis, all genes and all spatial patterns that are produced during a model simulation are recorded using hash tables. In order for spatial patterns beyond nearest neighbours (such as spaceships) to be recorded one needs a mechanism for segmenting the lattice. In this paper, we employ a rapid online connected component labelling algorithm to distinguish spatial patterns.

Transition Class Colouring. Transitions between states in genelife can firstly be classified as events of four types: death, survival, movement, birth. Combined events involving both death and movement or birth are possible if overwriting is permitted in the model. Furthermore, birth processes may be classified as clonal (exact inheritance) or with mutation. All these classes of events can further be divided into classes for different neighbourhood configurations depending on the symmetry of the model: using *s* for semi-totalistic symmetry, (*s, se*) for quarter totalistic *etc.* Alternatively, transitions can be classified as conforming to the GoL rule for that configuration.

Extended Neighbourhood Period-One Spaceships. Fast parallel bit mapping macros are employed to map the 7×7 array of up to third nearest (Moore) neighbouring live/empty states into a single 64-bit integer for local processing. These packed integers are then compared efficiently with those at the previous time step of their eight lattice neighbours (*i.e.* comparing overlapping offset-1 patterns in the directions NW, N, NE, E, SE, S, SW, W) to detect preserved or nearly preserved patterns (period 1 space-ships). The cells are coloured by the direction of travel with brightness depending on the quality of pattern preservation.

Connected Components. Rapid connected component labelling algorithms, as reviewed in [35], can be employed to distinguish spatial patterns at every step of the simulation. We implemented a modified linear two-scan equivalent-label resolving algorithm with 8-neighbourhood, employing rank union-find to resolve labels, the Suzuki decision tree [36] (Wu's enhancement [37] did not result in significant efficiency gains) and periodic BCs. The algorithm was adapted to work with both binary images (live/empty state) and with genetically differentiated images in which connected components must consist of the same genome or more permissively genomes with a common ancestor at some specified level or time (ancestors may be either global or clonal, see Sect. 3.4).

The connected components can then be extracted efficiently as quadtrees [38], i.e. as a 4-tree of sub-squares, storing all sub-patterns encountered in the hierarchical construction of a quadtree in a pattern hash table (using the same software *hashtable.h* as the genomes). Small patterns (8×8 pixels or smaller) are keyed directly by their 64-bit binary patterns while larger patterns are keyed by combining the four 64-bit addresses of their four square sub-image patterns {NW, NE, SE, SW} to a single 64-bit hash key with custom code minimizing collisions. This quadtree encoding is similar to but with a different handoff between large and small patterns to that employed in *hashlife* [39] for Gosper's algorithm [40] and our code development was aided by that implementation.

Although it would be an improvement for pattern recognition, we did not invest in reducing patterns to single representatives of their symmetry class (e.g. by rotation or reflection in the case of the isotropic rule sets of Sect. 2.5). The connected component patterns typically separated into a set of small frequently occurring patterns and larger patterns only found once in the simulation. This was more pronounced for the binary patterns. Larger connected components with the same genome are rarer. Since all patterns found in the simulation are saved in the hash tables, it is a single lookup to ascertain whether a pattern is novel, and to count reoccurrences of patterns. Thus, we enhanced the connected component labelling of different components by colour with an optional novelty filter, which darkens the colours of patterns that have already been encountered.

In order to track the information in spatial patterns over time, it is important to map the connected components at one time to those at the next time step. For unique assignment this is a linear assignment problem, and we initially used the LAPMOD algorithm [41] to find an optimal map between components. However, the more general problem of finding an (optimal incomplete) alignment matching components with weights determined by the pixel overlap between patterns, can be addressed as a maximal flow problem on bipartite graphs. A useful source of information on these algorithms is Tim Roughgarden's Stanford lectures (CS261). We modified the Hopcroft-Karp algorithm for maximal flow, with worst case execution time $O(|E|\sqrt{|V|})$ in terms of the number of edges $|E|$ and vertices $|V|$ in the bipartite graph, based on the implementation of Gupta [42]. Typically, connected components at one time step overlap with one or a few connected components at the next time step, so that a genealogy of connected components could be studied. However, we do not present this in the current paper. Instead, we use the mappings between connected components to provide continuity in tracking patterns over time and in colouring the cellular automata.

Displacement Genealogies. The above two methods are capable of labelling simple spaceships effectively which do not execute a complex periodic set of shape trans-formations. Here we introduce a novel dynamical pattern analysis tool, made possible by the genetic inheritance in the genelife model. We introduce a short-term dynamical memory packed into a 64-bit integer, in keeping with our general strategy of efficient machine integer-level processing. The novel feature is that this dynamical memory follows the genealogical inheritance path of live cell survival and ancestry, rather than sampling an expanding set of neighbour configurations. To be precise, any live cell at time t persists either by a survival or birth rule, and so at each time step and for each live cell, in the case of birth we first copy the integer dynamical memory (initially zero and termed *golr*) of the ancestor, and then in both cases we push (left shift and bitwise or) 4 bits of information to it: the four bits are a birth/survival bit and for birth a 3-bit displacement index 0..7 for {NW, N, NE, E, SE, S, SW, W} of the ancestor and for survival the 3-bit value s-1 mod 8. This short-term dynamical memory (*golr*) value thus records the ancestral displacement and survival configuration dynamics for the last 16 time-steps.

The displacement genealogy can then be used to identify various dynamical structures in the current CA. It has the advantage, compared with other dynamical records, of tracking the dynamics associated with the transmission of the live cell genetic information. For display we can further process this record by analysing the memory for periodicities and near periodicities, by calculating the minimal mismatch

4-bit byte shift (period) when comparing the dynamical memory with its shifted value and calculating the mean displacement of the dynamical memory for its optimal period. We use a colour representation to display important features of this dynamical memory, in which brightness corresponds to quality of match, one channel (blue) corresponds to the optimal period (1–15 or 0 if none above a matching threshold) and one channel (red) corresponds to the mean displacement at the optimal period.

We note that capturing the essential dynamics of information processing in dynamical systems has been a major challenge, with the two major approaches of information transfer entropy [22, 23, 43, 44] and ε-machines [25, 26, 28, 45, 46] proving increasingly computationally intractable as one moves from 1D CAs to 2D systems for larger periodicities. Facing these difficulties, neural networks have been used to extract statistically significant dynamical features (epsilon networks) in 2D [47].

3.2   Global Time Evolution of Genomes, Clones and Patterns

The global temporal evolution of the model can be captured by keeping track of the populations of all the genomes and patterns that occur. Although for natural systems a daunting proposition, it turns out that this is possible in the current framework using appropriate hash tables and segregation of patterns. For genomes we record each new genome that occurs in a simulation in a hash table. We use the efficient and self-contained C-package *hashtable.h* [48] with 64-bit hash keys: for genomes these are the genomes directly, for clones we use the x, y and t coordinates of the birth place and time of the clone and for spatial patterns we use a 64-bit quadtree hash code of the root of the tree or the patterns directly as hash keys for 8×8 bit patterns or smaller. See Sect. 3.1 for a description of the binary, genomic and ancestrally discriminated connected component decompositions. Note that these patterns are not aggregated corresponding to the symmetry of the transition rules in the model: although this would have been a further useful condensation.

In a single pass through the current state, we can count the populations of extant genomes and clones and once appropriately processed for connected components, we can assemble populations for the spatial patterns too, distinguished by binary state, genome or common ancestor. We identify the traces over time of these populations by an appropriate colour label corresponding to the hash key.

Population Scaling. In order to provide a robust visualization of populations of different magnitudes, we introduce a saturation scaling approach which is gleaned from the Michaelis-Menten biochemical kinetics of enzymatic reactions. The following rescaling of populations N_i^t using the mid-point parameter N_m (*cf.* Michaelis constant)

$$N_i^{\prime t} = N_i^t \frac{N_m}{(N_i^t + N_m)} \tag{1}$$

has the value $N_m/2$ when $N = N_m$, approximates to N_i^t at low values and saturates at N_m for high values of N_i^t. We also use this rescaling for activities in Sect. 3.2.

3.3   Evolutionary Activity

Evolutionary activity is a statistic designed to measure when components of an evolving population are persistent by virtue of their contributions to members of a population [49, 50]. The choice of component defines what aspect the statistics track; we will consider two examples, genomes and spatial patterns.

A component labelled by i has activity at time t given by

$$A_i^t = \sum_{t'=0}^t C_i^{t'} = A_i^{t-1} + C_i^t, \tag{2}$$

where C_i^t is a count of the component's presence at time t. We will refer to *live activity* as the activity of only the components that exist at the current time,

$$L_i^t = A_i^t \theta(C_i^t), \tag{3}$$

where $\theta(x) = 1$ if $x > 0$, and 0 otherwise. Even neutral evolution produces components that can persist for some time, and there are ways to construct neutral models to adjust activity measurement to signal only activity beyond neutral [50–52]. We will not require this in the present work, the main reason being that the case where all genes have no effect reduces to the GoL, which asymptotically produces no new activity because its dynamics relaxes to a field of fixed and low-periodicity local patterns.

Activities of genes or spatial patterns are stored in the relevant hash tables and updated efficiently using the recursion above, using the linear dependence of C_i^t on individual components to update only those component contributions that change in the current state.

From the component activities, we may form the time-dependent distribution of activity, for all activity and live activity,

$$P^t(A) = \sum_i \delta(A - A_i^t) \text{ and } P^t(L) = \sum_i \delta(L - L_i^t). \tag{4}$$

We will find it convenient to view activity in two ways, examples will be seen below, as a superposition of activity waves (one wave for each i), and as an evolution of the activity distribution, represented by the time trace of quantiles for each $P^t(A)$ (or $P^t(L)$). For visualizing the individual waves, we scale them as in Eq. (1) to see long-lived, high activity waves together with newly produced low-activity waves. Typical population and activity traces of genomes are shown in Fig. 2 and the probability distribution of activities is characterized in Fig. 3.

Gene Activities and Populations. When we consider components to be genes, we may label components with g (instead of i), and C_g^t is simply the number of genomes g present at time t (Figs. 2 and 3).

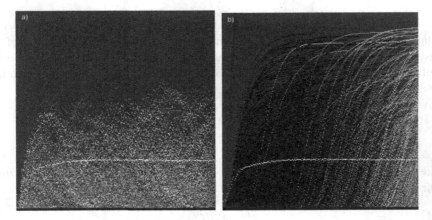

Fig. 2. Temporal evolution traces: (a) Population statistics of genomes P_g^t and (b) Activity waves A_g^t for $t = 0$ to 128. Populations, P_g^t, and live activity waves, L_g^t, are coloured with different shades of grey corresponding to different genomes g and activity waves for genomes that are extinct are shown in black. The global density is in white (on scale 0 to 1, bottom to top).

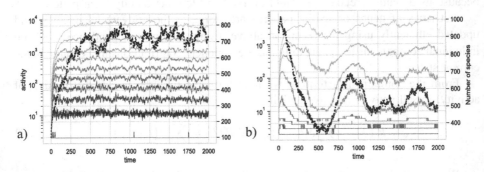

Fig. 3. Temporal evolution of deciles of the live activity distribution $P^t(L)$, for two examples of evolutionary dynamics, with different meta-parameters. The number of genetic species is shown with a dark dotted line. In (a) we see $P^t(L)$ converge to a rather stable distribution. Stable values of lower deciles imply that new genes are constantly being produced and are persisting in the population. In (b) we see a collapse of the genetic population for t < 500, followed by a recovery; persistence of new genomes in the following recovery is seen in a burst of new activity waves, reflected in the increase of low- and mid-level deciles from $t = 700$ to $t = 1000$.

Spatial Pattern Activities and Populations. As described above, connected spatial components may be rapidly detected for each time step. This enables the measurement of spatial pattern activity, which tells us whether there is an ongoing production of novel spatial patterns as a result of *genelife* evolution. The global record of spatial patterns can be traced via populations or activities (as shown in Fig. 4).

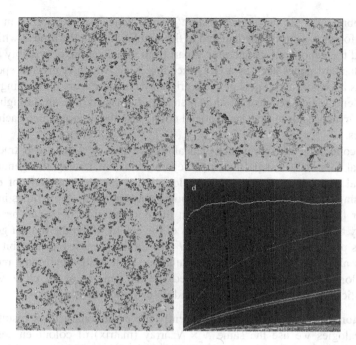

Fig. 4. Spatial pattern analysis and connection with genealogies. (a) The pattern of live cells after t = 256, coloured by genome identity; (b) The corresponding pattern of connected components, coloured by connected component identity – note that the connected components are often comprised of more than one genome; (c) Patterns coloured by common ancestor of clones at depth 2: The dark clones have root common ancestor, this is common at the early time shown; (d) Activity waves of connected components, each wave corresponding to a different connected component.

3.4   Genealogies: Global and Clonal

The study of inheritance in evolution has included genealogies and their statistics as an essential component in reconstructing the past, most recently and successfully in the form of coalescence theory [53–55], describing the statistics of the number of generations back to a common ancestor, applied to simple models of evolution [56] and the construction of evolutionary trees, the quality of which has been evaluated with statistical geometry [57]. Limited samples of sequences from current populations can be used to construct coalescence statistics and evolutionary trees. In genelife, inheritance is based on asexual reproduction, which simplifies genealogies since with a single parent the number of ancestors for an individual does not grow exponentially backwards in time. This allows a more complete record of ancestry to be recorded and updated at every timestep and the use of fast genealogical reconstruction to display the evolutionary development of a complete simulation.

Rather than consider every birth step, the majority of which do not introduce sequence changes (for the typically low mutation rates *ca.* 10^{-2} to 10^{-3} appropriate for evolving short genomes of length 64 employed here), we introduce two abbreviations of complete genealogies, both of which only record genetic changes. The first and most extreme abbreviation is the *first ancestor* (global) genealogy, recording in the hash table entry for each genome encountered in the simulation both the time at which it first appears and the genome of its ancestor. Apart from initialization, or possibly a random influx of standard genes such as a GoL-encoding gene, which is given a special root sequence as ancestor, every new genome arises by mutation from an existing gene, its ancestor. Genealogical reconstruction is then straightforward, tracing through the hash table from first ancestor to first ancestor and noting also the time at which each ancestor first appears.

The second type of abbreviated genealogy we use is clonal, also tracing only genealogical inheritance steps that involve mutation, but tracing the genealogy for every clonal population of a genome (a clone is the identical progeny of each new mutant arising in the population). Each genome may appear multiple times in separate spatially or temporally separated clones in the population. Clones can be identified uniquely by the time and space coordinates of the cell in which the mutant genome of the clone is produced. This so called *clonal birth-id* may be used as a 64-bit hash key for storing all clones that occur in a simulation: each hash table entry records the ancestral clone from which it was produced and the genome of the clone as well as other statistics like the size of the clone and its evolutionary activity.

Visualization. In order to visualize efficiently the evolutionary trees resulting from these genealogies we use the same $N \times N$ array (matrix) of colour entries used to display the spatial pattern of the genelife CA. Along the horizontal axis of the array, each column is devoted to an extant genome or clone in the current population, choosing the N most populated ones if there are more of them than can be displayed, and the time at which ancestors arise is displayed along the vertical axis, using discrete steps of length t_T/N, where t_T is the total simulation time. In a single trace back of ancestors for the extant genomes or clones, we place the hash colour-id of the genome for each ancestor in the row corresponding to the time at which the ancestor was produced. If multiple ancestors occur in the same discrete time interval, the genome of the oldest is displayed (*i.e.* overwritten in the matrix). Figure 8 shows examples of first ancestor (global) genealogical trees which can be displayed in real time during a simulation. Colour and video material for these genealogies is available in the online supplementary information. In addition to the temporal vertical axis, Fig. 8 also shows genealogical depth plots in which the vertical axis shows simply the number of ancestral mutation steps, instead of their duration.

3.5   Simulation and Analysis Software

A systematic interactive simulation and analysis tool was written primarily in C (over 7000 lines of custom code, with additional use of 700 lines of hashtable.h code [48]) and with a custom python front end (using numpy, matplotlib, pySDL2) for graphics, simulation control and analysis (*ca.* 2000 lines of code), with Jupyter notebooks documenting standard usage and recording results. The software is written to take advantage of parallel bit processing in long integers but does not yet take advantage of GPUs or other parallel processing architectures, nor the special acceleration provided for example by Gosper's algorithm [40]. Emphasis was on a flexible generic platform supporting online analysis tools with global recording of novel structures found during the simulation. The software is available on github at http://github.com/js1200/genelife.

4 Results

In this section we present some evidence for several key findings revealed by application of the analysis tools to the simulation platform genelife, which invests the computational universe of CAs with the capabilities of evolution. Only an initial sample of the kind of new insights and results afforded by *genelife* can be presented in this paper. We first demonstrate the purely deterministic evolution, with ongoing innovation of patterns, exhibited by the model in the absence of mutation. We then show how increasingly fine dissections of the transition between subcritical and supercritical proliferation can be achieved using the successive symmetry breakings in Sect. 2. We demonstrate how ongoing evolution is revealed by the tools of activity statistics and genealogies and extend this analysis to the domain of spatial patterns. We leave the exploration of the information potential in initial patterns for controlling computation to future work. Instead, in the final section we explore one of the novel possibilities for characterizing the natural information occurring in evolving dynamical systems by introducing dynamical genealogies and exploring their ability to capture systematic computational motifs arising in the simulation. This provides an efficient genetic alternative for 2D CAs to epsilon machines [25], which were applied successfully to 1D CAs [29].

4.1 Deterministic Dynamics of Evolution

Case of No Mutation. The deterministic extension of the GoL through genelife is illustrated for the case of s = 2, 3 with a non-well-ordered selection scheme as described in Sect. 2.1. The state of the 512×512 cell lattice after *ca.* 1000 timesteps is depicted in Fig. 5, both for genomes and connected spatial components, along with several filters identifying travelling spaceship structures including the displacement genealogies of Sect. 3.1. Novel localized spatial patterns continue to arise as documented both by the activity statistics comparing times 500–1000 with times 9500–10000, and by the novelty filtered components, a plot of number of live cells that are part of novel components over time (f). Using the global hash table for connected components, only the novel patterns are depicted in bright colours in Fig. 5c. The frequency of novel spatial patterns, occurring when spaceships collide giving birth to new spaceships, has not changed significantly even after 10x the simulation time. In contrast, only rarely are novel spaceships found after t = 1000.

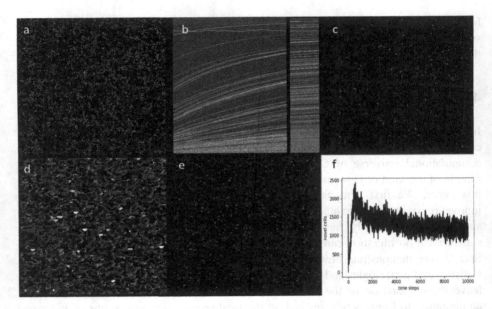

Fig. 5. Deterministic spatial evolution of ongoing novel patterns without mutation. (a–e) simulation status at t = 1002 (a) live cells coloured by genome (b) activity traces of connected patterns, left last 512 timesteps up to t = 1002, right same for t = 10066 (c) connected patterns with novelty filter darkening all non-novel patterns (d) fast spaceship detection using local 7 × 7 neighbourhood colouring cells moving in directions N, E, S, W with red, green, blue and white (e) displacement genealogies identifying moving locally periodic automata with period 1 in green and longer periods (rare) in bluer tones, static structures in dull red. (f) number of live cells in novel components. (Color figure online)

It is clear even from this simple example, which could be reproduced in all of the symmetry breaking extensions in Sect. 2, that allowing different species into the GoL enriches the dynamics – from generic relaxation to very simple static or low period structures with rare gliders from random initial conditions, to relaxation to a robust and diverse population of spaceships that continue to repopulate the space and produce novel patterns at much longer times than are typical for the relaxation of the GoL.

4.2   Symmetry Breaking from Semi-totalistic to Isotropic

As discussed in Sects. 1 and 2, the GoL decays too strongly for almost all initial conditions to support a spontaneous supply of patterns that could act as a substrate for evolution. The capability of genetically modified local rule tables to modulate the dynamics near to the GoL rules is limited by the number of variants with proliferation rates near to the threshold between proliferation to fill the lattice and decay to rare quiescent local periodic structures as in the GoL. This depends on the spatial symmetry of the rules. For example, the semi-totalistic rules are sub-critical in the GoL for S23B3 but supercritical for S_B23 so that with s = 2 or 3 rules no closer approach to criticality is achievable. As an example of the novel capabilities introduced by symmetry breaking, as discussed in Sects. 2.2, 2.3, 2.4 and 2.5, in Fig. 6 we examine the ability of the symmetry broken S_B23 rule sets to evolve closer to the critical threshold for proliferation. Yet finer differentiation is possible by including combinations with differentiated survival, and exhaustive exploration of this threshold must await a study dedicated only to this point, since there are 2^{60} isotropic combinations to investigate just for the three numbers of live neighbour rules s = 2, 3, 4.

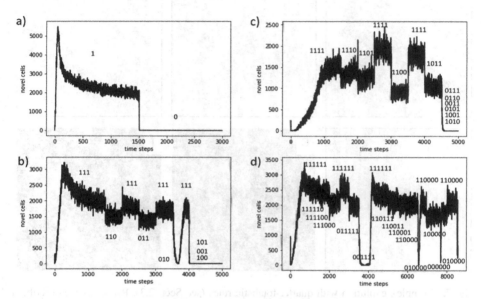

Fig. 6. Symmetry breaking of s = 2 rules near to proliferation threshold. The number of live cells that are part of novel connected components is shown for the four symmetry classes in Sects. 2.2–5 (a) semi-totalistic, (b) quarter-totalistic, (c) octavian and (d) isotropic. The simulations were run for no survival but with overwrite with the entire s = 3 rule sets allowed, but only the masked members of the s = 2 rule (as shown in the text labels) were allowed: these values changed as shown during each simulation run. The genome choice was neutral but different genomes were required for birth (mode 5).

4.3   Activities and Genealogies Show Ongoing Evolutionary Process

Evolutionary activity has long been a signal of ongoing evolution; if a population continuously produces new genetic variants that succeed in surviving and propagating in the population, the population continues to evolve. We have seen, in the case of deterministic evolution discussed in Sect. 4.1, that even when the genetic population is constrained to have no innovation (suppressing random mutation), evolutionary activity of spatial patterns reveals that evolution can proceed robustly nonetheless.

Evolution within the more simply defined rule spaces tends to produce a certain kind of open-endedness, with ongoing production of new genetic material that is successfully absorbed into the population. However, the dynamics appears to be quite similar, notwithstanding the new genes being absorbed into the population. This is a signal that these new genes are drawn from a genetic subspace that is neutral with respect to the dynamics, and hence the ongoing production of genetic activity does not produce new dynamical functionality.

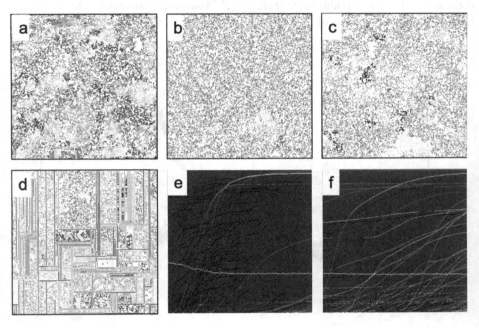

Fig. 7. Complex evolution with quarter-totalistic rules (see Sect. 2.3). Panes (a)–(c) describe a sequence proceeding from one dynamical phase (a) early expanding blooms (b) t ≈ 550 near collapse of the population to one dominant genome (c) t = 8000 successful invasion of new genomes that evolve and persist, with dynamics of competing domains that are more stable than the initial bloom dynamics. Pane (d) illustrates evolution in a similar universe of quarter-totalistic rules, producing an ecology that asymptotically evolves domains, with robust evolving dynamics within each domain. Temporal evolutionary activity waves A_g^t are traced in (e) and (f) at early and later times. Live activity waves, L_g^t, are coloured with different colours (shades of grey) corresponding to different genomes g and activity waves for genomes that are extinct are shown in black. The global density is shown in white (on scale 0 to 1, bottom to top).

This limitation on evolvability was in fact a motivation to consider more complex rule spaces obtained by breaking symmetries of the rule space as described in Sects. 2.3, 2.3, 2.4 and 2.5. Figure 7 illustrates a complex evolutionary sequence from the quarter totalistic rules of Sect. 2.3. In the evolutionary sequence illustrated, we see a 'major transition' in the evolution of the population, at about t = 550, when the population collapses toward a single dominant genome, but then is re-infected with genes that succeed in propagating and persisting for continued ongoing evolution.

The genealogies for the evolutionary sequence illustrated in Fig. 7 are shown in Fig. 8. The collapse drastically reduces the number of genomes present in the population, but recovery enables rebuilding of a genetically rich population. A movie showing the simulation dynamics is included as Supp. Fig. 6.

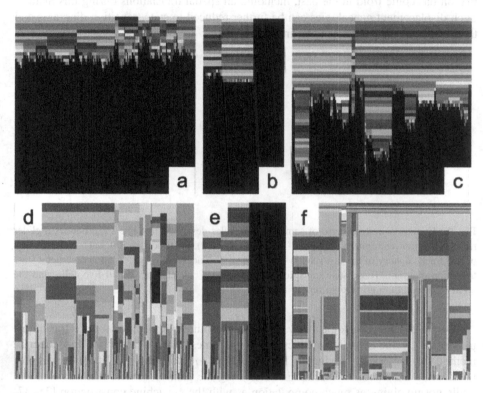

Fig. 8. Genealogies for the three phases of evolution in Fig. 7(a), (b), and (c), at the same time steps as those figures. These genealogies are colour coded by genome and successive generations occupy rows from the top (earliest time) to the present, coalescing backwards in time. The corresponding time-resolved genealogies are shown in (d), (e), and (f), with time between gene shifts represented as the vertical extent of each coloured patch representing a genome.

Evolutionary activity, both genealogical activity and spatial pattern activity, reveal the evolutionary dynamics to be open-ended. Activity associated with the evolution of new functionality remains, however, elusive. We see what may be interpreted as major transitions [19, 58] in the collapse and recovery illustrated in Fig. 7.

4.4 Displacement Genealogies, Computation and Selection

Computation is traditionally accomplished in the Game of Life by transmission of information using gliders, and locally oscillating and translating configurations. In other CAs, information is transmitted via traveling boundaries between phases [25]. Genelife has the additional feature that besides spatial patterns causing information transfer, genetic information is also transferred as a result of dynamics. In order to capture the genetic information transfer, we construct displacement genealogy histories, as in Sect. 3.1: every live cell has a short history of where the genome's information has come from in the past, including all spatial translations during this history. Such displacement genealogies can be further reduced to state transition diagrams and their statistics analysed as shown in Fig. 9.

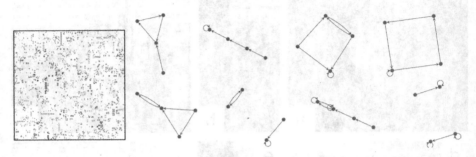

Fig. 9. Evolution in a universe of semi-totalistic rules described in Sect. 2.2 produces a glider rich population, continually evolving (shown on the left). At time $t = 500$, each live cell was polled for its history of the last sixteen timesteps of displacement genealogy, to construct a state transition diagram. These state transition diagrams were collected across all live cells, and the eight most common are shown on the right.

Displacement genealogies may be used to capture computational state transitions performed by the spatial dynamics of the genomes. This is a simple, but concrete method of empirically reducing the dynamics to computational state transitions, involving a 1D thread of information following the path of genetic transmission, and while not involving as much computation as with the ε-machine construction [25, 47] has advantages in 2D where the amount of information needing to be digested for the construction of ε-machines becomes prohibitive. It is well applicable for dynamics that produce many interacting periodic structures (gliders and spaceships). If the dynamics are too dense, spaceships travel only very short distances before collision and their displacement genealogies proliferate to the point that statistics are difficult to collect. At higher densities other regular structures of spatial genetic transmission may arise that can then also be captured by displacement genealogies. The local displacement genealogies can also be analysed for most prominent period and mean displacement at this period and coloured accordingly; an example is shown in Fig. 10.

4.5   Selection Based on Displacement Memory

As an extension of the model, without changing the relationship between genomes and rule tables, the choice of ancestors can be made dependent on the current displacement genealogy (in the same cell as genome). We made this step in order to examine whether an autonomous selection for genomes that modify the rules in such a way as to give rise to desirable local state genomic state machines (as depicted in Fig. 9) can occur. To this end we introduced a set of additional selection options that select for precise periodicity, for large or small periods, for large or diagonal displacements. Interestingly, rich repertoires of spaceships, as in the non-well-ordered selection model case of Sect. 4.1, were found generically in such models, demonstrating that local selection for dynamical traits is effective in genomic evolution, despite the indirect nature of the selection feedback (with multiple genomes determining local rules together). An example of such a simulation is shown in Fig. 10.

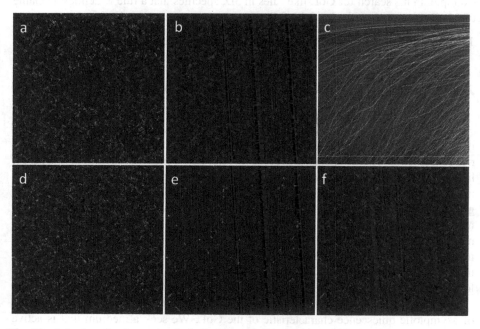

Fig. 10. Selection for longer period displacement histories resulting in rich populations of spaceships: complementary images at $t = 12772$. (a) colouring individual genomes by ID (b) visualizing the neighbour states for survival (blue) and birth (green), with brightness proportional to s (c) activity statistics of last 512 time steps (d) connected components (genetically distinguished) serving as the basis for pattern analysis (e) only novel patterns (occurring for first time as this step) retain bright colours, all others darkened (f) colour coding displacements genealogies: quality of periodicity is brightness, with static period 1 entities in red and longer periods in increasing blue. (Color figure online)

5 Discussion and Conclusions

We have created *genelife*, a new version of Conway's Game of Life that is evolutionary, in the sense that all live cells are endowed with a genome that can be passed on, possibly changed by mutation, to offspring during birth processes. The GoL is an intriguing version of active media because it has proven capability for universal computation, but computation does not arise in typical asymptotic dynamics on finite lattices. *Genelife's* evolutionary version of the GoL seeks to capitalize on the implicit computational capabilities of the GoL to provide an evolutionary system that can produce computation as an emergent property of the evolutionary dynamics.

One feature of cellular automata with complex dynamics that has been historically important is that the medium should be active, but have a natural relaxation to a quiescent state, as indeed is observed for the GoL. Only special and rare initial conditions lead to ongoing complex dynamics in the GoL, including expansive dynamics that can escape any finite bounded region, and these initial conditions are considered to be the carriers of complex natural (including universal) computation. Bays [59], for example, in his search for GoL-like rules in 3D, specifies that a rule R defines a "Game of Life" if and only if both of the following are true:

1. A glider must exist and must occur "naturally" if we apply R repeatedly to primordial soup configurations. (A *primordial soup* is any finite mass of arbitrarily dense randomly dispersed living cells.)
2. All primordial soup configurations, when subjected to R, must exhibit bounded growth.

In genelife, we could readily attain this criterion (or some more precise version of it) by making genes rare in sequence space that encode local rule departures that give rise to a live cell by a proper birth process (*i.e.* not a movement event in which a parent live cell gives rise to only one offspring and dies at its previous location). As we have implemented it here, however, we have simply accelerated the process of discovery for genes that can modify the local birth processes. We investigated the first two steps in making such genes rarer for the semi-totalistic case via the parameter n_c: increasing the number of bits to encode a LUT entry from 1 to 2 to 4. We maintain that it is not natural to assume that the probability of configurations that may give rise to complex or universal computation is much lower than the probability of configurations that may lead to proliferation.

In some sense, our goal of having a rich evolving system contrasts with the desire of asymptotic quiescence characteristic of the GoL. We seek a medium that is active enough to spontaneously produce complex evolutionary dynamics rather than quiescence. But for evolutionary progress to be observed, we must still have a constraint on the activity of the medium, otherwise chaos ensues.

It is important to stress that many of the innovations presented here can be generalized beyond the framework of nearest neighbour and binary CAs. The use of nearest neighbours only in the CA rules is clearly just a convenient starting point for genetic extension models as proposed here. GoL models have been extended to larger neighbourhoods [60] and 3D [59], to provide more differentiated rules near to the GoL configurations $s = 2, 3$, and non-discrete generalizations such as Smooth Life [61] have also been proposed. Larger neighbourhoods in CAs do result in new phenomena, such as making spiral waves commonplace [31, 33]. The insights and tools developed for *genelife* will be useful in the more general context of both less strictly local rules, other lattices and even continuous state dynamical systems such as coupled map lattices [62].

Likewise, our association of genomes with live states in binary CAs is compelling but is not a fundamental limitation of the domain of application of genetic extensions.

Firstly, the above approach can be used directly whenever it makes sense to distinguish two classes of states: the inanimate or physical states (devoid of biological information that can be inherited) and the live states (containing copyable or inheritable information). Secondly, one can also add ancillary information, differentiating inanimate states, in the same way as for live cells. The simplest example of this is the association of information strings also with 0 states in the current model. This could be viewed as extending the GoL with a more complex environment with differentiated resources, or put more simply, as adding a chemistry to the GoL. While transitions which copy long strings of such information would be equivalent to biological replication, which is not a property as yet found spontaneously in synthetic chemistry, there are a wealth of autocatalytic chemical reactions for simple substances that are formally equivalent to copy processes for limited information content.

In conclusion, we may regard *genelife* as a success, in the sense that it provides a rich evolutionary platform with a variety of mechanisms to exert control over evolutionary processes. We have also developed a novel coherent set of analytical tools reflecting both genetic and spatial information processing. Success might be considered limited, in the sense that emergence of increasingly complex computation within a genelife population remains an empirical challenge. *Genelife*'s ability to control evolution through constraints on genetic expression will enable the engineering of evolution's emergent properties. We look forward to exploring these directions in the future.

Acknowledgments. The authors would like to thank the Earth Life Science Institute (ELSI) Tokyo, Japan) for hosting them for a short visit as part of an EON Seed Grant in 2017 where this work began. The EON Seed Grant was supported by the John Templeton Foundation. Our thanks also to Nathaniel Virgo and Steen Rasmussen for helpful comments at an early stage in this work.

Supplementary Material

Deterministic Resolution of Neutral Selection

In general, if two genomes are different and a neutral outcome is sought, then some other mechanism must be invoked to choose an ancestor for the newly born genome. The conventional population genetics approach of choosing one of them randomly adds a major source of stochasticity to the otherwise deterministic GoL. It turns out there are a number of possible alternatives:

1. Random choice of live neighbours for birth
2. Distinguish live neighbours for birth by their position in the configuration
3. Examine the neighbourhoods of live neighbours to distinguish them.

Both 2. and 3. suffer from potential ambiguity if the live neighbours remain identical under the distinction. We obviously would wish to preserve a certain degree of spatial symmetry in both the alternatives 2. and 3. In the Supplementary Material figures Supp. Figs. 1, 2, and 3, we catalogue and illustrate the different configurations of live neighbours for the non-trivial cases of s = 2, 3, 4. The cases s = 0, 1 are very simple by comparison, and the cases 5, 6, 7, 8 can be obtained simply by exchanging zeros and ones in the figures. For the GoL B3 rule, we note that there is a very simple generic principle for choosing a single ancestor among the three live neighbours positionally, and one that does not break any of the spatial symmetries considered: choose the one at the "most different" position. This most different position is indicated in green in the figure in the appendix. Generally, it turns out that two of the three positions are related to each other by more symmetries than the different one. Now this is very good news, because it means that a deterministic inheritance scheme for neutral selection based on spatial position can be achieved without breaking spatial symmetries. Because approach 3. is incomplete for the many cases when the live neighbours themselves have equal numbers of live neighbours, and because a realization of 2. that works for B3 has been found, we do not pursue 3. further in this paper.

A somewhat weaker, but still valid procedure that generalizes 2. to other numbers of live neighbours (e.g. 2, 4, etc.) is to recognize that the choice of the most different position for B3 can be broken down into three steps: (a) find a canonical representation of the pattern of live neighbours which represents all symmetric versions of the pattern (under one of the chosen symmetries above) (b) specify the absolute position of the chosen position in this canonical representation (c) transform this position relative to the canonical representation back to the "orientation" of the particular starting configuration. It turns out that since the canonical rotation is mapped symmetrically to each possible instance that even making a simple choice such as the first position in the canonical representation gives rise to a positional inheritance rule with symmetry preserving properties. However non-trivial genetic dynamics such as genetic rotors for GoL oscillators or *still lifes* are possible.

We illustrate this principle first for the case of octavian symmetry (Sect. 2.4), which turns out to play a pivotal role in the analysis, and then extend it to other (more physical) symmetries. The distinguished configurations for s = 2, 3, 4 are shown in the left column of figures A1–A3 for the 4,7,10 canonical rotations. These are simply and efficiently defined as the 8-rotation of the 8-bit binary pattern of live neighbours that has the smallest numerical value. All the different configurations for s = 0–8 live neighbours given by the binomial coefficients ^8C_s (1, 8, 28, 56, 70, 56, 28, 8, 1) reduce to (1, 1, 4, 7, 10, 7, 4, 1, 1) configurations distinguishable up to 8-rotation symmetry. Note that these numbers only differ from $^8C_s/8$ for s = 0, 2, 4, 6, 8 and because of the 6 ambiguous canonical bit patterns 00000000, 00010001, 00110011 and 01010101, 01110111, and 11111111 (*i.e.* patterns that can be rotated into themselves with less than 8 single steps). For these patterns only, an alternative rule must be found to choose the ancestor if we allow B0, B2, B4, B6 or B8 rule extensions. In our implementation for these special cases, we coded the following 8 disambiguation options which are mostly deterministic but include one spatially and one genetically random option:

1. random choice: this involves a departure from determinism for these cases only
2. ignore problem and choose selected bit of canonical configuration: accepting minimal asymmetry induced by these comparatively infrequent (for s = 1–7) cases.
3. disallow birth: this effectively modifies the rules and is like excluding these rules from the table
4. choose lesser in value of genes if different (otherwise it makes no difference) i.e. revert to non-neutral genetic model in these (rare) cases only

5. similar to 4, choose gene with least number of ones and if same, then lesser in value
6. choose a recombinant AND of all genes involved in this case
7. choose a default ancestor such as the gene coding for the Game of Life in these cases only
8. generate a random gene to give birth to for these ambiguous instances.

The option 6 is potentially minimally disruptive, effectively just reducing the rate of departure from GoL dynamics and is better in most circumstances than option 5 that is also symmetric but creates a non-trivial correlation between dynamics and genetic change. However, depending on the investigation, each of the techniques has its strengths and weaknesses.

2-live-neighbour configurations

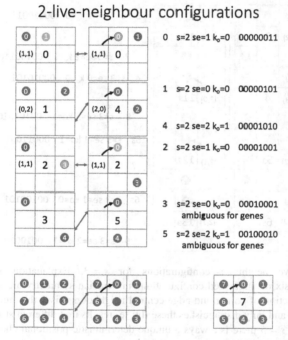

Supp. Fig. 1. Live neighbour configurations with $s = 2$. The figure shows the configurations distinguished in the four different symmetries, in their relation to the canonical octavian symmetry, which distinguishes the four in the left column: semi-totalistic (1: i.e. all equivalent), quarter-totalistic (3: different se), octavian (4) and isotropic (6). The canonical minimal binary string representations of the configurations are shown on the right. The deterministic positional choice of ancestor is shown in green, when this is possible without further information (see main text). In the bottom row, the numbering scheme for neighbours is shown, along with its rotation. (Color figure online)

3-live-neighbour configurations

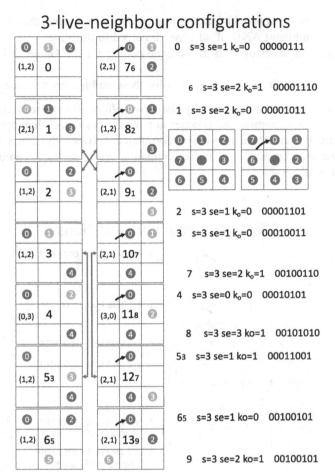

Supp. Fig. 2. Live neighbour configurations for $s = 3$. Explanation is analogous to Supp. Fig. 1. The six distinguished configurations in octavian symmetry are shown in the first column. The distinction of corner and edge-centred neighbours raises this number to 10 in the fully isotropic case and only distinguishes these (by se) results in 4 different structures. Note that in this case, as for $s = 5$ there is always a unique deterministic positional choice of neighbour, shown in green: the most different position (the other two have greater symmetry). (Color figure online)

4-live-neighbour configurations

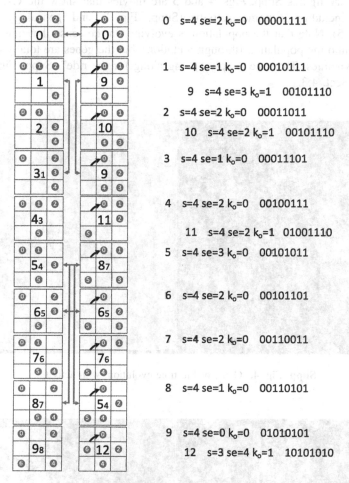

0 s=4 se=2 k₀=0 00001111

1 s=4 se=1 k₀=0 00010111

  9 s=4 se=3 k₀=1 00101110

2 s=4 se=2 k₀=0 00011011

  10 s=4 se=2 k₀=1 00101110

3 s=4 se=1 k₀=0 00011101

  9 s=4 se=2 k₀=0 (duplicate)

4 s=4 se=2 k₀=0 00100111

  11 s=4 se=2 k₀=1 01001110

5 s=4 se=3 k₀=0 00101011

6 s=4 se=2 k₀=0 00101101

7 s=4 se=2 k₀=0 00110011

8 s=4 se=1 k₀=0 00110101

9 s=4 se=0 k₀=0 01010101

  12 s=3 se=4 k₀=1 10101010

Supp. Fig. 3. Live neighbour configurations for s = 4. Here there are 10 distinguished configurations in the octavian symmetry, 5 in quarter-totalistic and 13 (0–12) in isotropic symmetry. The configurations 7 and 9(12) are the ones where it is not possible to unambiguously specify a particular choice of ancestor in way which is preserved under the symmetries and identifiable from the canonical binary representation. For all others a deterministic positional choice may be made.

Simulation Examples

Supplementary figures Supp. Figs. 4 and 5 are movies that show the Game of Life dynamics, including genome activity (Supp. Fig. 4) and genealogy evolution (Supp. Fig. 5). Note that the population is evolving, in the sense that new genes are introduced into the population (through mutation), but the genes are totally uncoupled from the dynamics. They are simply "going along for the ride". Supp. Fig. 6 is referenced in Sect. 4.3.

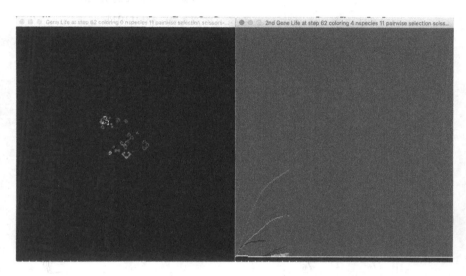

Supp. Fig. 4. Game of life time evolution, with activity.

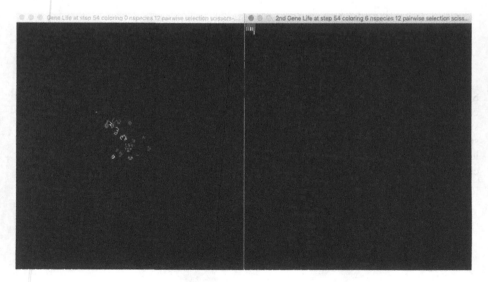

Supp. Fig. 5. Game of Life time evolution, with genealogies. First ancestor genealogies with the vertical axis genealogical depth, coloured by sequence type.

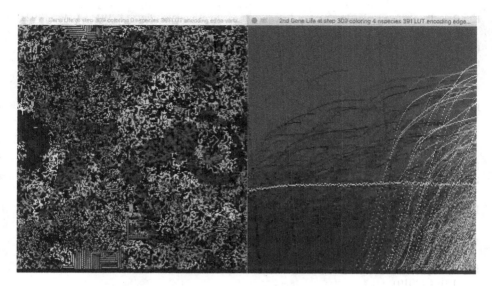

Supp. Fig. 6. Complex evolution discussed in Sect. 4.3 First phase: expanding blooms of competing domains, second phase is a collapse of the population, as it is almost taken over by a single genome, and the third phase is successful invasion of several new species, which continue to evolve for competing domains that have different dynamics from the original expanding bloom domains.

References

1. Von Neumann, J., Burks, A.W.: Theory of Self-reproducing Automata. University of Illinois Press, Urbana (1966)
2. Gardner, M.: Mathematical games –the fantastic combinations of John Conway's new solitaire game "life". Sci. Am. **223**, 120–123 (1970). https://doi.org/10.1038/scientificamerican1070-120
3. Wolfram, S.: Statistical mechanics of cellular automata. Rev. Mod. Phys. **55**, 601–644 (1983). https://doi.org/10.1103/revmodphys.55.601
4. Packard, N.H., Wolfram, S.: Two-dimensional cellular automata. J. Stat. Phys. **38**, 901–946 (1985). https://doi.org/10.1007/bf01010423
5. Rendell, P.: (2018). http://rendell-attic.org/gol/tm.htm
6. Pesavento, U.: An implementation of von Neumann's self-reproducing machine. Artif. Life **2**, 337–354 (1995). https://doi.org/10.1162/artl.1995.2.4.337
7. Conway, J.H.: On Numbers and Games. A K Peters/CRC Press United States (2000). ISBN 9781568811277
8. Johnston, N.: (2019). http://www.conwaylife.com/wiki/LifeWiki
9. Berlekamp, E.R., Conway, J.H., Guy, R.K.: Winning Ways for Your Mathematical Plays. vol. 4, pp. 1004. A. K. Peters, Natick, Mass (2001). 1568811446
10. Rendell, P.: A fully universal turing machine in conway's game of life. J. Cell. Autom. **8**, 19–38 (2013)
11. Bak, P., Chen, K., Creutz, M.: Self-organized criticality in the game of life. Nature **342**, 780–782 (1989). https://doi.org/10.1038/342780a0

12. Bak, P.: Self-organized criticality in nonconservative models. Phys. A **191**, 41–46 (1992). https://doi.org/10.1016/0378-4371(92)90503-I
13. Shapiro, A.: (2019). https://github.com/ShprAlex/SproutLife/wiki
14. Medernach, D., Kowaliw, T., Ryan, C., Doursat, R.: Long-term evolutionary dynamics in heterogeneous cellular automata. In: GECCO 2013: Proceedings of the 2013 Genetic and Evolutionary Computation Conference, pp. 231–238 (2013)
15. Ryan, C., Fitzgerald, J., Kowaliw, T., Doursat, R., Carrignon, S., Medernach, D.: Evolution of heterogeneous cellular automata in fluctuating environments. In: The 2019 Conference on Artificial Life, vol. 28, pp. 216–223 (2016). https://doi.org/10.1162/978-0-262-33936-0-ch041
16. Zamaraev, A.: (2019). https://github.com/a5kin/evolife
17. Suzuki, K., Ikegami, T.: Homeodynamics in the game of life. In: The 2nd Annual Conference of the Japanese Society for Artificial Intelligence, pp. 600–607 (2008)
18. Taylor, T.: Redrawing the boundary between organism and environment. In: Artificial Life IX: Proceedings of the Ninth International Conference on the Simulation and Synthesis of Living Systems, pp. 600. The MIT Press (2004). https://doi.org/10.7551/mitpress/1429.003.0045
19. Turney, P.D.: Modeling major transitions in evolution with the game of life. arXiv:1908.07034 (2019)
20. Eppstein, D.: Growth and decay in life-like cellular automata. In: Adamatzky, A. (ed.) Game of Life Cellular Automata, pp. 71–97. Springer, London (2010). https://doi.org/10.1007/978-1-84996-217-9_6
21. Mitchell, M., Hraber, P.T., Crutchfield, J.P.: Revisiting the edge of chaos: evolving cellular automata to perform computations. Complex Syst. **7**, 89–130 (1993)
22. Schreiber, T.: Measuring information transfer. Phys. Rev. Lett. **85**, 461 (2000)
23. Lizier, J.T.: Measuring the dynamics of information processing on a local scale in time and space. In: Wibral, M., Vicente, R., Lizier, J.T. (eds.) Directed Information Measures in Neuroscience. UCS, pp. 161–193. Springer, Heidelberg (2014). https://doi.org/10.1007/978-3-642-54474-3_7
24. Helvik, T., Lindgren, K., Nordahl, M.G.: Local information in one-dimensional cellular automata. In: Sloot, P.M.A., Chopard, B., Hoekstra, A.G. (eds.) ACRI 2004. LNCS, vol. 3305, pp. 121–130. Springer, Heidelberg (2004). https://doi.org/10.1007/978-3-540-30479-1_13
25. Crutchfield, J.P.: The calculi of emergence - computation, dynamics and induction. Phys. D **75**, 11–54 (1994). https://doi.org/10.1016/0167-2789(94)90273-9
26. Crutchfield, J.P., Ellison, C.J., James, R.G., Mahoney, J.R.: Synchronization and control in intrinsic and designed computation: an information-theoretic analysis of competing models of stochastic computation. Chaos **20**, 037105 (2010). https://doi.org/10.1063/1.3489888
27. Hanson, J.E., Crutchfield, J.P.: Computational mechanics of cellular automata: an example. Phys. D **103**, 169–189 (1997). https://doi.org/10.1016/s0167-2789(96)00259-x
28. Marzen, S.E., Crutchfield, J.P.: Statistical signatures of structural organization: the case of long memory in renewal processes. Phys. Lett. A **380**, 1517–1525 (2016). https://doi.org/10.1016/j.physleta.2016.02.052
29. Shalizi, C.R., Crutchfield, J.P.: Computational mechanics: pattern and prediction, structure and simplicity. J. Stat. Phys. **104**, 817–879 (2001). https://doi.org/10.1023/a:1010388907793
30. McCaskill, J.S., Packard, N.H., Rasmussen, S., Bedau, M.A.: Evolutionary self-organization in complex fluids. Philos. Trans. R. Soc. Lond. B Biol. Sci. **362**, 1763–1779 (2007). https://doi.org/10.1098/rstb.2007.2069

31. Boerlijst, M.C., Hogeweg, P.: Spiral wave structure in pre-biotic evolution: hypercycles stable against parasites. Phys. D: Nonlinear Phenom. **48**, 17–28 (1991). https://doi.org/10. 1016/0167-2789(91)90049-F

32. Nowak, M.A., May, R.M.: Evolutionary games and spatial chaos. Nature **359**, 826–829 (1992). https://doi.org/10.1038/359826a0

33. Lindgren, K., Nordahl, M.G.: Evolutionary dynamics of spatial games. Phys. D - Spec. Issue Constr. Complex. Artif. Reality Arch. **75**, 292–309 (1994). https://doi.org/10.1016/0167-2789(94)90289-5

34. Fraser, A.S.: An introduction to population genetic theory. By J. F. Crow and M. Kimura. Harper and Row, New York. 656 pp. 1970. Teratology **5**, 386–387 (1972) https://doi.org/10. 1002/tera.1420050318

35. He, L., Ren, X., Gao, Q., Zhao, X., Yao, B., Chao, Y.: The connected-component labeling problem: a review of state-of-the-art algorithms. Pattern Recogn. **70**, 25–43 (2017). https:// doi.org/10.1016/j.patcog.2017.04.018

36. Suzuki, K., Horiba, I., Sugie, N.: Linear-time connected-component labeling based on sequential local operations. Comput. Vis. Image Understand. **89**, 1–23 (2003). https://doi. org/10.1016/S1077-3142(02)00030-9

37. Wu, K., Otoo, E., Suzuki, K.: Optimizing two-pass connected-component labeling algorithms. Pattern Anal. Appl. **12**, 117–135 (2009). https://doi.org/10.1007/s10044-008-0109-y

38. Samet, H.: Connected component labeling using quadtrees. J. ACM **28**, 487–501 (1981). https://doi.org/10.1145/322261.322267

39. Rokicki, T.: (2019). http://golly.sourceforge.net

40. Gosper, R.W.: Exploiting regularities in large cellular spaces. Phys. D: Nonlinear Phenom. **10**, 75–80 (1984). https://doi.org/10.1016/0167-2789(84)90251-3

41. Volgenant, A.: Linear and semi-assignment problems: a core oriented approach. Comput. Oper. Res. **23**, 917–932 (1996). https://doi.org/10.1016/0305-0548(96)00010-X

42. Gupta, R.: (2018). https://www.geeksforgeeks.org/hopcroft-karp-algorithm-for-maximum-matching-set-2-implementation/

43. Liang, X.S.: Information flow and causality as rigorous notions ab initio. Phys. Rev. E **94** (2016). https://doi.org/10.1103/physreve.94.052201

44. Bossomaier, T.R.J.: An Introduction to Transfer Entropy: Information Flow in Complex Systems. Springer, Cham (2016). https://doi.org/10.1007/978-3-319-43222-9

45. Rupe, A., Crutchfield, J.P.: Local causal states and discrete coherent structures. Chaos **28**, 075312 (2018). https://doi.org/10.1063/1.5021130

46. Varn, D.P., Canright, G.S., Crutchfield, J.P.: Epsilon-machine spectral reconstruction theory: a direct method for inferring planar disorder and structure from X-ray diffraction studies. Acta Crystallogr. Sect. A **69**, 197–206 (2013). https://doi.org/10.1107/s0108767312046582

47. Sinapayen, L., Ikegami, T.: Online fitting of computational cost to environmental complexity: predictive coding with the ε-network. In: The 2019 Conference on Artificial Life, vol. 29, pp. 380–387 (2017). https://doi.org/10.1162/isal_a_065

48. Gustavsson, M.: (2017). https://github.com/mattiasgustavsson/libs/blob/master/hashtable.h

49. Bedau, M., Packard, N.: Measurement of evolutionary activity, teleology, and life. In: Artificial Life II, pp. 431–461. Addison Wesley (1991)

50. Bedau, M.A., Snyder, E., Packard, N.H.: A classification of long-term evolutionary dynamics. In: From Anim Animat, pp. 228–237. MIT Press (1998)

51. Channon, A.: Unbounded evolutionary dynamics in a system of agents that actively process and transform their environment. Genet. Program Evolvable Mach. **7**, 253–281 (2006)

52. Stout, A., Spector, L.: Validation of evolutionary activity metrics for long-term evolutionary dynamics. In: Proceedings of the 7th Annual Conference on Genetic and Evolutionary Computation, pp. 137–142. ACM (2005)

53. Kingman, J.F.C.: The coalescent. Stochast. Process. Appl. **13**, 235–248 (1982). https://doi.org/10.1016/0304-4149(82)90011-4
54. Blancas, A., Duchamps, J.J., Lambert, A., Siri-Jégousse, A.: Trees within trees: simple nested coalescents. Electron. J. Probab. **23**. https://doi.org/10.1214/18-ejp219
55. Hein, J., Schierup, M.H., Wiuf, C.: Gene Genealogies, Variation and Evolution: A Primer in Coalescent Theory. Oxford University Press, Oxford and New York (2005). 0-19-852995-3
56. Brunet, É., Derrida, B.: Genealogies in simple models of evolution. J. Stat. Mech. (2013). P01006. https://doi.org/10.1088/1742-5468/2013/01/p01006
57. Kay, N.-S.: Graphs in sequence spaces: a review of statistical geometry. Biophys. Chem. **66**, 111–131. https://doi.org/10.1016/s0301-4622(97)00064-1. PMID - 9362556
58. Smith, J.M., Szathmary, E.: The Major Transitions in Evolution. Oxford University Press (1997). ISBN 019850294X
59. Bays, C.: Candidates for the game of life in three dimensions. Complex Syst. **1**, 373–400 (1987). ISSN 0891-2513
60. Evans, K.M.: Larger than life: it's so nonlinear. Ph.D. thesis University of Wisconsin, Madison (1996). http://www.csun.edu/~kme52026
61. Rafler, S.: Generalization of Conway's "Game of Life" to a continuous domain - SmoothLife. arXiv:1111.1567 (2011)
62. Kaneko, K.: Overview of coupled map lattices. Chaos: Interdisc. J. Nonlinear Sci. **2**, 279–282 (1992). https://doi.org/10.1063/1.165869

Human-Inspired Socially-Aware Interfaces

Dominik Schiller(iD), Katharina Weitz(iD), Kathrin Janowski(iD),
and Elisabeth André(✉)(iD)

Human Centered Multimedia, Augsburg University, Augsburg, Germany
{schiller,weitz,janowski,andre}@hcm-lab.de

Abstract. Social interactions shape our human life and are inherently emotional. Human conversational partners usually try to interpret – consciously or unconsciously – the speaker's or listener's affective cues and respond to them accordingly. With the objective to contribute to more natural and intuitive ways of communicating with machines, an increasing number of research projects has started to investigate how to simulate similar affective behaviors in socially-interactive agents. In this paper we present an overview of the state of the art in social-interactive agents that expose a socially-aware interface including mechanisms to recognize a user's emotional state, to respond to it appropriately and to continuously learn how to adapt to the needs and preferences of a human user. To this end, we focus on three essential properties of socially-aware interfaces: Social Perception, Socially-Aware Behavior Synthesis, and Learning Socially-Aware Behaviors. We also analyze the limitations of current approaches and discuss directions for future development.

Keywords: Socially-interactive agents · Social signal processing · Affective computing

1 Introduction

Rosa [38] sees an essential aspect for a successful life in a resonant world relationship. By resonance, he understands the reaction of humans towards the world around them. In a world that has been strongly dominated by technology in recent decades, and after the great success of technical systems in industry, economy, and our daily life, these systems have become part of this human environment. Initially, the interaction between humans and machines did not seem very "social", but was characterized by the formal processing of tasks. Nowadays, machines are increasingly being used by non-expert users in domestic environments. Often machines are not just employed as tools, but can take on the role of assistants, consultants or even companions. Consequently, there is a need to design interaction technologies that allow humans and machines to interact with each other as naturally as possible. A prominent attempt to create a socially-interactive learning system that can communicate intuitively with the user is the

© Springer Nature Switzerland AG 2019
C. Martín-Vide et al. (Eds.): TPNC 2019, LNCS 11934, pp. 41–53, 2019.
https://doi.org/10.1007/978-3-030-34500-6_2

Baby-X-Project [25]. In addition to natural interaction, the developers also modeled the underlying mechanisms based on findings in the field of neuroscience. People can interact with the system that embodies a virtual baby as they would interact with a human toddler. One important aspect of human communication takes effect here: Interpersonal communication is inherently emotional. Human conversational partners usually try to interpret – consciously or unconsciously – the speaker's or listener's affective cues and respond to them accordingly. The willingness and ability to empathize with the attitudes and emotions of other people is not only important in interpersonal communication, but should also be considered in the development of socially-interactive agents.

This paper discusses the current state of the art in socially-aware interfaces that dynamically adapt to the affective state of an interlocutor and discusses current limitations and future perspectives of such systems. To this end, we focus on selected capabilities of socially-aware interfaces that fall into the following three categories: (1) Social Perception (2) Socially-Aware Behavior Synthesis and (3) Learning Socially-Aware Behaviors. We conclude this paper by summarizing the presented findings and pointing out potential directions for future developments.

2   Socially-Aware Interfaces

2.1   Social Perception

To incorporate social cues and non-verbal behavior into socially-aware interfaces, robust techniques are required to detect and analyze them. Since humans usually rely on multiple modalities to convey social cues including language, gestures or facial expressions, social cues can be recognized using a large variety of sensory equipment, such as microphones or cameras. Yet the recognition of such social signals is known to be a very hard problem and a real bottleneck on the path to improve human-computer interaction. This section presents a survey of research on automatically sensing and interpreting social signals.

Social Signal Sensing. Recent research in the area of social signal processing has focused on a large variety of modalities to determine the affective state of a user. Such modalities include facial expressions [29], gestures and postures [24], speech [46], and physiological measurements [23]. Since modern human-computer interfaces are often offering voice-based interaction, language is an obvious communication channel to explore. Emotions may be determined from the semantic meaning of utterances as well as the paralinguistic acoustic properties, such as jitter or pitch. Also, the recognition of spontaneous displays of emotion, such as sighs, laughs, or moans, have been examined [47].

In the recent past, significant effort has been made to determine an optimal set of such features for emotional speech recognition. As a result, modern frameworks like EmoVoice [45] or OpenSMILE [15] are able to extract thousands of features for this task. In an attempt to establish a generic baseline feature set that is easy to interpret and generalizes well over a magnitude of different tasks,

Eyben et al. [14] developed the Geneva Minimalistic Acoustic Parameter Set (GeMAPS). Besides manually engineered features, recent improvements in deep learning techniques are now providing the foundation for automatically learning a suitable representation of the data [44]. Wagner et al. [48], who compared hand-crafted acoustic features with automatically learned representations, concluded that hand-crafted features are still beneficial at the moment, but especially with recent improvements in deep learning, automatic feature extraction is gaining more and more importance.

Besides the analysis of paralinguistic features, the semantic content of spoken utterances may be exploited to determine the emotional content of an utterance [34]. Traditionally, affective word dictionaries, such as WordNet-Affect [42], are employed to determine the emotional content of a word. However, to obtain acceptable recognition rates, the linguistic context has to be taken into account. Negations represent a particular challenge. They may reverse the polarity of affect conveyed by an utterance as in "I'm not happy", but they may also serve as an amplifier of affect as in "Never have I been so happy." The examples indicate that hand-crafting rules for sentiment analysis is time-consuming. On the analogy of trends in the paralinguistic analysis of emotions, deep learning methods have been proven a promising approach to automatically learn linguistic representations for sentiment analysis [50]. To improve the results of emotion classifiers, the integration of data from multiple sources [27] has been researched. The fusion of multiple modalities usually leads to an improvement of classification reliability compared to a single modality. Though, fusion approaches typically achieve higher gains for acted than for spontaneous behavior [11].

Social Signal Understanding. As other areas, social signal sensing benefits from advances in deep neural networks learning. While the robustness of social signal sensing has improved, the use of visualization techniques to enhance the transparency of neural networks revealed that neural networks do not always focus on relevant input components to come up with an interpretation. For example, Weitz et al. [49] analyzed how a deep neural network distinguishes facial expressions of pain and emotions and observed that the deep neural network did not exclusively direct its attention to the face, but also on the (in this case expressionless) background of an image. Even though implausible behavior may lead to correct results, users may loose trust in a system if they find out that the system just attempts to convey the illusion of an understanding system.

To interpret social cues, it is important to equip a system with the ability to understand a user's behavior within the context of an interaction. For example, to determine whether an interaction is enjoyable or not, it does not suffice to look at the laughs of each individual separately. Rather, the temporal dynamics of the laughs within a dialogue has to be considered. In order to take account of the interplay of social cues, Baur et al. [4] developed a probabilistic framework that does not only explicitly model the interlocutors' social cues, but also how they depend on each other.

Furthermore, the interpretation of social cues depends on the situative context in which they occur. For example, a laugh is not always an indicator of joy, but may also allude to negative emotions, such as embarrassment. To interpret such social cues correctly, the situative context has to be taken into account. This task is a great challenge since it requires not only analyzing, but also reasoning about the interlocutor's situation. As a first step to deal with this task, Gebhard et al. [17] combined a framework for detecting multimodal social cues with a cognitive model of affect (see also Sect. 2.3). The basic idea of the framework is to relate expected emotional appraisal and regulation behaviors to observed social cues.

Overall, it may be said, however, that most approaches to social signal sensing focus on observable indicators of affect as opposed to aiming at deeper understanding of the user's psychological states.

2.2 Socially-Aware Behavior Synthesis

Rosa [38] describes the relationship to the world as fundamentally meaningful for humans, where the intertwining of human beings with their surroundings can be understood as constant mutual interaction. Therefore the environment affects human behavior, just as humans influence the world through their actions. While we have already addressed approaches for social signal perception in the previous section, we will now discuss how an agent should respond to such social signals to demonstrate that it is aware of the user.

Socially-Aware Navigation. Socially-aware behaviors include adequate navigation behaviors that follow proxemics conventions, such as maintaining a comfortable distance to nearby people.

Agents that are capable of moving freely in their environment may approximate human proxemic behavior by acting spatially, which in return unlocks a large variety of new possible (interaction) behaviors. Besides maintaining an appropriate distance to the interlocutor, agents may use their body orientation and gaze behavior (e.g., [5,35]). Proxemics is also expressed by conversational behaviors, such as choosing an appropriate topic in small talk that does not appear intrusive to the interlocutor [12].

Typically, the implementation of proxemics behaviors is inspired by studies with human users that interact with a robot in physical environment (see, e.g., [13,43]) or are placed with a synthetic agent in a virtual environment [36]. A particular challenge is to learn appropriate proxemics behaviors in real-time. An example includes the work by Mitsunaga et al. [31] who used comfort and discomfort as input for the reward function, which they calculated based on gaze duration and body movements.

Turn Management. Being able to understand and convey each other's turn-taking intentions is an important prerequisite for fluent, natural dialogue. In particular, people involved in a conversation monitor the other person's gaze direction to infer who or what has their attention at any given moment. This belief about their attentional state plays a major part in the constant negotiation of speaker and listener roles. Looking at an interaction partner is believed to signal that the communication channel is open and one is ready to receive information from the said partner, which is why human speakers establish eye contact when they want to elicit backchannel feedback or a full response from the listener [3]. Conversely, averted gaze is seen as a signal for the opposite, for example, when the speaker wants to take the turn, but is still planning what to say [3].

Bohus and Horvitz [7] used the gaze direction of human quiz players to determine whether a player was yielding the conversational floor to one of their team members or the virtual quiz master agent. Likewise, they directed the agent's gaze towards a certain player whenever the agent expected that player to start speaking, but had the agent avert its gaze while it was waiting for processing results to prevent the humans from taking the turn. Similar gaze aversion signals were applied to social robot behavior by Andrist et al. [2], causing the users to wait more patiently when the robot appeared to be busy thinking. Skantze et al. [41] observed similar effects when a robot was using turn hold signals, such as gaze aversion or filler sounds. They also observed that humans turned their gaze towards the robot when they were waiting for the next piece of information. From these observations, the authors concluded that detecting and correctly interpreting the corresponding behavioral cues from the human would allow social robots to time their responses more appropriately.

Interruptions. What timing is appropriate depends on more factors than the belief about the interaction partner's intentions. Deliberately ignoring or being overly sensitive to said intentions can send additional messages about the interaction context, the personality of a participant or their attitude towards the interlocutor. Studies with virtual agents have shown that interrupting and interruption handling behavior associated with specific human personality traits and attitudes also lead human observers to attribute similar characteristics to artificial beings. For instance, ter Maat et al. [28] found that agents who started to speak before the end of another agent's turn were perceived as less agreeable, whereas those who waited for a few seconds appeared less extraverted. Yielding the turn as soon as an overlap was detected led to lower dominance ratings than continuing. Gebhard et al. [19] later varied the interruption response timing for a virtual agent in an interactive dialogue system. Their study confirmed that the agent was perceived as more dominant when it continued talking for a longer time after the user had tried to interrupt it. The opposite was observed for the perceived closeness between user and agent, and the agent was also rated as more friendly when the overlap was minimal.

Turn-taking behavior is shaped by the arbitration between different, possibly conflicting interaction goals, such as being polite while also being assertive. Janowski and André [21] proposed a decision-theoretic model based on psychological theories about how a person's personality, interpersonal stance and different interaction goals relate to each other. One major objective of this research is to mimic human reasoning about timing one's dialogue contributions. This way, the behavior of social agents is intended to become more transparent to interaction designers and end users, as the causal relationships represented in the model can be used to explain the agent's decision. Furthermore, the same causal relationships can be used to interpret a human's surface behavior in terms of their intentions which, as stated above, the agent needs to understand in order to adapt its behavior. Evaluation results showed that the model could be used to generate interrupting and interruption handling behavior patterns in line with psychological literature and related works.

2.3 Modeling and Simulating Empathy

Various attempts have been made to implement empathic behaviors in computer-based dialogue systems. The simplest form of empathy, *Ideomotoric Empathy*, consists of imitating the emotional cues of the dialogue partner. Mirroring the users' expression is possible without understanding their emotional states. For example, if a user is distressed because he or she was not able to solve a task in a tutoring system, an artificial agent would simply imitate the user's facial expression without knowing why the user is distressed.

This is one of the behaviors realized by Bee et al. [6] with the attentive listener agent Alfred. They used EmoVoice [45] to detect emotional cues in the speaker's voice, from which they calculated the user's current mood tendency via the ALMA model of affect [16]. This mood was then reflected in the agent's facial expression. Another example has been realized by Janowski et al. [22] using the humanoid robot Zeno, developed by Hanson Robotics. The tone of voice as well as the user's facial expression are analyzed to infer the user's emotional state. Zeno then shows the recognized emotion in his face. The semantic content of the user's speech is not taken into account in either of these examples.

Higher forms of empathy can be generally divided into two concepts: *Cognitive* and *Affective Empathy*. While cognitive empathy refers to the ability to understand another person's perspective, affective empathy means the capacity to respond with an appropriate reaction to another's mental state.

Many approaches to simulate emotional processes are based on rules that are inspired by theories from the cognitive sciences. A popular theory is the OCC model by Ortony et al. [33] that includes detailed rules to explain the elicitation of 20 common emotions. On the basis of this model, several computer programs were developed that simulate emotional processes.

An example includes the work by Bee et al. [6] who implemented affective empathy for the virtual Alfred agent by appraising the emotional state inferred from the user's tone of voice. Based on the OCC model [33], the agent perceived negative emotions as "bad event for good other" and positive emotions as "good event for good other". Consequently, observing the user's state elicited the emotions "SorryFor" respectively "HappyFor" in the agent's own affect model, which would then be mapped to facial animations for the Alfred character.

Boukricha et al. [8] presented a computer model for affective empathy that considers the relationship between the single interlocutors when determining an agent's response to the emotional state of others. Their approach is illustrated by a scenario in which empathic behaviors for the agent Emma are automatically generated as a reaction to conversations between the agent Max and the agent Lisa. For example, Emma would get irritated based on her current mood and her relationship to Max if Lisa should offend Max.

2.4   Learning Socially-Aware Behaviors

In the previous section, we described analytic approaches to simulate socially-aware behaviors based on theories from the cognitive sciences. The question arises of to what extent it is possible to learn sensitive behaviors from recordings of human-human interactions or from life interactions with human interlocutors.

McQuiggan and Lester [30] followed an empirical approach and collected data of empathic interactions between two agents in a virtual environment that were controlled by human trainers. One trainer had to accomplish specific tasks while the other trainer had to observe the behavior and to select appropriate empathic behaviors. Based on these recordings, a computer model for empathic behaviors was created using methods from machine learning (Naïve Bayes and decision trees). The model was tested by having human users interact with virtual agents whose empathic behaviors were based on the learnt model. The study revealed that the human users found the empathic behaviors of the virtual agents appropriate.

While McQuiggan and Lester [30] learnt empathic behaviors from previously recorded computer-mediated interactions between humans, Leite [26] presented an approach to adjust empathic strategies of a robotic cat during the interaction with a child based on Reinforcement Learning (RL). The approach makes use of a reward function that takes into account how the emotional state of a user changes after the application of an empathic strategy. As time progresses, the system learns which strategies have proven promising. Using a sophisticated selection mechanism, the system ensures that successful strategies are selected with greater probability while enabling flexible adaptation to a new situation. For example, the child might require more help when the degree of difficulty of the chess game increases such that the robot needs to adjust in that case. An evaluation showed that the robot managed to keep children interested over a longer period of time, which the authors ascribe to its empathic behavior.

Ritschel et al. [37] presented an RL approach that adapts the linguistic style of a robot based on subliminal feedback provided by a human user: affective signals. RL is used for continuously learning the desired profile over time instead of asking the user explicitly, sticking to a fixed personality. The reward signal required for RL comes directly from the user's level of engagement, which is estimated based on multimodal affective cues. The system's ability to adapt its dialogue style was evaluated using simulation results and an interactive prototype. While an interactive prototype provides more realistic results, a significant amount of effort is required from the human user to provide the system with useful data. Lifelong reinforcement learning [40] represents a promising approach to enable a system to gradually learn appropriate social behaviors over its lifetime by treating novel situations as new tasks in the learning process.

2.5   Socially-Aware Conversational Systems

One form of human-technology interaction that benefits strongly from the integration of the previously presented techniques is natural-language dialogue with embodied conversational agents (see [1,20]). In the following, we will present representative research projects that are focusing on equipping such agents with socially-aware sensing capabilities to dynamically tailor their conversational behaviors to the affective state of a user.

Since listening is an important component to impart appreciation in dialogues, SEMAINE [39] has focused on the implementation of such a behavior. The empathic listeners in the SEMAINE project were characterized by agents with different personality profiles. These agents were able to conduct a conversation with a person and to recognize and respond to a human user's non-verbal behaviors in real-time. The goal of SEMAINE was to create a natural conversational dialogue with the focus on the non-verbal behavior of the human counterpart. To this end, the agent had to be able to produce natural and human-like listener behavior without addressing the challenges of speech recognition and deep natural language understanding.

Cavazza et al. [9] integrated the user's affective state in the dialogue management of an agent to improve the robustness of their speech recognition system. To this end, they inferred the emotion of a user by analyzing the paralinguistic aspects of spoken utterances as well as inferring the general sentiment from the transcription of the spoken statement. If the users employed words to express their emotional state that are unknown to the system, the system would still be able to recognize their emotions from the acoustics of speech. Furthermore, the results of this analysis were used to generate an immediate empathic response when the user stopped speaking.

Morency et al. [32] developed a virtual agent that interacts in a clinical setting with a patient to assess multimodal behaviors related to post-traumatic stress disorder and stress. The automatically analyzed cues by the patient are used for diagnostic purposes and for controlling the dialogue between the agent and the patient. For example, the agent motivates patients who took a lot of pauses to keep talking.

Gebhard et al. [18] implemented a virtual agent called EmmA running on the users' mobile phone and helping them cope with stress at work. The agent analyzes the users' psychological state based on behavioral data obtained from mobile sensors and a simulation of emotion regulation strategies [17] in order to select appropriate verbal intervention strategies if the stress level is at a critical stage.

Damian et al. [10] focused also on negative emotions, such as stress and nervousness, but in a different setting. They developed a game-like environment for job interview training. In this safe environment, trainees could experiment with different conversational strategies during a job interview with a virtual agent. During the job interview, the verbal and non-verbal signals of the trainee were recorded and analyzed to evaluate the trainee's multimodal behaviors and to regulate the flow of the dialogue.

3   Discussion and Conclusion

In this paper, we presented an overview of current state of the art research towards developing fully socially-aware interfaces. To this end, we identified three essential capabilities of socially-aware interfaces: Social Perception, Socially-Aware Behavior Synthesis and Learning Socially-Aware Behaviors.

A closer look at existing research reveals a clear timeline of progression. Initially, socially-aware interfaces made use of handcrafted features to infer a user's emotional state based on the input of the available sensory equipment, and interactions relied on scripted processes to simulate emotional behavior. Modern approaches are now working towards automatically learned representations of the input data in order to improve recognition results of social signal sensing. Other approaches are even going beyond plain recognition by modeling the dynamics of interpersonal social cues within the situative and conversational context of their occurrence. Such social sensing capacities are often used by the underlying systems to imitate human social behavior during interactions. This way modern agents are capable of displaying human-like interaction behavior, such as mirroring a user's emotion or deciding when to take a turn during a dialog. Finally, attempts are being made to continuously learn appropriate social behaviors from interactions with human users following the paradigm of lifelong learning.

While research endeavors have become increasingly more sophisticated and complex, one key question remains when it comes to determining the direction of future development: Are we creating systems that show true understanding of human social interactions and behaviors, or are we creating systems that pretend to do so by simulating social awareness at a surface level?

While a complete answer to this question is not within the scope of this paper, we argue that current state-of-the-art approaches are focusing rather on the simulation of behaviors as opposed to true understanding. In order to develop systems that are capable of executing not only scripted or isolated individual tasks, but also taking a step towards sensitive behaviors reflecting true understanding, we need to go beyond the pure analysis of observable social cues towards deeper reasoning processes that analyze the context in which they appear.

Acknowledgments. This work has been partially funded by the Bundesministerium für Bildung und Forschung (BMBF) within the project VIVA, Grant Number 16SV7960.

References

1. André, E., Pelachaud, C.: Interacting with embodied conversational agents. In: Chen, F., Jokinen, K. (eds.) Speech Technology, pp. 123–149. Springer, Boston (2010). https://doi.org/10.1007/978-0-387-73819-2_8
2. Andrist, S., Tan, X.Z., Gleicher, M., Mutlu, B.: Conversational gaze aversion for humanlike robots. In: ACM/IEEE International Conference on Human-Robot Interaction, (HRI), Bielefeld, Germany, pp. 25–32 (2014)
3. Argyle, M., Cook, M.: Gaze and Mutual Gaze. Cambridge University Press, Cambridge (1976)
4. Baur, T., Schiller, D., André, E.: Modeling user's social attitude in a conversational system. In: Tkalčič, M., De De Carolis, B., de Gemmis, M., Odić, A., Košir, A. (eds.) Emotions and Personality in Personalized Services. HIS, pp. 181–199. Springer, Cham (2016). https://doi.org/10.1007/978-3-319-31413-6_10
5. Bee, N., André, E., Tober, S.: Breaking the ice in human-agent communication: eye-gaze based initiation of contact with an embodied conversational agent. In: Ruttkay, Z., Kipp, M., Nijholt, A., Vilhjálmsson, H.H. (eds.) IVA 2009. LNCS (LNAI), vol. 5773, pp. 229–242. Springer, Heidelberg (2009). https://doi.org/10.1007/978-3-642-04380-2_26
6. Bee, N., André, E., Vogt, T., Gebhard, P.: The use of affective and attentive cues in an empathic computer-based companion. In: Wilks, Y. (ed.) Natural Language Processing, vol. 8, pp. 131–142. John Benjamins Publishing Company (2010)
7. Bohus, D., Horvitz, E.: Facilitating multiparty dialog with gaze, gesture, and speech. In: International ACM Conference on Multimodal Interfaces and the Workshop on Machine Learning for Multimodal Interaction (ICML-MLMI), Beijing, China, pp. 5:1–5:8 (2010)
8. Boukricha, H., Wachsmuth, I., Carminati, M.N., Knoeferle, P.: A computational model of empathy: empirical evaluation. In: 2013 Humaine Association Conference on Affective Computing and Intelligent Interaction, (ACII), Geneva, Switzerland, pp. 1–6. IEEE (2013)
9. Cavazza, M., de la Camara, R.S., Turunen, M.: How was your day?: a companion ECA. In: 9th International Conference on Autonomous Agents and Multiagent Systems, (AAMAS), Toronto, Canada, vol. 1, pp. 1629–1630, Richland (2010)
10. Damian, I., Baur, T., Lugrin, B., Gebhard, P., Mehlmann, G., André, E.: Games are better than books: in-situ comparison of an interactive job interview game with conventional training. In: Conati, C., Heffernan, N., Mitrovic, A., Verdejo, M.F. (eds.) AIED 2015. LNCS (LNAI), vol. 9112, pp. 84–94. Springer, Cham (2015). https://doi.org/10.1007/978-3-319-19773-9_9
11. D'Mello, S., Kory, J.: Consistent but modest: a meta-analysis on unimodal and multimodal affect detection accuracies from 30 studies. In: 14th ACM International Conference on Multimodal Interaction (ICMI), Santa Monica, CA, USA, pp. 31–38. ACM (2012)
12. Endrass, B., Rehm, M., André, E.: Planning small talk behavior with cultural influences for multiagent systems. Comput. Speech Lang. 25(2), 158–174 (2011)
13. Eresha, G., Häring, M., Endrass, B., André, E., Obaid, M.: Investigating the influence of culture on proxemic behaviors for humanoid robots. In: 2013 IEEE International Symposium on Robot and Human Interactive Communication, (RO-MAN), Gyeongju, South Korea, pp. 430–435 (2013)
14. Eyben, F., et al.: The Geneva minimalistic acoustic parameter set (GeMAPS) for voice research and affective computing. IEEE Trans. Affect. Comput. 7(2), 190–202 (2015)

15. Eyben, F., Weninger, F., Gross, F., Schuller, B.: Recent developments in open SMILE, the Munich open-source multimedia feature extractor. In: ACM Multimedia, Firenze, Italy, pp. 835–838 (2013)
16. Gebhard, P.: ALMA: a layered model of affect. In: 4th International Joint Conference on Autonomous Agents and Multiagent Systems (AAMAS), pp. 29–36 (2005)
17. Gebhard, P., Schneeberger, T., Baur, T., André, E.: MARSSI: model of appraisal, regulation, and social signal interpretation. In: 17th International Conference on Autonomous Agents and MultiAgent Systems (AAMAS), Stockholm, Sweden, pp. 497–506 (2018)
18. Gebhard, P., Schneeberger, T., Dietz, M., André, E., ul Habib Bajwa, N.: Designing a mobile social and vocational reintegration assistant for burn-out outpatient treatment. In: 19th ACM International Conference on Intelligent Virtual Agents (IVA), Paris, France, pp. 13–15 (2019)
19. Gebhard, P., Schneeberger, T., Mehlmann, G., Baur, T., André, E.: Designing the impression of social agents' real-time interruption handling. In: 19th ACM International Conference on Intelligent Virtual Agents (IVA), Paris, France, pp. 19–21 (2019)
20. Gratch, J., Rickel, J., André, E., Cassell, J., Petajan, E., Badler, N.I.: Creating interactive virtual humans: some assembly required. IEEE Intell. Syst. **17**(4), 54–63 (2002)
21. Janowski, K., André, E.: What if I speak now?: a decision-theoreticapproach to personality-based turn-taking. In: 18th International Conference on Autonomous Agents and MultiAgent Systems, (AAMAS), pp. 1051–1059, Richland (2019)
22. Janowski, K., Ritschel, H., Birgit, L., André, E.: Sozial interagierende Roboter in der Pflege. In: Bendel, O. (ed.) Pflegeroboter, pp. 63–87. Springer, Wiesbaden (2018). https://doi.org/10.1007/978-3-658-22698-5_4
23. Kim, J., André, E.: Emotion recognition based on physiological changes in music listening. IEEE Trans. Pattern Anal. Mach. Intell. **30**(12), 2067–2083 (2008)
24. Kleinsmith, A., Bianchi-Berthouze, N.: Affective body expression perception and recognition: a survey. IEEE Trans. Affect. Comput. **4**(1), 15–33 (2012)
25. Lawler-Dormer, D.: Baby X: digital artificial intelligence, computational neuroscience and empathetic interaction. In: ISEA 2013 Conference Proceedings, ISEA International (2013)
26. Leite, I., Pereira, A., Mascarenhas, S., Martinho, C., Prada, R., Paiva, A.: The influence of empathy in human-robot relations. Int. J. Hum Comput Stud. **71**(3), 250–260 (2013)
27. Lingenfelser, F., Wagner, J., Deng, J., Brueckner, R., Schuller, B., André, E.: Asynchronous and event-based fusion systems for affect recognition on naturalistic data in comparison to conventional approaches. IEEE Trans. Affect. Comput. **9**(4), 410–423 (2016)
28. ter Maat, M., Truong, K.P., Heylen, D.K.J.: How agents' turn-taking strategies influence impressions and response behaviors. Presence: Teleoperators Virtual Environ. **20**(5), 412–430 (2011)
29. Martínez, B., Valstar, M.F., Jiang, B., Pantic, M.: Automatic analysis of facial actions: a survey. IEEE Trans. Affect. Comput. **10**(3), 325–347 (2019)
30. McQuiggan, S.W., Lester, J.C.: Modeling and evaluating empathy in embodied companion agents. Int. J. Hum Comput Stud. **65**(4), 348–360 (2007)
31. Mitsunaga, N., Smith, C., Kanda, T., Ishiguro, H., Hagita, N.: Adapting robot behavior for human-robot interaction. IEEE Trans. Robot. **24**(4), 911–916 (2008)

32. Morency, L.P., et al.: SimSensei demonstration: a perceptive virtual human interviewer for healthcare applications. In: Twenty-Ninth AAAI Conference on Artificial Intelligence (2015)
33. Ortony, A., Clore, G.L., Collins, A.: The Cognitive Structure of Emotions. Cambridge University Press, Cambridge (1988)
34. Osherenko, A., André, E.: Lexical affect sensing: are affect dictionaries necessary to analyze affect? In: Paiva, A.C.R., Prada, R., Picard, R.W. (eds.) ACII 2007. LNCS, vol. 4738, pp. 230–241. Springer, Heidelberg (2007). https://doi.org/10.1007/978-3-540-74889-2_21
35. Peters, C., Asteriadis, S., Karpouzis, K.: Investigating shared attention with a virtual agent using a gaze-based interface. J. Multimodal User Interfaces 3(1–2), 119–130 (2010)
36. Petrak, B., Weitz, K., Aslan, I., André, E.: Let me show you your new home: studying the effect of proxemic-awareness of robots on users' first impressions. In: 28th IEEE International Conference on Robot and Human Interactive Communication (RO-MAN), New Delhi, India. IEEE (2019)
37. Ritschel, H., Baur, T., André, E.: Adapting a robot's linguistic style based on socially-aware reinforcement learning. In: 26th IEEE International Symposium on Robot and Human Interactive Communication (RO-MAN), Lisbon, Portugal, pp. 378–384. IEEE (2017)
38. Rosa, H.: Resonanz: Eine Soziologie der Weltbeziehung. Suhrkamp Verlag (2016)
39. Schröder, M., et al.: Building autonomous sensitive artificial listeners. IEEE Trans. Affect. Comput. 3(2), 165–183 (2012)
40. Silver, D.L., Yang, Q., Li, L.: Lifelong machine learning systems: beyond learning algorithms. In: Lifelong Machine Learning, Papers from the 2013 AAAI Spring Symposium, Palo Alto, California, USA, 25–27 March 2013 (2013)
41. Skantze, G., Hjalmarsson, A., Oertel, C.: Turn-taking, feedback and joint attention in situated human-robot interaction. Speech Commun. 65, 50–66 (2014)
42. Strapparava, C., Valitutti, A., et al.: Wordnet affect: an affective extension of wordnet. In: 4th International Conference on Language Resources and Evaluation, LREC, Lisbon, Portugal, pp. 1083–1086 (2004)
43. Takayama, L., Pantofaru, C.: Influences on proxemic behaviors in human-robot interaction. In: 2009 IEEE/RSJ International Conference on Intelligent Robots and Systems, IROS, St. Louis, MO, USA, pp. 5495–5502 (2009)
44. Trigeorgis, G., et al.: Adieu features? end-to-end speech emotion recognition using a deep convolutional recurrent network. In: 2016 IEEE International Conference on Acoustics, Speech and Signal Processing (ICASSP), Shanghai, China, pp. 5200–5204 (2016)
45. Vogt, T., André, E., Bee, N.: EmoVoice — a framework for online recognition of emotions from voice. In: André, E., Dybkjær, L., Minker, W., Neumann, H., Pieraccini, R., Weber, M. (eds.) PIT 2008. LNCS (LNAI), vol. 5078, pp. 188–199. Springer, Heidelberg (2008). https://doi.org/10.1007/978-3-540-69369-7_21
46. Vogt, T., André, E., Wagner, J.: Automatic recognition of emotions from speech: a review of the literature and recommendations for practical realisation. In: Peter, C., Beale, R. (eds.) Affect and Emotion in Human-Computer Interaction. LNCS, vol. 4868, pp. 75–91. Springer, Heidelberg (2008). https://doi.org/10.1007/978-3-540-85099-1_7
47. Wagner, J., Lingenfelser, F., André, E.: Using phonetic patterns for detecting social cues in natural conversations. In: Interspeech, Stockholm, pp. 168–172 (2013)

48. Wagner, J., Schiller, D., Seiderer, A., André, E.: Deep learning in paralinguistic recognition tasks: are hand-crafted features still relevant? In: Interspeech, Hyderabad, India, pp. 147–151 (2018)
49. Weitz, K., Hassan, T., Schmid, U., Garbas, J.U.: Deep-learned faces of pain and emotions: elucidating the differences of facial expressions with the help of explainable AI methods. tm-Technisches Messen **86**(7–8), 404–412 (2019)
50. Zhang, L., Wang, S., Liu, B.: Deep learning for sentiment analysis: a survey. Wiley Interdisc. Rev.: Data Min. Knowl. Disc. **8**(4), e1253 (2018)

Applications of Natural Computing

Stochastic Mechanisms of Growth and Branching in Mediterranean Coral Colonies

Ozan Kahramanoğulları[1]([envelope])([ORCID]), Lorenzo Bramanti[2]([ORCID]),
and Maria Carla Benedetti[2,3]([ORCID])

[1] Department of Mathematics, University of Trento, Trento, Italy
[2] Laboratoire d'Ecogéochimie des Environnements Benthiques, LECOB,
Observatoire Océanologique de Banyuls sur Mer, CNRS-Sorbonne Université,
Banyuls-sur-Mer, France
[3] Department of Biology, University of Pisa, Pisa, Italy
http://ozan-k.com

Abstract. *Corallium rubrum* is an octocoral species, endemic to Mediterranean and neighbouring marine habitats and plays a foundational role in these ecosystems. Due to extensive harvesting and increase in water temperature, this long-lived and slow-growing species is now endangered, and hence it is in the focus of conservation efforts. However, little is known about the mechanisms that govern growth and branching of their colony structures. To this end, we present a simple stochastic model that consists of three rules and accurately captures the phenotypic variability of the structures observed in the field. We show that the variations in structures due to the changes in model parameters are representative of the differences in environmental factors that affect the colony development. Repeated simulations on our model with varying parameters suggest that branching and growth are conflicting processes for the colony that may be prioritised in accordance with the environmental conditions. Our analysis provides an overview of how such stochastic models can provide insights into the structure and development of modular organisms.

Keywords: *Corallium Rubrum* · Systems biology · Rule-based models

1 Introduction

One of the fundamental questions in biology is concerned with the mechanisms that govern phenotype as a result of the interplay between the genetic material and the physical environment of the organisms. For the organisms that are characterised by bilateral symmetry, the morphology is mainly the product of the detailed encoding in the genome. However, in others, the environment can strongly influence the developmental process. In particular, in the growth of

© Springer Nature Switzerland AG 2019
C. Martín-Vide et al. (Eds.): TPNC 2019, LNCS 11934, pp. 57–69, 2019.
https://doi.org/10.1007/978-3-030-34500-6_3

marine sessile organisms such as seaweeds, sponges, and corals, there is a strong impact of the physical environment on the growth process, leading to a variety of structural forms [10].

The red coral *Corallium rubrum* is a gorgonian, endemic to the Mediterranean and adjacent Atlantic rocky bottoms, which can be found between 10 and 800 m depth. This slow-growing species has a life span that can exceed 100 years. The skeleton of branching colonies is composed of calcium carbonate deposited by the polyps. The colonies exhibit wide variability in growth forms, which are linked to local environmental conditions [1,3,7,8,16]. Its vibrant red color and the workability of its texture qualify the Mediterranean red coral as a marine species of high economic value due to its use as raw material for jewellery over the last two thousand years. Thus, the species has been extensively harvested, more so at depths up to 50 m, but also at depths reaching 150 m and deeper with the increasing economic accessibility of deep SCUBA technologies. As a consequence, this species, which has an important role in the three-dimensional structuring of coralligenous assemblages, is at risk of local extirpation in the coastal Mediterranean. Despite many conservation projects that focus on *Corallium rubrum*, little is known about the modular growth mechanisms of its colonies [1]. In particular, theoretical models, which can be used for restoration and guide conservation policies, are lacking.

We present a simple computational model of red coral colonies. Following the observations made on field data [1,3,7,8,16], our model, consisting of three rules, describes the growth and branching dynamics in Mediterranean coral colonies. This is done by adopting the notion that the growth process can be described as calcium carbonate deposition [10]. Similarly, branching structures are described as the deposition of calcium carbonate fork layers on top of the previously deposited layers. Consequently, we characterise the coral colonies as modular structures that are built from repeated units. As a result of this, and with the inclusion of stochasticity, the same processes, driven by the three rules of our model, result in an infinite number of different realisations of colony structures.

The compact representation of our model captures the structural properties of the species. However, growth and form in these sessile organisms are closely linked with the conditions of the physical environment [1,3,7,8,16]. This is because genetically identical colonies could show phenotypic variation under different conditions such as depth, prevalent currents, local available light intensities, and ease of accessibility for harvesting. These, in return, as well as their epigenetic consequences, such as polyp density on the colony, can influence the growth processes as they affect the intake and transport of food particles through diffusion and hydrodynamics, and vulnerability due to the availability of shelter. For example, the shallow populations that live between 10 and 50 m depth, have been long over-harvested, and they are mainly characterised by dense patches of small-size colonies. In our model, we use the stochastic rates of the model rules as abstractions of such environmental factors that determine the differentiation between different colonies in the same geographical location.

For the description of the model we use a rule-based language that extends
the languages such as BNG and Kappa [2,6] with species attributes. The implementation of the model for simulation is done by mapping the model rules to
the stochastic Pi-calculus, that is, SPiM [4,12,13,15]. In our model, the species
attributes become useful as they make it possible to modify various parametric
aspects of the model species. In particular, we use these attributes to describe
the geometry of the species that evolves throughout the simulation by encoding
the local modifications due to each rule instance. This allows us to display the
simulations as time-lapse visualisations to observe the spatial dynamics of the
emerging structures besides the common simulation outputs as time series[1].

2   The Model

We have previously defined a formal language, called M [11], which is a conser-
vative extension of rule based languages BNG and Kappa. Thus, the rules of
M extend the common chemical reaction notation used in systems biology with
constructs that involve complexation events. In addition, the language M allows
us to define attributes that are modified by the rule instances. For example,
let us consider the binding of a species P on its site p with a species Q on its
site q with rate λ. Let us further assume that the species Q is equipped with
a parameter n that is incremented as a result of this binding. Such a dynamics
can be modelled by a rule of the following form.

$$P(p) + Q(q, n) \xrightarrow{\lambda} P(p!1).Q(q!1, n + 1)$$

Here, the right-hand side of the rule describes the interaction of the species
P and Q. The dot '.' on the right-hand side denotes the complex formed by these
two species. The expressions $p!1$ and $q!1$ denote a unique bond, i.e., 1, between
P and Q at their sites p and q. The parameter n of Q becomes incremented on
the right-hand side as a result of the complexation, which is denoted by $n + 1$.

The semantics of the model is given by the continuous time Markov chain
(CTMC) interpretation of chemical reaction networks, implemented by the Gillespie algorithm [9]. This is done by generating the chemical reactions from the
rules at every state when they become applicable. This way, a model, that would
potentially require an infinite number of reactions, can be simulated with a finite
set of rules. Models that involve unbounded polymerization-like growth as in our
model are examples to such systems [4,5]. The SPiM language that we use for
simulating the model is equipped with a stochastic simulation engine that implements the Gillespie algorithm [9]. The simulation output consists of a trace of
rule instances with time stamps and the common time-series in csv format.

---

[1] A representative video can be found online at https://youtu.be/FAH1DgqUO8w.

2.1 Model Description

The model is given by a set of rules that describe the growth and branching dynamics of a colony, built up from discrete structural units. We distinguish the units that are at the extremities of the colony, denoted by Cx, from those that are in between, denoted by Cb. Each such unit models the calcium carbonate deposit that hosts polyps. The growth of the colony structure is then given by the addition of a unit to an extremity with an initial mass m_0.

$$\mathsf{Cx}(\boldsymbol{p}, \boldsymbol{v}, m, t) \xrightarrow{\alpha} \mathsf{Cb}(\boldsymbol{p}, m, t!1).\mathsf{Cx}(\boldsymbol{p} + \boldsymbol{v}, \boldsymbol{v}, m_0, b!1)$$

Each unit is equipped with a set of parameters that contain the position coordinates $\boldsymbol{p}$ of that unit, the growth direction vector $\boldsymbol{v}$, and its mass m. The growth rate α describes the speed of the growth. The expressions $t!1$ and $b!1$ denote a unique bond, i.e., 1, between Cb and Cx at their sites t and b. The sites and their states that are not distinguished by this rule are left implicit. For example, the site b of Cx on the left-hand side of the rule is left implicit since the rule does not distinguish the cases where this site is bound or unbound.

The accumulation of a constant mass, d, of calcium carbonate in each unit is given by a rule of the following form, whereby β is the accumulation rate.

$$\mathsf{Cb}(\boldsymbol{p}, m) \xrightarrow{\beta} \mathsf{Cb}(\boldsymbol{p}, d + m)$$

The branching is modelled by the addition of a fork unit, denoted by F, to an extremity of the colony with the branching rate γ.

$$\mathsf{Cx}(\boldsymbol{p}, \boldsymbol{v}, m, b!1) \xrightarrow{\gamma} \mathsf{F}(b!1, tp!2, tq!3).\mathsf{Cx}(\boldsymbol{p}, R(\theta).\boldsymbol{v}, m, b!2).\mathsf{Cx}(\boldsymbol{p}, R(-\theta).\boldsymbol{v}, m, b!3)$$

Here $R(\theta)$ denotes the rotation matrix for θ, which is required for rendering purposes. Thus, the parameter θ does not affect the simulation dynamics. In all the simulations depicted throughout the paper, we assume a rotation of $\theta = 30°$ on the $x = 0$ plane in the direction of the colony growth.

For the rendering, we use the simulation trace consisting of rule instances together with their time stamps. At each time step, we render the Cb units in the product of each rule instance in the three-dimensional coordinate system in proportion to the mass attribute of that unit. This is done by rendering a mass of m as a circle with the radius $\sqrt[3]{m}$ by resorting to the assumption that mass grows proportional to the cube of the radius. This way, we obtain time-lapse visualisations that display the growth of the three-dimensional structure.

3   Results

The colonies of Mediterranean coral *Corallium rubrum* have a life span that can exceed 100 years, whereby the shallow populations, between 10 and 50 m depth, have been reported to reach a maximum life span of about 40 to 60 years, depending on the region [3]. The shallow coral colonies that are reported in [3] have an average annual growth rate of 0.24 mm/*year* in diameter with a standard error of 0.06 mm. By relying on this, we have modelled 1 mm as 0.1 coordinate units, and adopted a growth rate $\alpha = 1\ year^{-1}$ with a growth vector of $(0, 0, 0.024)$. For the calcium carbonate accumulation, we have assumed a value of $m_0 = d = 1a.u.$, and instantiated the simulations with the corresponding seed, i.e., $Cx((0.5, 0.5, 0), (0, 0, 0.024), 1, b!0, t)$.

We have analysed colony development in relation to the variations in the parameters α, β and γ. The sample of 653 colonies in [3] reports on populations with balanced sex ratios and similar fertility and polyp fecundity. Therefore, we have assumed little or no genetic variation between the individuals of the same population, and used the model parameters as proxies for environmental factors such as depth, prevalent currents, colony density and ease of accessibility for harvesting as well as their epigenetic consequences. As a result of this, each simulation displays how the structural properties of the colonies are expressed as a function of their environmental factors as well as stochasticity.

In a set of individual simulations, we have first observed the changes in structure due to the changes in model parameters. In this setting, each rate α, β and γ quantifies the mean accumulation of an additional calcium carbonate layer per year. We have selected a spectrum for these parameters by ruling out the ones that result in structures not observed in nature. We have thus scanned the parameter values that result in a stem diameter different from the one at the tips after 20 years of age. With this consideration, we have taken $1.0\ year^{-1}$ as the centre of the parameter spectrum. The parameter values around this centre provided a calibration of the model that captures the significant negative correlation between the mean annual growth rate of the colonies and their age [3]. We have thus scanned the growth rate α within the range of $0.6\ year^{-1}$ to $1.4\ year^{-1}$, the calcium carbonate accumulation rate β within $0.1\ year^{-1}$ to $5.0\ year^{-1}$, and the branching rate γ within $0.025\ year^{-1}$ to $0.105\ year^{-1}$. The data in [3] indicate that the minimum harvestable size of 7 mm basal diameter in the sample is reached at 30–35 years age, and the percentage of colonies above it is less than 6.7%. We have thus taken representative snapshots of the simulated colonies at 40 years of age with the parameters scanned within their range.

Figure 1 displays the sample consisting of 81 simulations, where the parameters α and γ are varied in their respective spectrum. The structures that exhibit a more pronounced difference in diameter between the stem and the tips are localised on the broad diagonal from the lower-left to the upper-right corner,

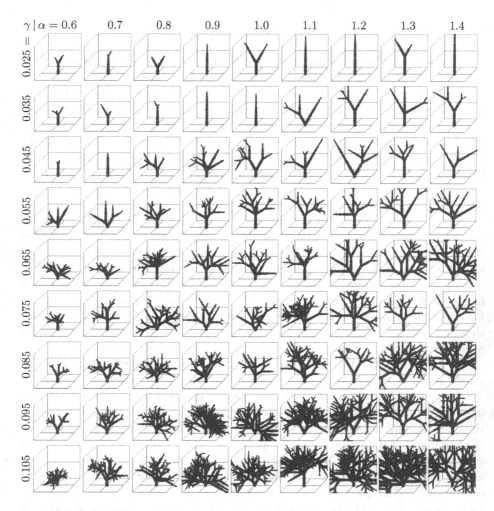

Fig. 1. Representative snapshots of the simulated colony at 40 years age in response to variations in the branching rate γ and the growth rate α.

whereby the lower values of α are coupled with the higher values of γ and vice versa. A similar situation is displayed in Fig. 2, where the parameters β and γ are varied in their respective spectrum. In these simulations, we again observe a negative correlation between branching and calcium carbonate accumulation in the structures that exhibit a more pronounced difference in diameter between the stem and the tips. The model response to concomitant variations in α and β displayed in Fig. 3 shows that the coupling of higher α values with lower β is less representative of the differentiation between the stem and the tip diameters.

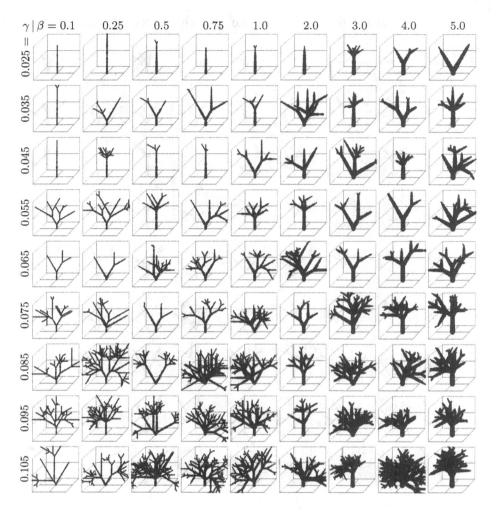

Fig. 2. Representative snapshots of the simulated colony at 40 years age in response to variations in the calcium carbonate accumulation rate β and the branching rate γ.

The average colony growth rate for shallow and deep populations is consistently reported to be centred around 0.24–0.26 mm $year^{-1}$ by various authors, e.g, [3,7,8]. However, the mean colony growth rate in the diameter of a population is related to the mean age of the colonies, whereby the mean colony growth rate in diameter in younger populations tend to be higher than the older populations. For example, intensively harvested populations show basal diameter values that are about twice as low on average and up to four times lower for maximum values in colony size in comparison to the non-harvested populations [8]. Moreover, there is evidence that the long-term harvesting pressure on shallow populations may have caused a shift in their structure towards higher colony densities and smaller size, e.g., [8,16]. Consistently with these findings,

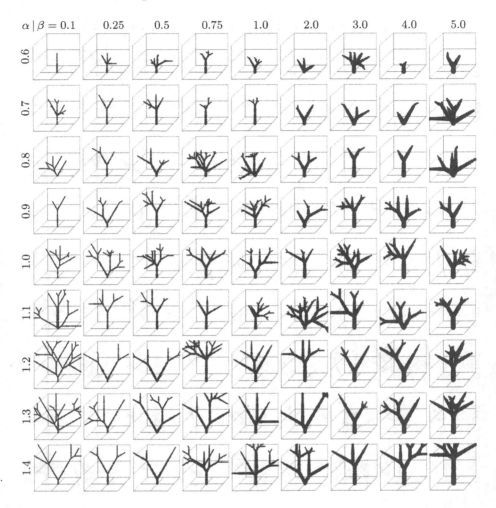

Fig. 3. Representative snapshots of the simulated colony at 40 years age in response to variations in the growth rate α and the calcium carbonate accumulation rate β.

our simulations indicate that colony development requires environmental conditions that provide shelter and sufficient levels of nutrients to sustain growth as well as calcium carbonate accumulation. In this regard, the model parameters reproduce the expected phenotypic variability in populations that show different demographic characteristics linked to the environmental conditions [3]. The observations on Figs. 1 and 2 indicate that branching and growth are conflicting processes that are prioritised by the colony according to the environmental conditions. In addition, our simulations indicate that early branching of the colony enhances further branching, which can explain the effects of the selective pressure that prevents shallow colonies from branching more frequently.

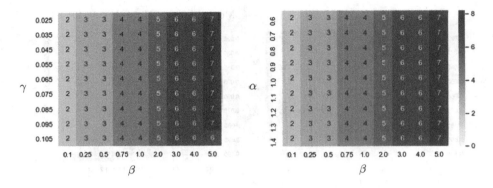

Fig. 4. The mean base diameter at 40 years age in 10 simulations in response to variations in model parameters α, β and γ. The diameter is measured as the cubic root of the volume in the first 10 Cb units in the stem, and rounded to the closest integer value. The left plot displays the model response to variations in the branching rate γ and the calcium carbonate accumulation rate β. The plot on the right displays the response to variations in the growth rate α and the accumulation rate β.

To better assess the demographic properties that are indicated by our model, we have recorded the mean effect of the variations on measurements in repeated simulations. For this, we have performed sets of 10 simulations for each of the 81×3 parameter combinations in Figs. 1, 2 and 3. We have first measured the mean base diameter at 40 years of age in these simulations. As expected, the resulting heatmaps in Fig. 4 indicate that basal diameter is a function of the rate β only, and it is not affected from the competition with other processes.

The average age of colonies at first branching has been reported to be 10 years with a standard deviation of 9 years, and the number of branches in each colony varies between 1 and 42 branches [1]. To assess our model in comparison to these observations, we have measured the mean first branching age and the number of branches at 40 years in sets of repeated simulations. The resulting heatmaps are shown in Fig. 5. These results indicate that our model remains consistent with the measurements in the field for most of the parameter values. Consistent with the observations on Figs. 1 and 2, branching rates that are greater than $0.085\,year^{-1}$ result in number of branches that are much greater than those observed in the field, and more so for larger growth parameters α and β. Similarly, branching rates that are more than $0.035\,year^{-1}$ result in a first branching age that is in agreement with the field data.

Field data collected by various authors indicate that morphological and growth parameters may differ significantly between samples from different patches, suggesting that these characteristics are affected by local environmental factors. Branch growth rate, age at first branching, proportional growth of colony bases, and the independence of linear growth from age appear to be constant features in colonies belonging to the same patch [1]. In this regard, stochastic noise

Mean first branching age   Mean number of branches at 40 years

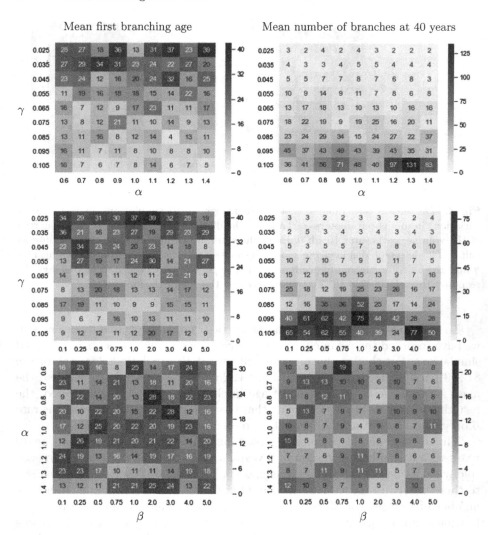

Fig. 5. The mean first branching age (left) and the mean number of branches at 40 years age (right) in 10 simulations in response to variations in model parameters α, β and γ. The branching age is measured as the simulation time at the production of the first F unit. The number of branches at 40 years age is measured as the number of F units plus one at simulation time 40.

remains a significant source of variability for the measurements, and the growth rates α and β of our model appear to have a noise enhancing role that may explain the variability within the populations exposed to similar environmental factors.

4   Discussion

We have presented a simple model of Mediterranean coral colonies consisting of three rules that are parameterised with stochastic rates. We have shown that the simulations with our model accurately capture the structural properties of this species [1,3,7,8,16]. In accordance with the notions in [10], variations of our model parameters provide a systematic abstraction that reflects the influence of various conditions that the marine environment can exert on individual colonies. The comparison of our simulation results with field data shows that our model is well-calibrated for representing the effects of the environment. However, the utility of models is not only to forecast the state of the studied system under different conditions, but also to explain and illustrate its working principles [17]. In this sense, our model suggests that the morphology of a *C. rubrum* colony can be the result of two conflicting processes, branching and growth, priority of which is regulated by environmental factors.

Although our model is equipped with features that make rendering possible, reproduction of high-fidelity time-lapse visualisations is secondary as it abstracts away from spatial constraints with the gain of simplicity. However, high-resolution reproduction of the time-lapse visualisations can be addressed independently. This can be done by exploiting the make-up of the model that uses an abstract representation of the coral structure, and keeps rendering external. Another related topic, which is left for future work, concerns introducing explicit mechanisms for resolving spatial constraints such as overlaps or those that model the more intricate structural aspects. Similarly, introducing elements of mechanical forces to our model may lead to more detailed representations, however this would drastically increase the model complexity.

Another direction of future work is using off-the-shelf optimisation methods for fitting the model parameters to field data, which can result in new insights. On the other end of the spectrum, knowledge about the genetic regulatory mechanisms can be integrated by using hierarchical modelling techniques, for example, in terms of components that dynamically alter model parameters. This can, in return, bridge the gap between the genetic information and the physical shape of the organism.

In silico modelling of corals, and other sessile marine organisms, is prone to providing new frontiers for marine biology and conservation ecology. This is partly because large-scale experiments on ecosystems are impractical or unethical at ecologically appropriate scales, and the demographic data on pristine populations is often lacking [14]. In this respect, simulation models can help us to better understand the complex mechanisms in these systems at various levels in a way that would complement, guide and accelerate the field work.

A   Appendix: SPiM Implementation

```
directive sample 60.0
directive plot Cx(); Cb(); F(); Cbb()
directive debug

(* Model Parameters *)
val alpha = 1.0
val beta = 1.0
val gamma = 1.0

(* Constants *)
val m0 = 1.0
val d = 1.0
(* 30 degrees *)
val CosTheta = 0.866
val SinTheta = 0.5
val CosThetaOp = 0.866
val SinThetaOp = - 0.5

let Cx(x:float,y:float,z:float,
       x0:float,y0:float,z0:float,
       m:float,lft:chan) =
      ( new rht@1.0:chan
        new rht1@1.0:chan
        new rht2@1.0:chan
       do delay@alpha;
         ( Cb(x,y,z, m, lft,rht)
         | Cx(x+x0,y+y0,z+z0, x0,y0,z0, m0, rht))
       or delay@gamma;
         ( F(lft,rht1,rht2) |
           Cx(x,y,z,
              x0,
              (y0 * CosTheta) + (z0 * -1.0 * SinTheta),
              (y0 * SinTheta) + (z0 * CosTheta), m0, rht1) |
           Cx(x,y,z,
              x0,
              (y0 * CosThetaOp) + (z0 * -1.0 * SinThetaOp),
              (y0 * SinThetaOp) + (z0 * CosThetaOp), m0, rht2)))

and F(lft:chan,rht1:chan,rht2:chan) = ()

and Cb(x:float,y:float,z:float, m:float, lft:chan, rht:chan) =
        delay@beta; Cb(x,y,z, m+d, lft, rht)

run 1 of ( new e@1.0:chan Cx(0.5,0.5,0.0,  0.0,0.0,0.024, 1.0, e))
```

References

1. Benedetti, M.C., Priori, C., Erra, F., Santangelo, G.: Growth patterns in mesophotic octocorals: timing the branching process in the highly-valuable Mediterranean *Corallium rubrum*. Estuar. Coast. Shelf Sci. **171**, 106–110 (2016)
2. Blinov, M.L., Faeder, J.R., Goldstein, B., Hlavacek, W.S.: BioNetGen: software for rule-based modeling of signal transduction based on the interactions of molecular domains. Bioinformatics **20**, 3289–3292 (2004)
3. Bramanti, L., et al.: Demographic parameters of two populations of red coral (*Corallium rubrum* L. 1758) in the North Western Mediterranean. Mar. Biol. **161**(5), 1015–1026 (2013)
4. Cardelli, L., Caron, E., Gardner, P., Kahramanoğulları, O., Phillips, A.: A process model of actin polymerisation. In: FBTC 2008. ENTCS, vol. 229, pp. 127–144. Elsevier (2008)
5. Cardelli, L., Zavattaro, G.: On the computational power of biochemistry. In: Horimoto, K., Regensburger, G., Rosenkranz, M., Yoshida, H. (eds.) AB 2008. LNCS, vol. 5147, pp. 65–80. Springer, Heidelberg (2008). https://doi.org/10.1007/978-3-540-85101-1_6
6. Feret, J., Danos, V., Krivine, J., Harmer, R., Fontana, W.: Internal coarse-graining of molecular systems. PNAS **106**(16), 6453–6458 (2008)
7. Gallmetzer, I., Alexandra, H., Velimirov, B.: Slow growth and early sexual maturity: bane and boon for the red coral *Corallium rubrum*. Estuar. Coast. Shelf Sci. **90**(1), 1–10 (2005)
8. Garrabou, J., Harmelin, J.G.: A 20-year study on life-history traits of a harvested long-lived temperate coral in the NW Mediterranean: insights into conservation and management needs. J. Anim. Ecol. **71**(6), 966–978 (2002)
9. Gillespie, D.T.: Exact stochastic simulation of coupled chemical reactions. J. Phys. Chem. **81**, 2340–2361 (1977)
10. Kaandorp, J.A., Kübler, J.E.: The Algorithmic Beauty of Seaweeds, Sponges and Corals. Springer, Heidelberg (2001). https://doi.org/10.1007/978-3-662-04339-4
11. Kahramanoğulları, O.: Simulating Stochastic dynamic interactions with spatial information and flux. In: Martín-Vide, C., Mizuki, T., Vega-Rodríguez, M.A. (eds.) TPNC 2016. LNCS, vol. 10071, pp. 149–160. Springer, Cham (2016). https://doi.org/10.1007/978-3-319-49001-4_12
12. Kahramanoğulları, O., Cardelli, L.: An intuitive modelling interface for systems biology. Int. J. Softw. Inf. **7**(4), 655–674 (2013)
13. Kahramanoğulları, O., Phillips, A., Vaggi, F.: Process modeling and rendering of biochemical structures: actin. In: Lecca, P. (ed.) Biomechanics of Cells and Tissues: Experiments, Models and Simulations, LNCVB, vol. 9, pp. 45–63. Springer, Heidelberg (2013). https://doi.org/10.1007/978-94-007-5890-2_2
14. Knowlton, N., Jackson, J.B.C.: Shifting baselines, local impacts, and global change on coral reefs. PLoS Biol. **6**(2), 215–220 (2008)
15. Phillips, A., Cardelli, L.: Efficient, correct simulation of biological processes in the stochastic Pi-calculus. In: Calder, M., Gilmore, S. (eds.) CMSB 2007. LNCS, vol. 4695, pp. 184–199. Springer, Heidelberg (2007). https://doi.org/10.1007/978-3-540-75140-3_13
16. Priori, C., Mastascusa, V., Erra, F., Angiolillo, M., Canese, S., Santangelo, G.: Demography of deep-dwelling red coral populations: age and reproductive assessment of a high valuable marine species. Estuar. Coast. Shelf Sci. **118**, 43–49 (2013)
17. Shannon, R.E.: Systems Simulation: The Art and Science. Prentice Hall, Upper Saddle River (1975)

Operation Insertion on the Conjugacy and Commutativity of Words

Kalpana Mahalingam and Hirapra Ravi$^{(\boxtimes)}$

Department of Mathematics, IIT Madras, Chennai 600 036, Tamil Nadu, India
hirapra.ravi@gmail.com

Abstract. In this paper, we do a theoretical study of some of the notions in combinatorics of words with respect to the insertion operation on words. We generalize the classical notions of conjugacy and commutativity of words to insertion-conjugacy and insertion-commutativity of words. We define and study properties of such words (i.e.) of words u, v and w such that $u \leftarrow v = v \leftarrow u$ and $u \leftarrow v = v \leftarrow w$.

Keywords: Conjugacy of words · Commutativity of words

1 Introduction

The study of combinatorial properties of words has meaningful applications in many fields. Word properties such as primitivity, periodicity and borderedness play important role in several areas that includes data compression [8,17], string searching algorithms [2,6,7] and sequence assembly in computational biology [16] to name a few.

Insertion is a word operation that was introduced in [12] as a generalization of catenation. The insertion operation is a binary operation on words. The insertion of v into u is obtained by inserting v into u in an arbitrary position. As opposed to the catenation operation, insertion of v into u is a set of words and hence catenation cannot be obtained as a particular case of the insertion operation. Given two words, u and v, v inserted into u, denoted by $u \leftarrow v$ is defined as

$$u \leftarrow v = \{u_1 v u_2 \; : \; u = u_1 u_2\}$$

Motivated by the mutagenesis performed by enzymatic activity in DNA, the concept of insertion was extended in [3–5,13]. In [13], authors have defined and studied the properties of k-suffix codes using the left-k-insertion operation and extended the concept of k-prefix and k-suffix codes to involution k-prefix and involution k-suffix codes. In [3–5], authors have introduced bio-inspired operations such as *site-directed deletion, outfix-guided insertion* and study some decision problems based on these operations.

Conjugacy and commutativity are two important relations on words. Several classical results about conjugacy of words and words that commute can be found in [9]. In [1], the authors extend certain combinatorial properties of conjugacy of

© Springer Nature Switzerland AG 2019
C. Martín-Vide et al. (Eds.): TPNC 2019, LNCS 11934, pp. 70–81, 2019.
https://doi.org/10.1007/978-3-030-34500-6_4

words to partial words with an arbitrary number of holes. In [14], these notions were extended to Watson-Crick conjugate and Watson-Crick commutative words that incorporate the notion of an involution function and related properties were discussed.

In this paper, we study conjugacy and commutativity properties of words with respect to the insertion operation, over any alphabet. If two words u and v commute with respect to the catenation operation, then it is well known that they must be powers of a common word. That is, if $uv = vu$, then u and v are of the form p^i for some word p and some integer i. Here, we study the implication of $u \leftarrow v = v \leftarrow u$ on words u and v. We also study the conjugacy relation on words with respect to the insertion operation.

The paper is organized as follows. Section 2 recalls some basic notions and results in combinatorics of words. In Sect. 3, we define the concept of ins-commutativity on words and give necessary and sufficient conditions on words u and v such that $u \leftarrow v = v \leftarrow u$. In Sect. 4, we introduce the concept of a word u being ins-conjugate to v and study the property of such words. We end with a few concluding remarks.

2 Basic Definitions and Preliminaries

An alphabet Σ is a finite set of symbols. A word over Σ is a finite sequence of symbols from it. The set of all words over Σ including the empty word λ and the set of all non-empty words over Σ are denoted by Σ^* and Σ^+ respectively. The i-th power of a word u is the catenation of the word u with itself i-times and is denoted by u^i. For a word u, u^* denotes the set of all words of the form u^i, $i \geq 0$ and u^+ denotes the set of all words of the form u^j, $j \geq 1$. The length of a word $w \in \Sigma^*$ is the number of symbol occurrences in w, denoted by $|w|$; i.e., if $w = a_1 a_2 \ldots a_n, a_i \in \Sigma$ then $|w| = n$. The length of an empty word λ is 0. $|w|_a$ denotes the number of occurrences of the symbol a in w. A language is a subset of Σ^*. For a word $w = w_1 w_2 \ldots w_n$, $w_i \in \Sigma$, the reversal of w denoted by w^R is the word $w_n \ldots w_2 w_1$.

A word w is called primitive if it is not a non-trivial power of another word; i.e., if $w = u^i$, then $w = u$ and $i = 1$. The primitive root of a word w is the shortest word u such that $w = u^i$ for some i, and is denoted by $\rho(w) = u$. It is well known that, for each word $w \in \Sigma^*$, there exists a unique primitive root.

We recall some well-known results from [15] and [9].

Lemma 1. Let $u, v \in \Sigma^*$.

1. If $uv = vw$ such that $u \neq \lambda$, then $u = xy$, $v = (xy)^i x$ and $w = yz$ for $x, y, z \in \Sigma^*$, $i \geq 0$.
2. If $uv = vu$, then u and v are powers of a common word.

Lemma 2. If $aw = wb$ for $a, b \in \Sigma$ and $w \in \Sigma^*$, then $a = b$ and $w \in a^*$.

Lemma 3. If p is primitive and $p^2 = p_1 p p_2$ with $p_1 p_2 = p$ then either $p_1 = \lambda$ or $p_2 = \lambda$.

Sequential insertion operation was first defined in [12]. For $L_1, L_2 \subseteq \Sigma^*$, the sequential insertion of L_2 into L_1 is defined as:

$$L_1 \leftarrow L_2 = \bigcup_{u \in L_1, v \in L_2} (u \leftarrow v)$$

where

$$u \leftarrow v = \{u_1 v u_2 \; : \; u_1 u_2 = u\}.$$

The i-th $\leftarrow$-power of a language L is defined as $L^{\leftarrow(0)} = \{\}$, $L^{\leftarrow(1)} = L$ and $L^{\leftarrow(i)} = L^{\leftarrow(i-1)} \leftarrow L$ for $i > 1$.

Example 4. Let $u = ab$, $v = c$ and $L = \{\lambda, ab\}$. Then,

1. $u \leftarrow v = \{cab, acb, abc\}$ and $v \leftarrow u = \{abc, cab\}$
2. $L^{\leftarrow(2)} = L \leftarrow L = \{\lambda, ab, abab, aabb\}$.

It was shown in [12], that the operation $\leftarrow$ is neither commutative nor associative.

A non-empty word w is called ins-primitive if $w \in u^{\leftarrow(i)}$ for some word u and $i \geq 1$, then $i = 1$ and $w = u$. It was shown in [10], that every ins-primitive word is primitive, but a primitive word need not be ins-primitive. For example, consider $ab^{\leftarrow(2)} = \{abab, aabb\}$. Here $aabb$ is primitive but not ins-primitive.

For a primitive word $u \in \Sigma^+$, u cannot be a factor of u^2 in a non-trivial way, i.e., if $u^2 = xuy$, then by Lemma 3, either $x = \lambda$ or $y = \lambda$. A similar result is not true for an ins-primitive word. For any word $u \in \Sigma^*$, u will be a proper factor of all the elements of $u^{\leftarrow(2)}$ other than u^2.

A non-empty word w is called ins-primitive if $w \in u^{\leftarrow^{(i)}}$ for some word u and $i \geq 1$ yields $i = 1$ and $w = u$. For a given word w, it is not necessary that there will be a unique word u such that $w \in u^{\leftarrow^{(i)}}$ [10] even though we have following theorem which forces $u = v$ and $m = n$ if $u^{\leftarrow(m)} = v^{\leftarrow(n)}$.

We first illustrate $u^{\leftarrow(m)}$ for a given u and m with the following example.

Example 5. For a word $u = a^3 bab$

$$u^{\leftarrow(2)} = \{a^3 baba^3 bab, a^4 baba^2 bab, a^5 bababab, a^6 babbab, a^3 ba^3 babab, a^3 ba^4 babb\}.$$

Note that all elements of $u^{\leftarrow(2)}$ are of the form $a^k bw$ with $k \geq 1$ and some $b \in \Sigma$, $w \in \Sigma^*$.

Theorem 6. *For words $u, v \in \Sigma^* \backslash a^+$, if $u^{\leftarrow(m)} = v^{\leftarrow(n)}$ for some $m, n \geq 1$, then $u = v$ and $m = n$.*

Proof. Let $u^{\leftarrow(m)} = v^{\leftarrow(n)}$ with $u, v \in \Sigma^* \backslash a^+$. Since $u, v \in \Sigma^* \backslash a^+$, more than one letter will appear in u and v both. Also note that first letter of both u and v are equal since $u^{\leftarrow(m)} = v^{\leftarrow(n)}$. Thus $u = a^i bw$ and $v = a^j b'w'$ for some $i, j \geq 1$ and some $a, b, b' \in \Sigma$, $w, w' \in \Sigma^*$.

Now we have two possible cases while comparing im and jn.
Case 1: $im = jn$

As $u = a^i bw$, we can find an element in $u^{\leftarrow(m)}$ which has a^{im} as prefix. That element must be $a^{im}(bw)^m$. Since $u^{\leftarrow(m)} = v^{\leftarrow(n)}$, There must be a matching element for $a^{im}(bw)^m$ in $v^{\leftarrow(n)}$. That element must be $a^{jn}(b'w')^n$. Thus $a^{im}(bw)^m = a^{jn}(b'w')^n$. Since $im = jn$, $(bw)^m = (b'w')^n$. Thus $b = b'$.

We claim that $i = j$.

Note that all elements in $u^{\leftarrow(m)}$ and $v^{\leftarrow(n)}$ are also of the form $a^k bw$ with $k \geq 1$ and some $b \in \Sigma$, $w \in \Sigma^*$.

Let $z_1 \in u^{\leftarrow(m)}$ and $z_2 \in v^{\leftarrow(n)}$ are such that $z_1 = a^r bw$ $z_2 = a^s bw'$ for some $r, s \geq 1$, $b \in \Sigma$, $w, w' \in \Sigma^*$ and r and s are least. Since $u^{\leftarrow(m)} = v^{\leftarrow(n)}$, we get $r = s$. Also $u^m \in u^{\leftarrow(m)}$ and $v^n \in v^{\leftarrow(n)}$ have prefix $a^i b$ with least power i and $a^j b$ with least power j respectively. Thus $i = r$ and $j = s$. As $r = s$, we get $i = j$.

Since $im = jn$, we get $m = n$. As $(bw)^m = (b'w')^n$, we get $w = w'$ and thus $u = v$.

Case 2: $im \neq jn$

In this case, without loss of generality, assume that $im > jn$. Then the element $a^{im}(bw)^m$ is in $u^{\leftarrow(m)}$ but there is no matching element in $v^{\leftarrow(n)}$ as any element in $v^{\leftarrow(n)}$ can not have a prefix a power of a with power more than jn. Thus $u^{\leftarrow(m)} \neq v^{\leftarrow(n)}$ which is contradiction. $\square$

3   Commuting Under Insertion

Two words u and v are said to commute if $uv = vu$. (For interesting properties of such words, we refer the reader to [9]). In this section, we deduce properties of words that commute under the insertion operation (i.e.) study the properties of u and v such that $u \leftarrow v = v \leftarrow u$. In [11], several particular properties of words that belong to $u \leftarrow u$ or $u \leftarrow u \cap v \leftarrow v$ were discussed. Here, we give necessary and sufficient conditions on words that satisfy the relation $u \leftarrow v = v \leftarrow u$. We begin the section with the following result.

Lemma 7. *Let $u, v \in \Sigma^+$ such that $u \leftarrow v = v \leftarrow u$. Then, for a primitive word p, if p is a proper prefix (suffix) of u, then p is a prefix (suffix) of v.*

Proof. Let $u, v \in \Sigma^*$ be such that $u \leftarrow v = v \leftarrow u$ and let p be a primitive proper prefix of u. Then, there exists a non-empty word r such that $u = pr$. Thus, we have $pr \leftarrow v = v \leftarrow pr$. Since, $pvr \in pr \leftarrow v$, there must be a matching element in $v \leftarrow pr$. Let the matching element be $v_1 prv_2$ with $v_1 v_2 = v$. We have two possible cases for v_1. We have the following cases.

Case 1: Let $v_1 \neq \lambda$. Using the fact that $pvr = v_1 prv_2$, we have $pvr = pv_1 v_2 r = v_1 prv_2$. Thus, we get $pv_1 = v_1 p$. Since $v_1 \neq \lambda$ in this case, we get $\rho(v_1) = \rho(p) = p$ and p is a prefix of v as required.

Case 2: Let $v_1 = \lambda$. Then, we get $v_2 = v$ as $v_1 v_2 = v$. Using the fact that $pvr = v_1 prv_2$, we get $pvr = prv$. This implies $vr = rv$. As neither of v or r is an empty word, we get $\rho(v) = \rho(r)$. Let q be the primitive root of v and r. Then, we have $u = pq^i$ and $v = q^j$ for some $i, j > 0$. Thus, $pq^i \leftarrow q^j = q^j \leftarrow pq^i$.

Since $j > 0$, we have the following cases:

Case 2.1: If $j = 1$, then we have $pq^i \leftarrow q = q \leftarrow pq^i$. We further distinguish this case into the following sub-cases:

Case 2.1.1: $|p| = 1$. Let $p = a$ for some $a \in \Sigma$. Since $|v| > 1$ and $q = v$, we can consider an element $aq_1qq_2q^{i-1} \in aq^i \leftarrow q$ with $q_1q_2 = q$ and $q_1, q_2 \neq \lambda$. As we have $pq^i \leftarrow q = q \leftarrow pq^i$, there must be a matching element for $aq_1qq_2q^{i-1}$ in $q \leftarrow pq^i$. Let the matching element in $q \leftarrow aq^i$ be $q'_1aq^iq'_2$ with $q'_1q'_2 = q$. Then $aq_1qq_2q^{i-1} = q'_1aq^iq'_2$.

If $q'_1 = \lambda$, then $q'_2 = q$ and $aq_1qq_2q^{i-1} = aq^{i+1}$. Note that aq_1qq_2 is the prefix of first term and aq^2 is the prefix of second term which are of same length. Comparing both of them, we get $aq_1qq_2 = aq^2$. Thus, $q_1qq_2 = q^2$. Since q is primitive, we conclude by Lemma 3, that either $q_1 = \lambda$ or $q_2 = \lambda$, which is contradiction to our assumption that $q_1, q_2 \neq \lambda$.

If $q'_1 \neq \lambda$, then let w be the common prefix of q_1 and q'_1. Since $aq_1qq_2q^{i-1} = q'_1aq^iq'_2$, we get $aw = wb$ for some $b \in \Sigma$ and by Lemma 2, we have $w \in a^+$. Since $p = a$ and w is prefix of v, we get p as a prefix of v as required.

Case 2.1.2: $|p| > 1$. Since, we have from hypothesis that $|v| > 1$, and $v = q^j$ with $j = 1$, we conclude that $|q| > 1$. Let q be of the form $q = q'd$ for some $d \in \Sigma$ and $q' \in \Sigma^+$. Now consider an element $pq'qdq^{i-1} \in pq^i \leftarrow q$. Since $pq^i \leftarrow q = q \leftarrow pq^i$, there must be a matching element for $pq'qdq^{i-1}$ in $q \leftarrow pq^i$. Let this element be $q_1pq^iq_2$ with $q_1q_2 = q$ and $q_1, q_2 \in \Sigma^*$. If $q_1 = \lambda$ then $pq'qdq^{i-1} = pq^{i+1}$ and thus, $pq'qd = pq^2$. Thus, $q'qd = q^2$ which is a contradiction by Lemma 3. If $q_2 = \lambda$, then $q_1 = q$ and $pq'qd = qpq$. Comparing the suffix of length $|q| + 1$ on both sides, we get $qd = p'q$, where p' is the suffix of p of length one. Then, by Lemma 2, $q \in d^+$ which is a contradiction since q is a primitive word and $|q| > 1$.

Thus, $pq'qdq^{i-1} = q_1pq^iq_2$ such that both q_1, q_2 are non-empty. We now prove that p is a prefix of q. Since $q = q'd$ and $q_1 \neq \lambda$, we get q_1 to be a prefix of q'. Now comparing the prefix of length $|pq_1|$ from both sides of equation $pq'qdq^{i-1} = q_1pq^iq_2$, we get $pq_1 = q_1p$. As $q_1 \neq \lambda$ and p is a primitive word, we get $p \in q_1^+$. Thus, p is a prefix of q_1 and hence a prefix of q.

Case 2.2: Let $j > 1$. Consider the element $qpq^{i+j-1} \in q^j \leftarrow pq^i$. Since $pq^i \leftarrow q^j = q^j \leftarrow pq^i$, there must be a matching element for qpq^{i+j-1} in $pq^i \leftarrow q^j$. The possible cases for matching element are:

(1) q^jpq^i
(2) $p_1q^jp_2q^i$ with $p_1p_2 = p$
(3) $pq^{n_1}q_1q^jq_2q^{n_2}$ with $q_1q_2 = q$ and $n_1 + n_2 + 1 = i$.

For case (1), we have $qpq^{i+j-1} = q^jpq^i$. Then, $pq^{j-1} = q^{j-1}p$ and $\rho(p) = \rho(q^{j-1})$. Since both p and q are primitive, we get $p = q$. Thus, p is a prefix of v.

For case (2), we have $qpq^{i+j-1} = p_1q^jp_2q^i$ with $p_1p_2 = p$ which implies that $qpq^{j-1} = p_1q^jp_2$. Then, $qp_1 = p_1q$ and $p_2q^{j-1} = q^{j-1}p_2$. Thus, $\rho(q) = \rho(p_1)$ and $\rho(q^{j-1}) = \rho(p_2)$ and hence, $p_1, p_2 \in q^+$ which implies $p \in q^+$. Since p and q are both primitive, $p = q$ and hence, p is prefix of v.

For case (3), we have $qpq^{i+j-1} = pq^{n_1}q_1q^jq_2q^{n_2}$ with $q_1q_2 = q$ and $n_1 + n_2 + 1 = i$. If $n_1 \geq 1$ then $qp = pq$ and thus, $p = q$ and p is a prefix of v as required.

Let $n_1 = 0$. Then, we get $qpq^{i+j-1} = pq_1q^jq_2q^{i-1}$. Thus, $qpq^j = pq_1q^jq_2$. Since $j \geq 2$, comparing the suffix of both terms, we get $q^2 = wqq_2$. We know that for a primitive word q, q can not be a non-trivial factor of q^2. Thus, $q_2 = \lambda$ or $q_2 = q$ and $qpq^j = pq^{j+1}$. Thus, $pq = qp$ which implies that $\rho(p) = \rho(q)$. Since p and q both are primitive, we get $p = q$. Therefore, p is a prefix of v as required.

When p is primitive and proper suffix of u, with similar arguments as above we get p as a suffix of v. $\square$

We recall the following result from [18].

Theorem 8. *If $a \in \Sigma$ and $u \in \Sigma^+ \setminus a^+$, then either ua or u is primitive.*

It is clear from the above result that for such a u, either u^R or au^R is primitive. Using Theorem 8, we also deduce the following.

Result 1. *If a word $w = ua \in \Sigma^+ \setminus a^+$, then either u or ua is primitive.*

We now deduce structures of words u and v such that they commute under the insertion. We first discuss the case when $u = a^i$, $a \in \Sigma$ (Proposition 9) and then, for any $u \in \Sigma^*$ (Theorem 10).

Proposition 9. *Let $u = a^i$ for some $i \geq 1$ and some $a \in \Sigma$. Then $u \leftarrow v = v \leftarrow u$ if and only if the following conditions holds:*

(1) if $i = 1$, then either $v = b$ or $v = a^j$ for some j and for some $b \in \Sigma$,
(2) if $i > 1$, then $v = a^j$ for some j.

Proof. Let $u = a^i$ for some i and $a \in \Sigma$.

Given that $u \leftarrow v = v \leftarrow u$. It is clear that for $v = a^j$, $u \leftarrow v = v \leftarrow u$. Let us assume that v is such that $v \neq a^j$. Then, $v = v_1 v_2 \ldots v_j$ such that $v_i = b$ for some i and $b \neq a$, $v_i \in \Sigma$. We have the following cases:

Case 1: $|v| = 1$. In this case $v = b$ and

$$u \leftarrow v = a^i \leftarrow b = \{ba^i, aba^{i-1}, a^2ba^{i-2}, \ldots, a^ib\}$$

and $v \leftarrow u = b \leftarrow a^i = \{ba^i, a^ib\}$. Since $u \leftarrow v = v \leftarrow u$, comparing the above two sets, we get $i = 1$. Thus, $u = a$ and $v = b$, which is of the form as in condition (1).

Case 2: Let $|v| > 1$ and let k be the least positive index such that $v_k = b$. Note that $k \neq 1$ and $k \neq j$. If $k = 1$ or $k = j$, b is either a prefix or a suffix of v and by Lemma 7, b is also a prefix or a suffix of u, which implies that $b = a$, a contradiction.

Thus, $v_1 v_2 \ldots v_k$ is a proper primitive prefix of v with $v_k = b$ and by Lemma 7, it is also prefix of u. Thus, the k-th symbol of u is b, which is a contradiction.

The converse is straightforward and we omit the proof. $\square$

It is well known that (see [9,15]), if words u and v commute under the catenation operation, then they must be powers of a common word. However, this is not true for words that commute under the insertion operation. We now give necessary and sufficient conditions on words u and v such that they commute under the insertion operation.

Theorem 10. *Let $u, v \in \Sigma^+$ and $a, b \in \Sigma$, $u \leftarrow v = v \leftarrow u$ if and only if at least one of the following conditions holds:*

(1) $u = v$
(2) $u = a, v = b$
(3) $u = a^i, v = a^j$
(4) $u = a^i b,\ v = a^j b$ or $u = ab^i,\ v = ab^j,\ |i - j| \leq 1$.
(5) $u = (ab)^i a,\ v = (ab)^j a,\ |i - j| \leq 1$.

Proof. We first prove the converse. Suppose u and v satisfy the given conditions, then we show that $u \leftarrow v = v \leftarrow u$. For conditions $(1), (2)$ and (3), it is straightforward to see that $u \leftarrow v = v \leftarrow u$.

Let $u = a^i b$, $v = a^j b$ with $|i - j| \leq 1$. Since $|i - j| \leq 1$, either $i = j$ or $i = j + 1$ or $j = i + 1$. If $i = j$, then $u = v$ and by condition (1), $u \leftarrow v = v \leftarrow u$. Assume that $i = j + 1$. Then,

$$
\begin{aligned}
u \leftarrow v = a^{j+1} b \leftarrow a^j b \\
= \{a^k a^j b a^{j+1-k} b\ :\ k = 0, 1, \ldots, j+1\} \cup \{a^{j+1} b a^j b\} \\
= \{a^{k+j} b a^{j+1-k} b\ :\ k = 0, 1, \ldots, j+1\}
\end{aligned}
$$

$$
\begin{aligned}
v \leftarrow u = a^j b \leftarrow a^{j+1} b \\
= \{a^k a^{j+1} b a^{j-k} b\ :\ k = 0, 1, \ldots, j\} \cup \{a^j b a^{j+1} b\} \\
= \{a^{k+j} b a^{j+1-k} b\ :\ k = 0, 1, \ldots, j+1\}
\end{aligned}
$$

Thus, $u \leftarrow v = v \leftarrow u$. Similar argument holds for $j = i + 1$. Same is true when $u = ab^i$, $v = ab^j$ with $|i - j| \leq 1$.

Similarly, one can show that, when $u = (ab)^i a$, $v = (ab)^j a$ and $|i - j| \leq 1$.

$$
\begin{aligned}
u \leftarrow v = (ab)^i a \leftarrow (ab)^j a \\
= \{(ab)^k (ab)^j a (ab)^{i-k} a\ :\ k = 0, 1, \ldots, i\} \\
\cup \{(ab)^k a (ab)^j ab (ab)^{i-k-1} a\ :\ k = 0, 1, \ldots, i-1\} \\
\cup \{(ab)^i a (ab)^j a\} \\
= \{(ab)^{k+j} a (ab)^{i-k} a\ :\ k = 0, 1, \ldots, i\} \\
\cup \{(ab)^k a (ab)^{j+i-k} a\ :\ k = 0, 1, \ldots, i-1\} \\
\cup \{(ab)^i a (ab)^j a\} \\
= \{(ab)^k a (ab)^{j+i-k} a\ :\ k = 0, 1, \ldots, i-1, i, j, j+1, \ldots, j+i\}
\end{aligned}
$$

Similarly, $v \leftarrow u = \{(ab)^k a(ab)^{j+i-k}a : k = 0, 1, \ldots, j-1, j, i, i+1, \ldots, i+j\}$. If $i = j$, then $u = v$ and the result follows from condition (1). When $i = j+1$ we get,

$$u \leftarrow v = \{(ab)^k a(ab)^{j+i-k}a ; k = 0, 1, \ldots, j, j+1, \ldots, 2j+1\} = v \leftarrow u$$

Similarly, one can observe that for $j = i+1$, $u \leftarrow v = v \leftarrow u$.

We now assume that for a given $u, v \in \Sigma^*$ $u \leftarrow v = v \leftarrow u$. Let $u = x_1 x_2 \ldots x_n$ and $v = y_1 y_2 \ldots y_m$, where $x_i, y_j \in \Sigma$. There are three cases while comparing the length of u and v.

Case 1: We first assume that $m = n$ and show that $u = v$.

Case 1.1: $n \leq 2$. If $n = 1$, then $u = a$ and $v = a$ or $v = b$ which is of the form as in condition (1) or (2). If $n = 2$, then u is either a^2 or ab. If $u = a^2$, then by Proposition 9, $v = a^2$. If $u = ab$, then a is the proper primitive prefix and b is the proper primitive suffix of u and hence by Lemma 7, a is a prefix of v and b is a suffix of v. Since $|v| = 2$, $v = ab$. Thus, $u = v$ in both cases.

Case 1.2: $n > 2$. If $u = a^n$ then by Proposition 9, $v = a^n$ and hence, $u = v$. If $u \in \Sigma^* \setminus a^+$, then we have the following sub-cases.

Case 1.2.1: If $x_1 x_2 \ldots x_{n-1} = a^{n-1}$ for some a, then $u = a^{n-1}x_n$. Since, a is a primitive proper prefix of u, by Lemma 7, we conclude that a is also a prefix of v. Thus, $y_1 = a$. Also, note that $a^{n-2}x_n$ is a proper primitive suffix of u and by Lemma 7, $a^{n-2}x_n$ is a suffix of v. Thus, $y_2 y_3 \ldots y_n = a^{n-2}x_n$ and hence, $v = a^{n-1}x_n = u$.

Case 1.2.2: If $x_1 x_2 \ldots x_{n-1} \neq a^{n-1}$, then by Theorem 8, either $x_1 x_2 \ldots x_{n-2}$ or $x_1 x_2 \ldots x_{n-1}$ is primitive. By Lemma 7, $x_1 x_2 \ldots x_{n-2}$ is a prefix of v and hence, $y_1 y_2 \ldots y_{n-2} = x_1 x_2 \ldots x_{n-2}$.

We now show that $x_{n-1} = y_{n-1}$ and $x_n = y_n$. Since, x_n is primitive and is a proper suffix of u, by Lemma 7, we have that x_n is a suffix of v. Thus, we have $x_n = y_n$. Also since, $u \in \Sigma^* \setminus a^+$, either $x_2 x_3 \ldots x_n$ is primitive or u is of the form ab^{n-1} for some $a, b \in \Sigma$. If $x_2 \ldots x_n$ is primitive, then by Lemma 7, $x_2 \ldots x_n$ is a suffix of v and hence, $u = v$. If u is of the form ab^{n-1}, then ab^{n-2} is a primitive prefix of u and by Lemma 7, a primitive prefix of v and hence, $x_{n-1} = y_{n-1}$. Thus, we have $u = v$.

Case 2: We now assume that $n > m$. Here we consider three sub-cases : $n = m+1$, $n = m+2$ and $n > m+2$.

Case 2.1: Let $n = m+1$ and let $u = x_1 x_2 \ldots x_{m+1}$, $v = y_1 y_2 \ldots y_m$.

Case 2.1.1: If $x_1 x_2 \ldots x_m = a^m$, then $u = a^m x_{m+1}$. If $x_{m+1} = a$, then $u = a^{m+1}$ and by Proposition 9, $v = a^m$ as in condition (3). If $x_{m+1} \neq a$, then $a^{m-1}x_{m+1}$ is a proper primitive suffix of u and hence a suffix of v by Lemma 7. Since $|v| = m$, we have $v = a^{m-1}x_{m+1}$ as in condition (4).

Case 2.1.2: If $x_1 x_2 \ldots x_m \neq a^m$, then by Theorem 8, either $x_1 x_2 \ldots x_{m-1}$ or $x_1 x_2 \ldots x_m$ is a primitive proper prefix of u. In either case, by Lemma 7 we get,

$$x_1 x_2 \ldots x_{m-1} = y_1 y_2 \ldots y_{m-1}$$

If $x_2 \ldots x_{m+1} = a^m$ for some symbol a, then $u = x_1 a^m$. As $x_1 \ldots x_m \neq a^m$ in this case $x_1 a^{m-1}$ is a primitive prefix of u and thus, a prefix of v. Thus,

$v = x_1 a^{m-1}$ as required (condition (4)). If $x_2 \ldots x_{m+1} \neq a^m$ for any symbol a, then by Theorem 8, either $x_2 \ldots x_{m+1}$ or $x_3 \ldots x_{m+1}$ is primitive and in either case, by Lemma 7, $x_3 \ldots x_{m+1}$ is a suffix of v. Thus, we have

$$x_3 \ldots x_m x_{m+1} = y_2 y_3 \ldots y_m$$

and hence, we get $u = y_1 y_2^{m-1} y_m$ and $v = y_1 y_2^{m-2} y_m$. If $y_1 = y_2$, then $u = y_1^m y_m$ and $v = y_1^{m-1} y_m$. If $y_1 \neq y_2$, then $y_1 y_2^{m-1}$ is a primitive prefix of u and by Lemma 7, it is a prefix of v. Thus, $y_2 = y_m$ and hence, $u = y_1 y_2^m$, $v = y_1 y_2^{m-1}$ as required.

Case 2.2: Let $n = m + 2$ and let $u = x_1 x_2 \ldots x_{m+2}$ and $v = y_1 y_2 \ldots y_m$.

Case 2.2.1: Let $x_1 x_2 \ldots x_m = a^m$. If $x_{m+1} x_{m+2} = a^2$, then $u = a^{m+2}$ and by Proposition 9, $v = a^m$ which is of the form as in condition (3). If $x_{m+1} x_{m+2} \neq a^2$, then $x_2 x_3 \ldots x_{m+2}$ is a primitive proper suffix of u, since $x_1 x_2 \ldots x_m = a^m$. Hence, $x_2 x_3 \ldots x_{m+2}$ is also suffix of v by Lemma 7. As $|x_2 x_3 \ldots x_{m+2}| = m + 1$ and $|v| = m$ we get contradiction.

Case 2.2.2: If $x_1 x_2 \ldots x_m \neq a^m$, then by Theorem 8, either $x_1 x_2 \ldots x_m$ or $x_1 x_2 \ldots x_{m+1}$ is primitive and in either case, by Lemma 7, $x_1 x_2 \ldots x_m$ is a prefix of both u and v. Thus,

$$x_1 x_2 \ldots x_m = y_1 y_2 \ldots y_m$$

If $x_3 \ldots x_{m+2} = a^m$, then either $x_1 x_2 = a^2$ or $x_1 x_2 \neq a^2$ and the case is similar to that of Case 2.2.1.

If $x_3 \ldots x_{m+2} \neq a^m$, then either $x_2 x_3 \ldots x_{m+2}$ or $x_3 x_4 \ldots x_{m+2}$ is primitive and in either case, by Lemma 7, $x_3 x_4 \ldots x_{m+2}$ is a suffix of both u and v. Thus,

$$x_3 x_4 \ldots x_{m+2} = y_1 y_2 \ldots y_m = x_1 x_2 \ldots x_m$$

and hence, $x_i = y_i = x_{i+2}$ for $1 \leq i \leq m$. If m is odd, then $u = (y_1 y_2)^k y_1$ and $v = (y_1 y_2)^{k-1} y_1$ for some k which is of the form as in condition (5). If m is even, then $u = (y_1 y_2)^k$ and $v = (y_1 y_2)^{k-1}$ for some k. If $y_1 = y_2$, then $u = y_1^{2k}, v = y_1^{2k-2}$ which is of the form as in condition (3). If $y_1 \neq y_2$, then $(y_1 y_2)^{k-1} y_1$ is a primitive proper prefix of u. Thus $(y_1 y_2)^{k-1} y_1$ is also prefix of v using Lemma 7. Here $|(y_1 y_2)^{k-1} y_1| = 2k - 1$ and $|v| = y_1^{2k-2} = 2k - 2$. Thus we get contradiction.

Case 2.3: Let $n > m + 2$.

Case 2.3.1: Let $x_1 x_2 \cdots x_{n-2} = a^{n-2}$ for some $a \in \Sigma$. If $x_{n-1} x_n = a^2$, then $u = a^n$ and by Proposition 9, $v = a^m$.

If $x_{n-1} x_n \neq a^2$, then $a^{n-2} x_{n-1} x_n$ is a primitive word. Note that, $n - 4 \geq 0$ as $m \geq 1$ and $n > m + 2$.

Consider the word $a v a^{n-3} x_{n-1} x_n \in a^{n-2} x_{n-1} x_n \leftarrow v$. Let the matching element in $v \leftarrow a^{n-2} x_{n-1} x_n$ be $v_1 a^{n-2} x_{n-1} x_n v_2$ with $v_1 v_2 = v$.

If $v_2 = \lambda$, then we get $a v a^{n-3} x_{n-1} x_n = v a^{n-2} x_1 x_2$ and hence by comparing the prefix of length $|av|$, we get $av = va$. Thus, $v \in a^+$. By Proposition 9, $u \in a^+$ which is a contradiction as $x_{n-1} x_n \neq a^2$.

If $v_2 \neq \lambda$, then by comparing the suffix of length $|v_2| + n - 1$, we get $v_2 a^{n-3} x_{n-1} x_n = a^{n-3} x_{n-1} x_n v_2$. Since $a^{n-3} x_{n-1} x_n$ is primitive, we get $v_2 \in$

$(a^{n-3}x_{n-1}x_n)^+$ and hence, $|v_2| \geq n-1$ which is a contradiction, as length of v is m and $n > m+2$ in this case.

Case 2.3.2: If $x_1 \ldots x_{n-2} \neq a^{n-2}$, then either $x_1 \ldots x_{n-2}$ or $x_1 \ldots x_{n-1}$ is primitive. With arguments similar to the above case, we get $|v| > n-2$ or $|v| > n-1$ which is a contradiction as $n > m+2$.

Case 3: The case when $n < m$ is similar to case 2 and can be proved similarly by interchanging the roles of u and v. □

4 Conjugacy with Insertion

A word u is a conjugate (see [9,15]) of another word v if there exists a word z such that $uz = zw$. An equivalent condition for u to be a conjugate of v is the existence of words x and y such that $u = xy$ and $v = yx$. In this section, we define the notion of a word u to be a conjugate of another word v with respect to the insertion operation and study properties of such words. We begin the section with the following observation.

Lemma 11. *For a word $w \in \Sigma^*$ and symbols $a, b \in \Sigma$, if wa and wb are conjugate of each other, then $a = b$.*

Proof. Given that wa is a conjugate of wb, there exists words x and y such that $xy = wa$ and $yx = wb$. Note that $|xy|_a = |wa|_a = |yx|_a = |wb|_a$ and hence, $|wa|_a = |w|_a + 1 = |wb|_a = |w|_a + |b|_a$, which implies that $b = a$.

We define the following:

Definition 12. *A word u is said to be an ins-conjugate of another word v if there exists a word z such that $u \leftarrow z = z \leftarrow v$.*

We now give conditions on the words u and v such that u is an ins-conjugate of v.

Theorem 13. *For words $u, v \in \Sigma^*$, if there exists a word z such that $u \leftarrow z = z \leftarrow v$, then $u = v$.*

Proof. All words in the set $u \leftarrow z$ have length $|u| + |z|$ and words in set $z \leftarrow v$ have length $|z| + |v|$. Since $u \leftarrow z = z \leftarrow v$, we get $|u| + |z| = |z| + |v|$. Thus, $|u| = |v|$.

Let w be the common prefix of u and v of maximum length. If $w = u$, then $w = v$ since length of u and v are equal. If w is a proper prefix of u, then let $u = wax$ and $v = wby$ for some words $x, y \in \Sigma^*$. Consider the word $wazx \in u \leftarrow z$. Let the matching element for $wazx$ in $z \leftarrow v$ be $z_1 v z_2$ with $z_1 z_2 = z$. Thus, $wazx = z_1 v z_2$ and $waz_1 z_2 x = z_1 wbyz_2$. By comparing the common prefix of length $|w| + |z_1| + 1$ on both side, we get $waz_1 = z_1 wb$ and by Lemma 11, we get $a = b$. Thus, w is not the common prefix of u and v of maximum length which is a contradiction. Hence, $u = v$. □

It is well known [9] that, for $u, w, v, q \in \Sigma^*$, if $uv = vq$ and $qv = wu$, then $q = u$ and $w = v$. We have an analogous result that is also true when concatenation is replaced with insertion operation.

Corollary 14. *Let $u, w, v, q \in \Sigma^*$. If $u \leftarrow v = v \leftarrow q$ and $q \leftarrow v = w \leftarrow u$, then $q = u$ and $w = v$.*

5   Conclusion

In this paper, we extended the relations conjugacy and commutativity on words with respect to the insertion operation. We then investigated the properties of words that satisfy these relations. A future research direction is to generalize the Fine and Wilf theorem and study several word equations involving insertion operation. It would also be interesting to look in to the conjugacy and commutativity relations with respect to the deletion operation.

References

1. Blanchet-Sadri, F., Luhman, D.: Conjugacy on partial words. Theor. Comput. Sci. **289**, 297–312 (2002)
2. Boyer, R., Moore, J.: A fast string searching algorithm. Commun. ACM **20**, 762–772 (1977)
3. Cho, D.-J., Han, Y.-S., Kim, H., Salomaa, K.: Site-directed deletion. In: Hoshi, M., Seki, S. (eds.) DLT 2018. LNCS, vol. 11088, pp. 219–230. Springer, Cham (2018). https://doi.org/10.1007/978-3-319-98654-8_18
4. Cho, D.-J., Han, Y.-S., Salomaa, K., Smith, T.J.: Site-directed insertion: decision problems, maximality and minimality. In: Konstantinidis, S., Pighizzini, G. (eds.) DCFS 2018. LNCS, vol. 10952, pp. 49–61. Springer, Cham (2018). https://doi.org/10.1007/978-3-319-94631-3_5
5. Cho, D., Han, Y., Ng, T., Salomaa, K.: Outfix-guided insertion. Theor. Comput. Sci. **701**, 70–84 (2017)
6. Crochemore, M., Perrin, D.: Two-way string matching. J. Assoc. Comput. Mach. **38**, 651–675 (1991)
7. Crochemore, M., Rytter, W.: Jewels of Stringology. World Scientific, Singapore (2003)
8. Crochemore, M., Mignosi, F., Restivo, A., Salemi, S.: Text compression using anti-dictionaries. In: Wiedermann, J., van Emde Boas, P., Nielsen, M. (eds.) ICALP 1999. LNCS, vol. 1644, pp. 261–270. Springer, Heidelberg (1999). https://doi.org/10.1007/3-540-48523-6_23
9. Dömösi, P., Ito, M.: Context-Free Languages and Primitive Words. World Scientific, Singapore (2005)
10. Hsiao, H.K., Yeh, Y.T., Yu, S.S.: A note of Ins-primitive words. Int. J. Comput. Math. **81**(8), 917–929 (2004)
11. Hsiao, H.K., Yu, S.S., Zhao, Y.: Word-paired insertions of languages. Int. J. Comput. Math. **81**(2), 169–181 (2004)
12. Kari, L.: On insertion and deletion in formal languages, Ph.D. thesis, University of Turku (1991)

13. Kari, L., Mahalingam, K.: Insertion and deletion for involution codes. In: Proceedings of Conference of Algebraic Informatics, CAI, pp. 207–219 (2005)
14. Kari, L., Mahalingam, K.: Watson-Crick conjugate and commutative words. In: Garzon, M.H., Yan, H. (eds.) DNA 2007. LNCS, vol. 4848, pp. 273–283. Springer, Heidelberg (2008). https://doi.org/10.1007/978-3-540-77962-9_29
15. Lyndon, R.C., Schützenberger, M.P.: The equation $a^M = b^N c^P$ in a free group. Mich. Math. J. **9**(4), 289–298 (1962)
16. Margaritis, D., Skiena, S.: Reconstructing strings from substrings in rounds. In: Proceedings of the 36th Annual Symposium on Foundations of Computer Science, pp. 613–620 (1995)
17. Storer, J.A.: Data Compression: Methods and Theory. Computer Science Press, Rockville (1998)
18. Yu, S.S.: Languages and Codes, pp. 112–113. Tsang-Hai Co., Taichung (2005)

Boolean Recombinase-Based Devices

Guillaume Pérution-Kihli[1], Sarah Guiziou[2,3], Federico Ulliana[1], Michel Leclère[1]($\boxtimes$), and Jérôme Bonnet[2]

[1] LIRMM, CNRS UMR 5506, University of Montpellier, Montpellier, France
michel.leclere@umontpellier.fr
[2] CBS, INSERM U154, CNRS UMR 5048, University of Montpellier, Montpellier, France
[3] Department of Biology, University of Washington, Seattle, WA 98195, USA

Abstract. This paper relates to a central problem in synthetic biology, which is that of designing *Recombinase-based biological devices* by matching a functional specification expressed as a Boolean function. This task is challenging as exploring the space of possibilities is typically unfeasible, and therefore many non-trivial design alternatives remain unexplored. Also, the issue has been so far regarded mainly from a practical perspective and is still lacking of formal foundations on which the definition of algorithms for assisting the biologists in their design tasks can be based. In this work, we present the first formal study of the problem, and give a formal semantics for a family of Recombinase-based biological devices. We then exhibit a set of semantic properties leading to the definition of *representative devices*, a notion that allows one to express infinitely large classes of design possibilities in a *finite* way. Building on this, we then provide a terminating algorithm for generating representative devices for n-input Boolean functions. An open online database of 18M design solutions for 4-inputs devices generated with our method has been released at http://recombinator.lirmm.fr.

Keywords: Boolean devices · Synthetic biology

1 Introduction: The Design Issue

One of the main targets of the field of synthetic biology is that of designing new biological systems (also called *devices*) by matching a functional specification with state of the art techniques in biological engineering. As a concrete example, a novel type of bacteria can be assembled for clinical diagnosis purposes to react to the presence of a combination of molecules by exhibiting a fluorescence recognizable via microscopy [9]. This is a challenging task as, when designing a new biological device, the space of possibilities rapidly becomes too large to be explored and the biological reliability of each of them impossible to be experimentally tested. This implies that biological engineering solutions often fall back to best-practices and established architecture patterns, and many non-trivial design alternatives remain unexplored. Synthetic biology has nowadays

© Springer Nature Switzerland AG 2019
C. Martín-Vide et al. (Eds.): TPNC 2019, LNCS 11934, pp. 82–94, 2019.
https://doi.org/10.1007/978-3-030-34500-6_5

key applications in health, environment, and manufacturing, and there is therefore a huge need for tools assisting biologists in best engineering their biological
devices [6].

The specification of a new biological device includes (1) its intended
behaviour and (2) the biotechnologies to be used to implement it. The biologist formalizes the behaviour of a device as a function of its inputs. Intuitively,
the purpose of this is to precisely describe how the device must react to the
substances in the environment where it will be deployed. Many approaches are
today used for synthetic biology. Among them, we mention transcriptional regu-
lators [10], RNA molecules [13], proteins [5], and Recombinases [3]. In this work,
we focus on the problem of assisting the design of biological systems whose
behaviour is (1) specified as *Boolean functions* and (2) based on (single-layer
single-cell) *Recombinases*.

Boolean functions affirmed as an intuitive means for biologists to precisely
define the device behaviour [3]. Inputs serve to acquire the environment stimuli.
A biological system with a binary output means that it emits a signal (or not)
depending on the inputs. In biological terms, such a "signal" corresponds to the
outcome of a well understood biological process called *gene expression*, which
is the natural process by which living cells produce proteins. In other words,
gene expression is the natural process exploited by biotechnologists to artificially
assemble living organisms implementing logic functions [3].

Our interest in *Recombinase-based* devices stems from their importance in
biological engineering. It is worth mentioning that Recombinase-based devices
are named after *Recombinases* [11], which are the enzymes used to control gene
expression. This type of devices offer several design advantages. First, they can
be adapted to various species of living organisms with minimal modifications
[2,12]. Then, and most importantly for the study conducted here, they are modular and compact. *Modular* means among other that the device inputs can be
easily interchanged. From a biological engineering point of view, this implies
that the same device architecture can be *reused* to implement different logic
functions (by simply interchanging the inputs). This is reminiscent of the notion
of *P*-class introduced for analogous problems in circuit-logic design [1]. *Compact*
means that this type of devices allow the biologists to minimize the number of
living cells implementing together a certain logic function, hence increasing the
device reliability. It is known that any Boolean function can be implemented
over multicellular [8] or multi-layer devices [4] (i.e., where distinct "parts" of the
Boolean function are implemented separately). Here, we will focus on the study
of the capacity of *single-layer single-cell* devices whose expressivity limits, that
is, the Boolean functions they can implement in a "monolithic" way (i.e., without distributing the Boolean function in several parts), are still unknown. From
a computational point of view, recombinase-based devices enable two types of
operations, named *inversion* and *excision*, on the elements controlling the process of gene expression. Hence, abstracting away, biological devices can be seen
as programs, written in a specific formal language allowing for inversion and
excision like operations on word expressions, that implement a logic function.

Despite the importance of recombinase-based devices in synthetic biology, the development of most design solutions mainly follows best-practices and fixed architecture patterns which limit the possibilities of such type of devices. Indeed, so far mostly 2-input functions only have been considered [3] with the exception of [12] that considered 3-input functions implemented with excisions only (that is, all designs using inversions have not been considered). Also, at the best of our knowledge, no foundational study of the properties of devices has been done.

The first goal of this paper is to present a formal study of recombinase-based devices (presented in Sect. 2) which can serve as foundations of the development of new biological engineering solutions for this type of devices. Precisely, we present the first formal semantics allowing one to compare them from a computational point of view (Sect. 3). From this, a set of minimality properties naturally emerge, which lead us to the notion of *canonical and representative* devices, by which infinitely large classes of design solutions can be expressed in a *finite* way (Sect. 4). The second goal of this paper is to actually compute devices that can help biologists defining their engineering solutions. We then present a terminating algorithm which allows one to generate all representative canonical devices for n-input systems (Sect. 5). Then, since each device has an associated Boolean function, the output of this algorithm can be used by biologist as a starting point to design new devices starting from a Boolean logic specification. An online platform for search and detailed comparison of 18M canonical and representative design solutions of up to 4-input devices generated with our method has been released (http://recombinator.lirmm.fr). Finally, our results also indicate some interesting expressivity limits for *single-layer single-cell* devices (Sect. 6). Indeed, the generation process shows that 8% among all 4-input Boolean functions cannot be implemented. We also show that they cannot implement all n-input Boolean functions, for every $n \geq 7$.

2   Recombinase-Based Devices

This section presents the main biological aspects of Recombinase-based devices [11]. The notions presented here are intended to introduce the reader to the formal semantics presented next. In biological terms, a device is a DNA construct in a living cell capable of gene expression. The DNA is artificially assembled thereby controlling gene expression according to the stimuli of the environment where the cell is. Roughly speaking, the two macro steps of gene expression are called *transcription* and *translation*. First, the cell DNA is copied to RNA (*transcription*). Then, the RNA is used to manufacture proteins (*translation*). By this process, a bacteria can for instance express a protein triggering a fluorescence.

To control gene expression, the main goal is to *control the transcription phase* of the device, i.e., which segment of the DNA is transcribed in RNA. Towards this goal, the DNA sequence of a cell is assembled by concatenating DNA segments called *biological parts*. As DNA, every biological part has a forward (F) or reverse (R) orientation, and therefore the transcription of a gene (and hence gene expression) *can succeed in both directions*. As a convention, we assume the forward orientation to run from left to right, opposed to the reverse orientation.

The two basic types of biological parts are *promoters* and *terminators*, which are responsible to start and stop the transcription phase, respectively. Then, the *genes* encode the information transcribed for the manufacturing of a protein at the end of the translation phase (and hence of gene expression).

$$P \ (\textit{F-promoter}) \qquad T \ (\textit{F-terminator}) \qquad G \ (\textit{F-gene})$$
$$d \ (\textit{R-promoter}) \qquad \bot \ (\textit{R-terminator}) \qquad \Im \ (\textit{R-gene})$$

Note at this point that whether a protein is transcribed from a device with only promoters, terminators, and genes, does not depend from the environment stimuli. Gene transcription directionally occurs if and only if a promoter starts a transcription (of course, without this being stopped by a terminator) that transcribes a gene. For instance, gene expression occurs for the device PLG but not for PTG. In principle, many distinct genes can be expressed by the same device. Here, we consider the case where a single gene can be expressed.

Recombinase-based devices use a third type of parts, namely the attachment *sites*, which enable the rearrangement of the DNA segments. We assume that there is a unique pair of sites for every input. Every rearrangement occurs between a pair of sites, and is triggered by an input i, so every site is labeled by its corresponding input. These rearrangements perform either the *inversion* which reverses the segment between two sites (e.g., PLG becomes $\Im$Td) and the *excision* which suppresses the segment between two sites. The modified DNA is likely to behave differently after the DNA rearranging. In practice, what happens is that a transcription process can be started or stopped. Also, a gene can be suppressed or transcribed thereby changing the outcome of the process.

3   Syntax and Transcriptional Semantics

This section presents a formalization of Recombinase-based devices. A Device is defined starting from an architecture and a naming of the inputs. A *biological architecture* A is an expression obtained from (1) biological parts, (2) the concatenation of expressions and finally (3) the nesting of expressions between excision and inversion marks. Two types of delimiters are marking excision and inversion operations. The excision marks are denoted by a pair of square brackets [] while the inversion marks are denoted by a pair of round brackets (). The set of architectures we consider is thus defined by the following grammar.

$$A ::= \epsilon \mid P \mid AA \mid [\,A\,] \mid (\,A\,) \qquad P ::= P \mid T \mid G \mid d \mid \bot \mid \Im$$

Here, ϵ is the empty architecture, P the set of parts, and AA the concatenation of two architectures. Note that the grammar generates only balanced parenthesized expressions, whose backbone are Dyck words with two types of delimiters. An architecture with n excisions or inversions is called a n-input architecture; 0-input architectures are special expressions also called *elementary sequences* and will be denoted by E. An architecture obtained by suppressing (at least) one biological part of an architecture A is called a *part-erasure* of A. An architecture obtained by suppressing (at least) one pair of marks denoting an excision or inversion of an architecture A is called an *input-erasure* of A. Note that architectures are closed for erasure, that is, any erasure of an architecture is still an architecture. A *device* is a couple $D = (A, \rho)$ where A is a n-input architecture and ρ is a bijective labeling function which associates every pair of companion delimiters of A to its corresponding input, i.e. an integer in $\{1, \ldots, n\}$. For example the architecture $A = [\text{P}](\text{G})$ can be used to build the devices $D = [\text{P}]_1(\text{G})_2$ and $D' = [\text{P}]_2(\text{G})_1$. Hence, there exists $n!$ devices for a given architecture. We denote by $D_{[i]}$ the sub-device of D delimited by the pair of marks corresponding to input i. For instance, $D_{[1]} = [\text{P}]_1$ and $D_{[2]} = (\text{G})_2$. The notions of part and input erasures are naturally extended to devices.

3.1 Device Activation and Architecture Rearrangement

The underlying architecture of a device is rearranged depending on the excisions and inversions activated by the environment stimuli. Let us denote by $\mathbf{B} = \{0, 1\}$ the Boolean domain. We define a possible configuration of the environment where a n-input device D is deployed as a tuple $\mathbf{c} \in \mathbf{B}^n$. Then, the activation function, we denote by $\text{activ}(D, \mathbf{c})$ yields an elementary sequence by rearranging D as the result of successively performing all excisions and inversions according to $\mathbf{c}$. For every elementary sequence $\text{activ}(E, \mathbf{c}) = E$, no rearrangement happens. Otherwise, let $\mathbf{c}[i]$ be the i-th element of the tuple $\mathbf{c}$ and D the sequence on which the activation of the i-th input is performed. If $D_{[i]}$ is an excision, i.e. $D_{[i]} = [D']_i$, the rearrangement of input i consists at substituting $D_{[i]}$ with D' if $\mathbf{c}[i] = 0$ and with ϵ if $\mathbf{c}[i] = 1$. Moreover, if $D_{[i]}$ is an inversion, i.e. $D_{[i]} = (D')_i$, the rearrangement of input i consists at substituting $D_{[i]}$ with D' if $\mathbf{c}[i] = 0$ and with $\text{inverse}(D')$ if $\mathbf{c}[i] = 1$, where the $\text{inverse}()$ function is defined as follows.

$$\text{inverse}(\epsilon) = \epsilon \qquad \text{inverse}(A\,A') = \text{inverse}(A')\,\text{inverse}(A)$$
$$\text{inverse}([A]_i) = [\,\text{inverse}(A)\,]_i \qquad \text{inverse}((A)_i) = (\,\text{inverse}(A)\,)_i$$
$$\text{inverse}(\text{P}) = \text{d} \quad \text{inverse}(\text{d}) = \text{P} \quad \text{inverse}(\text{T}) = \text{L} \quad \text{inverse}(\text{L}) = \text{T}$$
$$\text{inverse}(\text{G}) = \text{D} \quad \text{inverse}(\text{D}) = \text{G}$$

The result of $\text{activ}(D, \mathbf{c})$ consists at performing all architecture rearrangements, in any order, for all inputs $i \in \{1, \ldots, n\}$. Note that the result of the activation is an elementary sequence where all marks have been removed. The result of the rearrangement function is unique, and does not depend on the order on which elements are activated. Finally, note that for any two devices with the same architecture produce the same set of elementary sequences.

To illustrate, $[\text{P}(\text{L})]\text{G}$ is a 2-input architecture yielding two devices $D_1 = [\text{P}(\text{L})_2]_1\text{G}$ and $D_2 = [\text{P}(\text{L})_1]_2\text{G}$. So, $\text{inverse}(D_1) = \text{D}[(\text{T})_2\text{d}]_1$ and $\text{inverse}(D_2) = \text{D}[(\text{T})_1\text{d}]_2$. Consider now the possible input configurations. If no input is activated, then both devices transcribe the gene $\text{activ}(D_1, 00) = \text{PLG} = \text{activ}(D_2, 00)$. In all other cases no gene is transcribed as $\mathrm{activ}(D_1, 01) = \mathrm{PTG} = \mathrm{activ}(D_2, 10)$, and $\mathrm{activ}(D_1, 10) = \mathrm{activ}(D_1, 11) = \mathrm{G} = \mathrm{activ}(D_2, 01) = \mathrm{activ}(D_2, 11)$.

P		T		G	
s_0	$s_\mathbb{P}$	s_0	s_0	s_0	s_0
$s_\mathbb{P}$	$s_\mathbb{P}$	$s_\mathbb{P}$	s_0	$s_\mathbb{P}$	s_1
s_1	s_1	s_1	s_1	s_1	s_1

0		1		S	
s_0	s_0	s_0	s_1	s_0	$s_\mathbb{P}$
$s_\mathbb{P}$	$s_\mathbb{P}$	$s_\mathbb{P}$	s_1	$s_\mathbb{P}$	s_1
s_1	s_1	s_1	s_1	s_1	s_1

$\circ$	0	P	T	G	S	1
0	0	P	T	G	S	1
P	P	P	P	S	S	1
T	T	T	T	G	G	1

$\circ$	0	P	T	G	S	1
G	G	1	T	G	1	1
S	S	1	P	S	1	1
1	1	1	1	1	1	1

Fig. 1. Transcriptional function of parts (left). Neutral and composed functions (center). Composition of characteristic functions (right).

3.2 The Transcriptional Semantics of a Device

We formalize in this section the transcriptional semantics of devices, a notion which defines the computation that they perform. We model this as a transcription state function running over a finite number of states: *neutral* (s_0), *transcription* ($s_\mathbb{P}$), and *gene transcribed* (s_1). We denote this set of states $\{s_0, s_\mathbb{P}, s_1\}$ by S. In the neutral state no transcription is started and no gene is transcribed. In the transcription state no gene is transcribed but a transcription is started. The final state is reached when the gene is transcribed.

We will present first the transcriptional semantics of elementary sequences and then turn to that of general devices. We define the transcriptional semantics $\tau()$ for a sequence of parts without a specific orientation (again, we write in the forward orientation merely for readability).

$$\tau(\epsilon) = 0 \qquad \tau(EE') = \tau(E') \circ \tau(E) \qquad \tau(\mathrm{P}) = \mathbb{P} \quad \tau(\mathrm{T}) = \mathbb{T} \quad \tau(\mathrm{G}) = \mathbb{G}$$

For each part P, T, and G we define a characteristic transition function $\mathbb{P}$, $\mathbb{T}$, and $\mathbb{G}$, respectively, reported in Fig. 1. We now briefly comment on these. A system which is in the neutral state s_0 moves to the transcription state $s_\mathbb{P}$ when a promoter part starts the transcription. All other parts do not modify the s_0 state. When a system is in the transcription state $s_\mathbb{P}$ the gene part lifts it to the gene expressed state s_1. However, a terminator part gets it back to state s_0. Finally, the state s_1 is the final state of the computation as no part can further impact it. Figure 1 also presents a neutral transition function 0 which behaves as the identity and models the empty architecture ϵ.

More interestingly, the concatenation of any two biological parts (in the same orientation) and thus the composition of any of the previously mentioned functions, yields only two new composite functions $\mathbb{S}$ and $\mathbb{1}$, reported in Fig. 1. The function $\mathbb{1}$, denoting gene expression, results from a promoter (function $\mathbb{P}$) followed by a gene (function $\mathbb{G}$). The function $\mathbb{S}$ describes the effect of a sequence containing an expressible gene (function $\mathbb{G}$) followed by a promoter (function $\mathbb{P}$). We denote by $\mathcal{C}$ the set of *characteristic functions* $0, \mathbb{P}, \mathbb{T}, \mathbb{G}, \mathbb{S}, \mathbb{1}$. To illustrate, $\tau(\mathrm{PG}) = \mathbb{1}$, $\tau(\mathrm{TGPT}) = \mathbb{T}$ and $\tau(\mathrm{GPPTGP}) = \mathbb{S}$.

Proposition 1. *Characteristic functions are closed under composition.*

An elementary sequence E with parts on both orientations can be seen as a pair of distinct elementary sequences (E_F, E_R), containing only the parts in each orientation in the order of the original sequence. For example dTG can be seen as the pair (TG, d). The transcriptional semantics can then be described by a function $T : P^* \to C \times C$ yielding a characteristic functions for each orientation. Formally, we define $T(E) = \langle \tau(E_F), \tau(\text{inverse}(E_R)) \rangle$. We are ready to define the semantics of general devices, which depends on the environment configuration.

Definition 2 (Transcriptional Semantics). *Let D be a n-input device. The transcriptional semantics of D is a function $\delta_D : \mathbf{B}^n \to C \times C$ such that, for any configuration $\mathbf{c} \in \mathbf{B}^n$, $\delta_D(\mathbf{c}) = T(E)$ where $E = \text{activ}(D, \mathbf{c})$.*

To illustrate, consider again $D_1 = [\text{P}(\text{L})_2]_1\text{G}$. The configuration 00 gives the elementary sequence $E = \text{PLG}$, thus $E_F = \text{PG}$ and $E_R = \text{L}$. Then $\delta_{D_1}(00) = (\mathbb{1}, \mathbb{T})$, $\delta_{D_1}(01) = (\mathbb{0}, \mathbb{0})$, and $\delta_{D_1}(10) = \delta_{D_1}(11) = (\mathbb{G}, \mathbb{0})$.

Note that with six characteristic functions, for an elementary sequence we have 36 possible bidirectional transcriptional semantics. From this it follows that the number of possible logical semantics of a n-input device is $2^n \cdot 36$.

4   The Logical Semantics of Gene Transcription

The purpose of this section is to establish a connection between devices and the Boolean functions modeling gene transcription they implement. Boolean functions are important as they constitute a starting point for the biologist willing to design a new device that implements a certain logic.

A Boolean function is a function $\varphi : \mathbf{B}^n \to \mathbf{B}$, where n denotes its arity. We associate to each device a Boolean function. The goal of a Boolean function is to model the fact that gene transcription occurs after a certain activation of the inputs. Importantly, the function should not make any distinction regarding the orientation on which gene transcription succeeds. This leads to the following definition.

Definition 3. *Let D be a n-input device. The Boolean function of gene transcription $\varphi_D : \mathbf{B}^n \to \mathbf{B}$ associated with D is such that, for any configuration $\mathbf{c} \in \mathbf{B}^n$, $\varphi_D(\mathbf{c}) = 1$ if $\delta_D(\mathbf{c}) = \langle \mathbb{1}, \mathbb{C} \rangle$ or $\delta_D(\mathbf{c}) = \langle \mathbb{C}, \mathbb{1} \rangle$ with $\mathbb{C} \in C$.*

One first important observation is that two devices can be different from a transcriptional semantics point of view, yet implement the same Boolean function. To see that consider $E = \text{PG}$ and $E' = \text{ƎdP}$. In this case $\delta_E = (\mathbb{1}, \mathbb{0})$ and $\delta_{E'} = (\mathbb{P}, \mathbb{1})$ but $\varphi_E = 1 = \varphi_{E'}$. The same holds for the devices $D = [E]_1$ and $D' = [E']_1$ with different transcriptions but such that $\varphi_D = \varphi_{\neg i_1} = \varphi_{D'}$.[1]

We wish now to have a mean to compare devices on the basis of the Boolean functions they implement, so as to propose to the biologists a set of viable

---

[1] φ also denotes the Boolean function associated with the logic formula built with the inputs. For instance, $\varphi_{(\neg i_1 \wedge i_2)} = \{00 \mapsto 0, 01 \mapsto 1, 10 \mapsto 0, 11 \mapsto 0\}$.

design alternatives. As already explained, by means of input permutations one has access to the implementation of different Boolean functions with the same architecture. Also, we should take into account the fact that architectures with a different number of inputs may turn out to implement the same logics. The rest of the section is dedicated to the formalization of such notions of equivalence.

The P and M Classes of Boolean Functions. A classical notion for Boolean functions, introduced in the context of circuit design, is that of P-class [1].

Definition 4. *Two n-input Boolean functions φ and φ' belong to the same permutation class (or simply P-class) if $\varphi' = \varphi \circ \rho$, where ρ is an input permutation.*

For example, the functions $\varphi_{(i_1 \wedge \neg i_2)} \neq \varphi_{(\neg i_1 \wedge i_2)}$ belong to the same P-class by the permutation that interchanges the two inputs. Therefore, the permutation class of a function $\varphi_{(A,\rho)}$ contains all Boolean functions modeling gene transcription that can be implemented by using a given architecture A and a permutation of its inputs. This is the case for instance for $D_1 = \mathsf{P[T]}_1(\mathsf{G})_2$ and $D_2 = \mathsf{P(T(D)}_2)_1$ simply because $\varphi_{D_1} = \varphi_{(i_1 \wedge \neg i_2)} = \varphi_{D_2}$. However, also $D_3 = [\mathsf{P(D)}_2]_1$ yields functions in the same permutation class because $\varphi_{D_3} = \varphi_{(\neg i_1 \wedge i_2)}$. Finally $D_4 = \mathsf{PD[TL]}_1(\mathsf{Gd})_2$ is also such that $\varphi_{D_4} = \varphi_{(i_1 \wedge \neg i_2)}$ but it does not uses a minimal number of part, as the gene is transcribed in both directions here, and can hence be simplified to again obtain D_1.

The notion of P-class does not allow however to compare functions that have a different number of inputs. To do so, we now define the notion of M-class, which allows one to group Boolean functions with a different number on inputs, but that are equal once they have reached their minimal form, i.e., where all redundant inputs have been removed. We formalize this as follows. We say that a n-input function φ is the jth-input minimization of a $(n+1)$-input function φ', when given the mapping removing the jth input of φ, namely $\pi_j : \mathbf{B}^{n+1} \to \mathbf{B}^n$, which is defined as $\pi_j(i_1, \ldots, i_{n+1}) = (i_1, \ldots, i_{j-1}, i_{j+1}, \ldots, i_{n+1})$ we have that $\varphi \circ \pi_j = \varphi'$. We say that φ is a *minimization* of φ' if φ is obtained as the result of a sequence of input minimizations from φ'. A function that cannot be minimized is said to be in *minimal form*. The minimal form of a Boolean function φ is unique, and we denote it by $min(\varphi)$.

Definition 5. *Two Boolean functions φ and φ' belong to the same* minimization class *(or simply M-class) if $min(\varphi) = min(\varphi')$.*

To illustrate, the function $\varphi_{(i_2 \wedge \neg i_3 \wedge (i_1 \vee \neg i_1))}$ (where the input i_1 is redundant) belongs to the same M-class as $\varphi_{(i_2 \wedge \neg i_3)}$, which is its minimal form, but not to the same P-class. The function $\varphi_{(i_2 \wedge \neg i_3 \wedge (i_1 \vee \neg i_1))}$ is implemented for instance by the 3-input device $D_5 = \mathsf{P([T]}_2[\mathsf{G}]_3)_1\mathsf{d}$. It turns out that D_1, D_2, D_3, D_4, D_5 are all viable design alternatives (albeit D_4, D_5 are not minimal in the number of parts and inputs and shall be avoided). We can now define equivalent devices.

Definition 6. *Two devices D and D' are* equivalent for gene transcription, *denoted $D \equiv_{\mathsf{GenTran}} D'$, if φ_D and $\varphi_{D'}$ belong both to the same P-class or M-class.*

Note that $\equiv_{\mathsf{GenTran}}$ is an equivalence relation that partitions every set of devices with at most n inputs in a finite number of classes. Still, every class has an infinite number of elements, which makes the space of design configurations impossible to explore for the biologist willing to compare all n-input architectures implementing the same logic. For example, there is a class which contain all sequences PG, PPG, PPPG, etc. Furthermore, it may be interesting to consider only devices that satisfy some minimality criteria concerning their inputs and number of parts.

The remainder of the section is dedicated to answering the following questions.

1. Is it possible to characterize the devices which are *representative of all elements* of an equivalence class defined by $\equiv_{\mathsf{GenTran}}$?
2. Are such representative device finite in number ?
3. Are all n-input Boolean functions implementable with this type of devices ?

Representative Devices. We say that a device is representative if it is minimal in regard of the number of parts and inputs it uses. It is said *irreducible* if none of its parts can be erased without affecting gene expression. It is said *irredundant* when reducing its input set does affect gene expression.

Definition 7. *A device D is* representative *when the following holds.*

1. *if for any of its part-erasures D' holds $D' \not\equiv_{\mathsf{GenTran}} D$*   (IRREDUCIBILITY)
2. *if for any of its input-erasures D' holds $D' \not\equiv_{\mathsf{GenTran}} D$*   (IRREDUNDANCY)

Note that if a device is not irreducible then there exists another equivalent one in the same P-class that uses less parts. Similarly, if a device is not irredundant then there exists another equivalent device in the same M-class that uses less inputs. It is not difficult to see that for every device D there exists an equivalent device D' which is irredundant and irreducible.

Theorem 8. *The number of representative devices in an equivalence class defined by $\equiv_{\mathsf{GenTran}}$ is finite.*

Take the minimum number of inputs n for a device in a class defined by $\equiv_{\mathsf{GenTran}}$. All devices with more than n inputs are redundant, and hence not representative. Then, a n-input device architecture is a well-parenthesized expression with n pairs of marks. The parenthesis themselves (we call architecture skeleton) constitute Dyck words with two types of delimiters of size $2 \times n$. There are $2^n \times C(n)$, where $C(n)$ is the n-th Catalan number. This means that an architecture interleaves such a word with $2 \times n + 1$ elementary sequences. One can check that there are only 53 irreducible (representative) elementary sequences, which implies that the number of representative devices is bounded by $m!$ where $m = 2^n \times C(n) \times 53^{2n+1}$. We also derive the following on the device expressivity.

Proposition 9. *There is a n-input Boolean function which is not implementable for every $n \geq 7$.*

We know that $2^n \times C(n) \times 53^{2n+1}$ is an upper bound for the number of n-input architectures yielding representative devices. Since the number of n-input Boolean functions is 2^{2^n}, and the number maximum of n-input Boolean functions belonging to a n-input P-class is bounded by $n!$ (corresponding to the number of permutations of its n inputs), then $(2^{2^n}/n!)$ is a lower bound for the number of n-input P-classes. It follows that from 7 inputs the upper bound of n-input architectures yielding representative devices is strictly lower than the number lower bound for the number of n-input P-classes.

5   Generating Canonical Representative Architectures

Theorem 8 directly allows us to define a terminating algorithm for generating all n-input representative devices. Importantly, the generation method rather works on *generating the architectures* leading to the representative devices.

1. Generate all possible architecture skeletons with n inputs
2. Fill the architecture skeletons with $2n+1$ representative elementary sequences
3. Filter the architectures that don't yield representative devices

Once an architecture is generated, the devices are obtained by input permutation. Note that the third step of the algorithm is necessary because by assembling irreducible elementary sequences we are not guaranteed to build an architecture yielding a representative device. For example, P, G, and PG taken alone are irreducible elementary sequences but the device $P[PG]_1G$ is not representative as equivalent to PG. In this respect, it is important to see that to test if all devices obtained from one architecture are representative it suffices to test only one device with that architecture. Indeed, it holds that any device D from A is representative if and only all devices obtained from A are representative.

Removing Mirror Structures. An important optimization of the method we just presented accounts for the bidirectionality of architectures. Since the orientation of the architecture is merely conventional, there is no difference between an architecture and its inverse. We call a *mirror architecture* an architecture A such that inverse(A) = A. Hence, we can optimize step (1) by discarding one among a pair of distinct mirror skeletons that have been generated. For example we keep one between the skeletons [] () and () []. This almost drops by half the number of architectures generated. For the special case of skeletons that are mirror of themselves, like [], we can then optimize step (2) by carefully avoiding to generate pair of equivalent mirror architectures like [P]G and Ɔ[d]. The correctness of this optimization is stated as follows.

Proposition 10. *Let A be an architecture and D a device obtained from A. Let D' be a device obtained from the architecture* inverse(A). *Then, $D \equiv_{\mathsf{GenTran}} D'$.*

Using Canonical Elementary Sequences. We know that with respect to gene transcription all elementary sequences whose transcriptional semantics contains 𝟙 in one of the two orientations are equivalent.

Definition 11. *Two elementary sequences E and E' are gene transcription equivalent, denoted $E \equiv_1 E'$, if either (i) $\varphi_E = 1 = \varphi_{E'}$ or (ii) $\delta_E = \delta_{E'}$.*

Therefore, for each equivalence class defined by $\equiv_1$ we can consider only one irreducible elementary sequence, we call *canonical*. This optimization is key because in practice biologists prefer to work with a single canonical elementary sequence per semantics. This allows us to further limit the number of irreducible elementary sequence to consider in step (2), which drops from 53 to 26 (as all elementary sequences E such that $\varphi_E = 1$ have a unique canonical). The correctness of the optimization is now stated.

Table 1. Generation results up to 4-inputs.

# Inputs	Generation time	# Canonical architectures	# Implemented functions vs. # Possible functions
0	-	2	2/2 (100%)
1	3 s	10	2/2 (100%)
2	3 s	724	10/10 (100%)
3	5 min	96,981	218/218 (100%)
4	87 min	18,065,512	59,590/64,594 (92.25%)

Proposition 12. *Let D be a representative device and E an irreducible elementary sequence. For any irreducible elementary sequence E' such that $E \equiv_1 E'$ and D' obtained by substituting some occurrence of E with E' in D, we have that $D \equiv_{\mathsf{GenTran}} D'$. Moreover, D' is also a representative device.*

6   Implementation and Results

We implemented our method for generating all n-input architectures without mirror structures in C++(version 17), which allows us to have an optimized implementation. Our tool has been run on a High Performance Computer (HPC) cluster to generate all representative architectures from 1 to 4-input. The HPC processor is an Intel Xeon E5-2680 v4, 2.40GHz, 14 physical cores, with 128Go RAM DDR4 2400Mhz. Our implementation features a parallelization of the generation method which exploits multi-threading to fully use the 28 logical cores of the machine.

Table 1 reports the results of the generation. The generation time (column 2) follows the number of architectures leading to canonical representative devices (column 3) which, as already outlined, have an exponential growth in the number of inputs. Recall that each architecture allows to produce $n!$ different canonical devices. The last column indicates the number of Boolean functions searchable by biologists which are implemented by *at least* one architecture, over the total number of Boolean functions without redundant inputs (those that are not in minimal form are excluded). The results for 4-inputs functions complement Proposition 9, as they show that already for $n = 4$ some Boolean functions cannot be implemented with the devices considered here, while for every $0 \leq n \leq 3$ all functions are implemented.

The Recombinator Web Platform. To help biologists in their design tasks, a database containing the results of the generation have been made openly available on the *Recombinator* Web platform http://recombinator.lirmm.fr. The application offers an interface allowing the biologist to identify, for a given Boolean function, the set of canonical devices which implement it. The Web interface also offers a number of filters with relevant criteria for biologists that can be applied for a detailed search. For instance, it is possible to control the size of the device, as well as the number of promoters, terminators, genes, excisions, and inversions, in the sequence, and finally their relative positioning. The database has also been used to carry a statistical analysis of the relationships between devices and Boolean functions [7].

7   Conclusions and Perspectives

In this paper, we carried a formal study of a type of Recombinase-based devices an important family of biotechnologies used in synthetic biology. We presented a formal semantics for such type of devices and outlined a generation method for listing all representative and canonical n-input devices. We believe that the notions presented here can be used for further developments of design methods in synthetic biology. Our method has been implemented and the result of the generation published in a platform for detailed search of devices implementing a certain Boolean functions. Our results also show some limits in the expressivity of devices, in terms of the Boolean functions they implement. Future work will focus on the precise characterization of the (non-)implementable Boolean functions. The framework can also be extended with a probabilistic time-dependent activation of the inputs to express more complex logics within living organisms.

References

1. Astola, J., Stankovic, R.: Fundamentals of Switching Theory and Logic Design A Hands on Approach. Springer, Cham (2006). https://doi.org/10.1007/0-387-30311-1
2. Bischof, J., Maeda, R.K., Hediger, M., Karch, F., Basler, K.: An optimized transgenesis system for drosophila using germ-line-specific φc31 integrases. Proc. Natl. Acad. Sci. **104**(9), 3312–3317 (2007)
3. Bonnet, J., Yin, P., Ortiz, M.E., Subsoontorn, P., Endy, D.: Amplifying genetic logic gates. Science **340**(6132), 599–603 (2013)
4. Chiu, T.Y., Jiang, J.H.R.: Logic synthesis of recombinase-based genetic circuits. Sci. Rep. **7**(1), 12873 (2017)
5. Dueber, J.E., Yeh, B.J., Chak, K., Lim, W.A.: Reprogramming control of an allosteric signaling switch through modular recombination. Science **301**(5641), 1904–1908 (2003)

6. Endy, D.: Foundations for engineering biology. Nature **438**(7067), 449 (2005)
7. Guiziou, S., Pérution-Kihli, G., Ulliana, F., Leclère, M., Bonnet, J.: Exploring the design space of recombinase logic circuits. bioRxiv (2019). https://doi.org/10. 1101/711374
8. Guiziou, S., Ulliana, F., Moreau, V., Leclère, M., Bonnet, J.: An automated design framework for multicellular recombinase logic. ACS Synth. Biol. **7**(5), 1406–1412 (2018)
9. Kumari, A., Pasini, P., Daunert, S.: Detection of bacterial quorum sensing n-acyl homoserine lactones in clinical samples. Anal. Bioanal. Chem. **391**(5), 1619–1627 (2008)
10. Nielsen, A.A., et al.: Genetic circuit design automation. Science **352**(6281), aac7341 (2016)
11. Wang, Y., Yau, Y.Y., Perkins-Balding, D., Thomson, J.G.: Recombinase technology: applications and possibilities. Plant Cell Rep. **30**(3), 267–285 (2011). https:// doi.org/10.1007/s00299-010-0938-1
12. Weinberg, B.H., et al.: Large-scale design of robust genetic circuits with multiple inputs and outputs for mammalian cells. Nat. Biotechnol. **35**(5), 453 (2017)
13. Win, M.N., Smolke, C.D.: Higher-order cellular information processing with synthetic RNA devices. Science **322**(5900), 456–460 (2008)

Card-Based Protocol Against Actively Revealing Card Attack

Ken Takashima[1] , Daiki Miyahara[1,2] , Takaaki Mizuki[3] ,
and Hideaki Sone[3]

[1] Graduate School of Information Sciences, Tohoku University,
6–3–09 Aramaki-Aza-Aoba, Aoba-ku, Sendai 980–8579, Japan
{ken.takashima.q4,daiki.miyahara.q4}@dc.tohoku.ac.jp
[2] National Institute of Advanced Industrial Science and Technology,
2–3–26, Aomi, Koto-ku Tokyo 135-0064, Japan
[3] Cyberscience Center, Tohoku University, 6–3 Aramaki-Aza-Aoba, Aoba-ku,
Sendai 980–8578, Japan
mizuki+lncs@tohoku.ac.jp

Abstract. In 1989, den Boer presented the first card-based protocol, called the "five-card trick" that securely computes the AND function using a deck of physical cards via a series of actions such as shuffling and turning over cards. This protocol enables a couple to confirm their mutual love without revealing their individual feelings. During such a secure computation protocol, it is important to keep any information about the inputs secret. Almost all existing card-based protocols are secure under the assumption that all players participating in a protocol are semi-honest or covert, i.e., they do not deviate from the protocol if there is a chance that they will be caught when cheating. In this paper, we consider a more malicious attack in which a player as an active adversary can reveal cards illegally without any hesitation. Against such an actively revealing card attack, we define the t-secureness, meaning that no information about the inputs leaks even if at most t cards are revealed illegally. Subsequently, we design a 1-secure AND protocol. Thus, our contribution is the construction of the first formal framework to handle actively revealing card attacks and their countermeasures.

Keywords: Cryptography · Card-based protocols · Active Security ·
Secure multiparty computations

1 Introduction

In 1989, den Boer presented the first card-based protocol, called the *five-card trick* that securely computes the AND function using a deck of physical cards [1]. Assuming that Alice has a private bit $a \in \{0,1\}$ and Bob has a private bit $b \in \{0,1\}$, the five-card trick, which uses five cards ♣♣♡♡♡, proceeds as follows.

C. Martín-Vide et al. (Eds.): TPNC 2019, LNCS 11934, pp. 95–106, 2019.
https://doi.org/10.1007/978-3-030-34500-6_6

1. According to the encoding rule:

$$\boxed{\clubsuit}\,\boxed{\heartsuit} = 0 \text{ and } \boxed{\heartsuit}\,\boxed{\clubsuit} = 1, \tag{1}$$

Alice commits her private bit a to two face-down cards of different colors ($\clubsuit, \heartsuit$) without anyone seeing the order of the two cards:

$$\underbrace{\boxed{?}\,\boxed{?}}_{a}.$$

Such a pair of face-down cards is called a *commitment* to a. Similarly, Bob places a commitment to b on the table. Therefore, together with the remaining red card $\boxed{\heartsuit}$, the initial sequence of the five cards is

$$\underbrace{\boxed{?}\,\boxed{?}}_{a}\,\underbrace{\boxed{?}\,\boxed{?}}_{b}\,\boxed{\heartsuit}.$$

2. Move the rightmost red card to the center and turn it over:

$$\underbrace{\boxed{?}\,\boxed{?}}_{a}\,\boxed{\heartsuit}\,\underbrace{\boxed{?}\,\boxed{?}}_{b} \rightarrow \underbrace{\boxed{?}\,\boxed{?}}_{a}\,\boxed{?}\,\underbrace{\boxed{?}\,\boxed{?}}_{b}.$$

3. Swap the first and second cards (from the left), namely the two cards constituting the commitment to a; owing to the encoding (1), this action performs the NOT operation such that a commitment to the negation $\bar{a}$ of a can be obtained:

$$\underbrace{\boxed{?}\,\boxed{?}}_{\bar{a}}\,\boxed{?}\,\underbrace{\boxed{?}\,\boxed{?}}_{b}.$$

It is noteworthy that only when $a = b = 1$, the three cards in the middle will be $\boxed{\heartsuit}\,\boxed{\heartsuit}\,\boxed{\heartsuit}$.

4. Apply a *random cut*, denoted by $\langle \cdot \rangle$; it is a shuffle action to cyclically shift the sequence of cards at random:

$$\left\langle \boxed{?}\,\boxed{?}\,\boxed{?}\,\boxed{?}\,\boxed{?} \right\rangle \rightarrow \boxed{?}\,\boxed{?}\,\boxed{?}\,\boxed{?}\,\boxed{?}.$$

The shift offset is uniformly distributed on $\{0, 1, 2, 3, 4\}$, and nobody knows the offset[1].

5. Open all the five cards.
   - If three consecutive red cards $\boxed{\heartsuit}\,\boxed{\heartsuit}\,\boxed{\heartsuit}$ (apart from cyclic rotation) appear, we have $a \wedge b = 1$.
   - If $\boxed{\heartsuit}\,\boxed{\heartsuit}\,\boxed{\heartsuit}$ do not appear, we have $a \wedge b = 0$.

---

[1] It is well known that humans can implement a random cut securely [13].

This is the five-card trick, which securely computes the AND function, i.e., it reveals only the value of $a \wedge b$. As an application, for instance, this card-based protocol enables Alice and Bob to confirm their mutual love without revealing their individual feelings.

During such a secure computation protocol, it is important to keep any information about the inputs secret. As seen above, the five-card trick preserves the secrecy of the inputs a, b by virtue of the face-down cards, and the shuffle action eliminates the individual values of the inputs aside from the exact value of $a \wedge b$. In other words, the five-card trick is secure provided that all players obey the protocol. Similar to the five-card trick, almost all existing card-based protocols (e.g., [2, 4, 6, 10, 11]) are secure under the assumption that all players are *semi-honest* or *covert*, i.e., they do not deviate from the protocol if there is a chance that they will be caught when cheating. In most cases, a card-based protocol is executed completely publicly with all eyes fixed on how the cards are manipulated, and hence, any illegal actions by the players (or others) will be noticed [8]; thus, any semi-honest or covert player always follows the protocol.

By contrast, this paper considers a more malicious attack: We assume that one player (e.g., Alice) is an active adversary who may possibly reveal face-down cards illegally without any hesitation. For example, if Alice suddenly reveals the commitment to b at Step 3 during the execution of the five-card trick, Bob's private input will be leaked immediately. We call such a malicious attack the *actively revealing card attack*.

To prevent face-down cards from being revealed illegally, we may place each card into an envelope, as indicated by Koch and Walzer [3]. However, using envelopes is not convenient; hence, we solicit another solution that does not rely on any additional tools such as envelopes. Thus, we have to devise a method to keep individual players' inputs secret even if some of the face-down cards are revealed maliciously. To this end, we borrow an idea from secret sharing schemes [12] such that each input commitment will be split into several "share" commitments. Specifically, as the "revealing-card tolerance," we introduce the concept of "t-secureness" in which any information regarding the inputs will be preserved even if at most t cards are revealed maliciously. Subsequently, we design a 1-secure AND protocol. Thus, our main contribution is to construct the first formal framework to handle actively revealing card attacks and their countermeasures.

This paper focuses on *non-committed format* protocols that specify the output value by revealing some face-down cards, as shown in the five-card trick (or in others, e.g., [6]). By contrast, there are *committed format* protocols that produce commitments (consisting of face-down cards) as the output (e.g., [2, 10, 11]): Because the output is hidden owing to the face-down cards, during such a committed format protocol, information regarding the input as well as output will not be leaked. Meanwhile, committed format protocols have been formalized well; no formal treatment of non-committed format protocols has been reported (note that because a committed format protocol does not leak any information, it suffices to consider perfect secrecy; meanwhile, a non-committed format protocol needs to leak some information regarding the input to reveal the output value, and hence, a more careful treatment is required). Herein, we first formalize a non-committed format protocol. This formalization is one of our major results.

It is noteworthy that Mizuki and Shizuya [8] previously adopted a similar idea to deal with the situation where some of the cards may be flawed, i.e., the cards may have scuff marks on their backs (undoubtedly, the problem of flawed cards is different from that of the actively revealing card attack, but they may share some common features). Because this previous work [8] considered only committed format protocols, it is interesting future work to apply the technique proposed herein to design "scuff-proof" non-committed format protocols.

The remainder of this paper is organized as follows. In Sect. 2, we briefly introduce a formal approach for describing a card-based protocol. In Sect. 3, we formally define a non-committed format protocol. In Sect. 4, we define the t-secureness against the actively revealing card attack. In Sect. 5, we construct a 1-secure AND protocol and confirm its security. Finally, the paper is concluded in Sect. 6.

2   Preliminaries

In this section, the way to formally describe a card-based protocol is presented.

The computational model of card-based protocols has been formalized via abstract machine [3,4,7,9]. Roughly speaking, a protocol consists of a series of three actions: turn, perm, and shuf actions, along with a sequence of cards.

Consider a sequence of d cards. A turn action is specified by a set $T \subseteq \{1, 2, \ldots, d\}$ of positions of cards; the action (turn, T) turns over every card whose position is in T. A perm action is specified by a permutation $\pi \in S_d$, where S_d denotes the symmetric group of degree d; the action (perm, π) rearranges the positions of d cards according to π. A shuf action is specified by a set $\Pi \subseteq S_d$ of permutations; the action (shuf, Π) probabilistically rearranges the positions of d cards according to a permutation π uniformly drawn from Π. We call a protocol using exactly d cards a d-card protocol.

To illustrate, recall the execution of the five-card trick [1] presented in the previous section. It uses two types of cards, ♣ and ♡ , whose backs are ? . All cards of the same type are indistinguishable. The five-card trick, which is a 5-card protocol, starts with a sequence of five cards:

$$\underbrace{?\ ?}_{a}\ \underbrace{?\ ?}_{b}\ ♡.\tag{2}$$

Step 2 of the five-card trick is formally captured by (perm, (3 4 5)) along with (turn, {3}). Step 3 is (perm, (1 2)). In Step 4, we apply a random cut that can be written as (shuf, RC_5), where $RC_5 = \{(1\ 2\ 3\ 4\ 5)^i | 1 \leq i \leq 5\}$. Step 5 is (turn, {1, 2, 3, 4, 5}).

To discuss the correctness and security of protocols, we use the concept of *statuses* of a protocol. For example, the initial status of the five-card trick (as in (2)) is described as follows:

$$\clubsuit\heartsuit\clubsuit\heartsuit\heartsuit \quad (p_{00}, 0, 0, 0)$$
$$\clubsuit\heartsuit\heartsuit\clubsuit\heartsuit \quad (0, p_{01}, 0, 0)$$
$$\heartsuit\clubsuit\clubsuit\heartsuit\heartsuit \quad (0, 0, p_{10}, 0)$$
$$\heartsuit\clubsuit\heartsuit\clubsuit\heartsuit \quad (0, 0, 0, p_{11}),$$

where p_{ij} denotes the probability that input (a, b) is equal to (i, j) for every $(i, j) \in \{0, 1\}^2$; in other words, $(p_{00}, p_{01}, p_{10}, p_{11})$ denotes a probability distribution on the input set $\{0, 1\}^2$. The status above consists of four *entries*, each of which is a pair of a symbol sequence (such as $\clubsuit\heartsuit\clubsuit\heartsuit\heartsuit$) and a *probability trace* (such as $(p_{00}, 0, 0, 0)$); the first entry means that the symbol sequence $\clubsuit\heartsuit\clubsuit\heartsuit\heartsuit$ and the event $(a, b) = (0, 0)$ occur with a probability of p_{00} (and $\clubsuit\heartsuit\clubsuit\heartsuit\heartsuit$ with $(a, b) \neq (0, 0)$ never occurs), the second entry means that $\clubsuit\heartsuit\heartsuit\clubsuit\heartsuit$ and $(a, b) = (0, 1)$ occur with a probability of p_{01}, and so on. The initial status (and succeeding statuses) are transformed into another status by an action as shown in Fig. 1. In particular, the turn action results in ten "leaf" statuses.

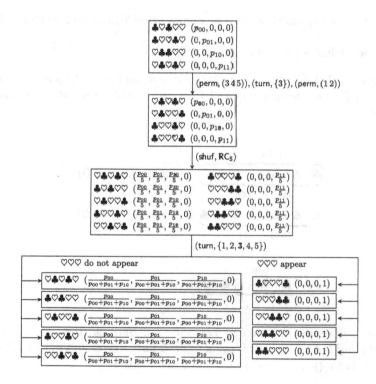

Fig. 1. The (modified) KWH-tree of the five-card trick

The expression of protocols in Fig. 1 was established by Koch and Walzer [3] where a tree structure specifies a protocol. We modify it slightly using the probability traces introduced by Mizuki and Komano [5]. We call such a tree the *(modified) KWH-tree* of a protocol. Borrowing a terminology in graph theory, we call the bottom statuses in a KWH-tree the *leaf* statuses.

Note that in each of the first three statuses (namely, "non-leaf" statuses) depicted in Fig. 1, the (coordinate-wise) sum of all probability traces is equal to $(p_{00}, p_{01}, p_{10}, p_{11})$; this guarantees that no information regarding the input (a, b) will be leaked. Regarding the ten leaf statuses, each of them has only one probability trace, which is either $(\frac{p_{00}}{p_{00}+p_{01}+p_{10}}, \frac{p_{01}}{p_{00}+p_{01}+p_{10}}, \frac{p_{10}}{p_{00}+p_{01}+p_{10}}, 0)$ or $(0, 0, 0, 1)$; this implies that any information other than the value of $a \wedge b$ will not be leaked.

To the best of our knowledge, Fig. 1 is the first attempt to depict the KWH-tree of the five-card trick. Because a formal treatment for non-committed format protocols does not exist, we will create such a formal framework, as will be explained in the next section.

3   Formalizing Non-committed Format Protocols

In this section, we formally define a non-committed format protocol for a Boolean function.

First, we define an n-input protocol.

Definition 1. *Let $d \geq 2n$ for an integer $n \geq 2$, and let $\mathcal{P}$ be a d-card protocol. We say that $\mathcal{P}$ is an n-input protocol if its initial status consists of the following 2^n entries:*

$$\overbrace{\clubsuit\heartsuit\clubsuit\heartsuit\clubsuit\heartsuit\cdots\clubsuit\heartsuit\clubsuit\heartsuit}^{2n\ symbols}\ \alpha \quad (p_0, 0, 0, \ldots, 0, 0)$$
$$\underbrace{}_{000\ldots 00_2}$$

$$\clubsuit\heartsuit\clubsuit\heartsuit\clubsuit\heartsuit\cdots\clubsuit\heartsuit\heartsuit\clubsuit\ \alpha \quad (0, p_1, 0, \ldots, 0, 0)$$
$$\underbrace{}_{000\ldots 01_2}$$

$$\vdots$$

$$\heartsuit\clubsuit\heartsuit\clubsuit\clubsuit\heartsuit\clubsuit\cdots\heartsuit\clubsuit\heartsuit\clubsuit\ \alpha \quad (0, 0, 0, \ldots, 0, p_{2^n-1})$$
$$\underbrace{}_{111\ldots 11_2}$$

where α is any symbol sequence of length $d - 2n$. Here, p_i, $0 \leq i \leq 2^n - 1$, is the probability that the n-bit input is equal to the binary expression of i. Furthermore, we call the tuple $(p_0, \ldots, p_{2^n-1})$ an input distribution.

As shown in Definition 1, we implicitly assume a one-to-one mapping between $\{0, 1\}^n$ and $\{0, 1, \ldots, 2^n - 1\}$. Thus, throughout this paper, if we write q_b for $b \in \{0, 1\}^n$ and a tuple $(q_0, \ldots, q_{2^n-1})$, we regard the subscription b as the corresponding decimal number.

Next, we define some properties regarding the statuses.

Definition 2. *Let $\mathcal{P}$ be an n-input protocol with an input distribution $(p_0, \ldots, p_{2^n-1})$, and consider a Boolean function $f : \{0,1\}^n \to \{0,1\}$.*

- *A status S of $\mathcal{P}$ is called an* opaque status *if the (coordinate-wise) sum of its probability traces is equal to $(p_0, \ldots, p_{2^n-1})$.*
- *We say that a status S is an* output-0 status *if the sum of its probability traces $(q_0, \ldots, q_{2^n-1})$ satisfies*

$$\begin{cases} q_b = \frac{p_b}{\sum_{i \in f^{-1}(0)} p_i} & \text{if } f(b) = 0 \\ q_b = 0 & \text{if } f(b) = 1 \end{cases}$$

for every $b \in \{0,1\}^n$, where $f^{-1}(0)$ is the preimage of 0 under f.
- *We say that a status S is an* output-1 status *if the sum of its probability traces $(q_0, \ldots, q_{2^n-1})$ satisfies*

$$\begin{cases} q_b = 0 & \text{if } f(b) = 0 \\ q_b = \frac{p_b}{\sum_{i \in f^{-1}(1)} p_i} & \text{if } f(b) = 1 \end{cases}$$

for every $b \in \{0,1\}^n$.

We are now ready to formally define a non-committed format protocol.

Definition 3. *Let $\mathcal{P}$ be an n-input protocol, and let $f : \{0,1\}^n \to \{0,1\}$ be a Boolean function. We say that $\mathcal{P}$ works for f in a non-committed format if the following holds:*

- *every leaf status is either an output-0 status or an output-1 status, and all other statuses are opaque;*
- *the expected height of its KWH-tree is finite.*

One can easily verify that the five-card trick satisfies Definition 3.

4   Defining Revealing-Card Tolerance

As mentioned before, this paper considers an active attack where an adversary can reveal some cards without obeying a protocol. Because the execution of a protocol is conducted publicly, it is difficult for an adversary to illegally reveal many cards simultaneously. Thus, we assume that such a malicious adversary can reveal at most t cards at most once when the protocol is executed.

Note that any n-input protocol (defined in Definition 1) cannot be "secure" against the actively revealing card attack because the adversary can reveal some cards that constitute the input commitments to obtain the secret values immediately after the protocol starts. Therefore, the input commitments must be masked. To achieve this, we borrow an idea from secret sharing schemes. Hence, instead of directly placing commitments to their private bits, Alice places two commitments to $a^1, a^2 \in \{0,1\}$ such that $a = a^1 \oplus a^2$, where Alice's private bit a is split into a^1 and a^2 randomly, and Bob places two commitments similarly:

$$\boxed{?}\,\boxed{?}\;\boxed{?}\,\boxed{?}\quad\boxed{?}\,\boxed{?}\;\boxed{?}\,\boxed{?}\,.$$

$$\underbrace{}_{a^1}\;\underbrace{}_{a^2}\quad\underbrace{}_{b^1}\;\underbrace{}_{b^2}$$

For such an input sequence, even if at most one card is revealed illegally, the values of a and b will not be leaked. By further extending this, we have an $(n, t+1)$-input protocol, as in the following Definition 4. Hereinafter, for $b \in \{0,1\}^n$, $b[i]$ denotes the i-th bit (of the n-bit sequence b).

Definition 4. *Let $d \geq 2n(t+1)$ for integers $n \geq 2$ and $t \geq 1$, and let $\mathcal{P}$ be a d-card protocol. We say that $\mathcal{P}$ is an $(n, t+1)$-input protocol if its initial status consists of all entries in $\bigcup_{b \in \{0,1\}^n} \mathcal{E}_b$ such that*

$$\mathcal{E}_b = \left\{ (x_1^1 \ldots x_1^{t+1} x_2^1 \ldots x_2^{t+1} \ldots x_n^1 \ldots x_n^{t+1} \alpha, \ (0, \ldots, 0, \frac{p_b}{n2^t}, 0, \ldots, 0)) \right.$$
$$\left. \left| \bigoplus_{j=1}^{t+1} x_i^j = b[i], 1 \leq i \leq n \right\} \right.$$

for every $b \in \{0,1\}^n$, where $x_i^j \in \{0,1\}$ is interpreted as a pair of symbols based on the encoding: $0 = \clubsuit\heartsuit$ and $1 = \heartsuit\clubsuit$, and α is any symbol sequence of length $d - 2n(t+1)$.

We are now ready to define the "t-secureness" as in the following Definition 6 along with Definition 5.

Definition 5. *Let $\mathcal{P}$ be an $(n, t+1)$-input protocol, and let $f : \{0,1\}^n \to \{0,1\}$ be a Boolean function. We define opaque, output-0, and output-1 statuses similarly as in Definition 2. Additionally, we define "working for f" similarly to Definition 3.*

Definition 6. *Let $\mathcal{P}$ be an $(n, t+1)$-input protocol working for a Boolean function f in a non-committed format. We say that $\mathcal{P}$ is t-secure if any resulting status from applying any action (turn, T) with $|T| \leq t$ to every status of $\mathcal{P}$ is either an opaque status, an output-0 status, or an output-1 status.*

5 Our 1-Secure AND Protocol

We describe the construction of a 1-secure AND protocol in this section. In Sect. 5.1, we present its outline; our protocol consists of the setup, first, second, and third phases. In Sects. 5.2, 5.3, and 5.4, we provide the details of the first, second, and third phases, respectively.

5.1   Outline of Our Protocol

Because we wish to design a 1-secure AND computation of two variables (namely, $n = 2$ and $t = 1$), we should use a $(2, 2)$-input protocol. Therefore, Alice and Bob create $a^1, a^2, b^1, b^2 \in \{0, 1\}$ such that $a = a^1 \oplus a^2$ and $b = b^1 \oplus b^2$ as input. Thus, it suffices to compute $(a^1 \wedge b^1) \oplus (a^1 \wedge b^2) \oplus (a^2 \wedge b^1) \oplus (a^2 \wedge b^2) = a \wedge b$. To this end, our protocol proceeds as follows.

Setup Phase. Satisfying Definition 4, Alice places two commitments to a^1, a^2, and Bob places two commitments to b^1, b^2:

$$\underbrace{\boxed{?}\,\boxed{?}}_{a^1}\ \underbrace{\boxed{?}\,\boxed{?}}_{a^2}\ \underbrace{\boxed{?}\,\boxed{?}}_{b^1}\ \underbrace{\boxed{?}\,\boxed{?}}_{b^2}.$$

First Phase. Make two copied commitments to each of b^1 and b^2 using the existing COPY protocol [10]:

$$\underbrace{\boxed{?}\,\boxed{?}}_{a^1}\ \underbrace{\boxed{?}\,\boxed{?}}_{a^2}\ \underbrace{\boxed{?}\,\boxed{?}}_{b^1}\ \underbrace{\boxed{?}\,\boxed{?}}_{b^2} \rightarrow \underbrace{\boxed{?}\,\boxed{?}}_{a^1}\ \underbrace{\boxed{?}\,\boxed{?}}_{a^2}\ \underbrace{\boxed{?}\,\boxed{?}}_{b^1}\ \underbrace{\boxed{?}\,\boxed{?}}_{b^1}\ \underbrace{\boxed{?}\,\boxed{?}}_{b^2}\ \underbrace{\boxed{?}\,\boxed{?}}_{b^2}.$$

Second Phase. From the commitments to a^1, b^1, b^2, make commitments to $a^1 \wedge b^1, a^1 \wedge b^2$ using the existing AND protocol [8]; similarly, from the commitments to a^2, b^1, b^2, make commitments to $a^2 \wedge b^1, a^2 \wedge b^2$:

$$\underbrace{\boxed{?}\,\boxed{?}}_{a^1}\ \underbrace{\boxed{?}\,\boxed{?}}_{b^1}\ \underbrace{\boxed{?}\,\boxed{?}}_{b^2}\ \underbrace{\boxed{?}\,\boxed{?}}_{a^2}\ \underbrace{\boxed{?}\,\boxed{?}}_{b^1}\ \underbrace{\boxed{?}\,\boxed{?}}_{b^2} \rightarrow \underbrace{\boxed{?}\,\boxed{?}}_{a^1 \wedge b^1}\ \underbrace{\boxed{?}\,\boxed{?}}_{a^1 \wedge b^2}\ \underbrace{\boxed{?}\,\boxed{?}}_{a^2 \wedge b^1}\ \underbrace{\boxed{?}\,\boxed{?}}_{a^2 \wedge b^2}.$$

Third phase. Compute $(a^1 \wedge b^1) \oplus (a^1 \wedge b^2) \oplus (a^2 \wedge b^1) \oplus (a^2 \wedge b^2)$.

Here, we analyze the security of the setup phase. There are 16 possibilities for $(a^1, a^2, b^1, b^2) \in \{0, 1\}^4$, and hence, the initial status can be written as the first four columns and the last column in Table 1. (Note that any action (turn, $\{i\}$) reveals at most one bit among four bits.) One can easily confirm that any action (turn, $\{i\}$) results in an opaque status.

5.2   First Phase

In this phase, we duplicate the commitments to b^1 and b^2. To this end, we use the existing COPY protocol [10], which performs the following (refer to [10] for the details):

$$\underbrace{\boxed{?}\,\boxed{?}}_{x}\ \boxed{\clubsuit}\,\boxed{\clubsuit}\,\boxed{\heartsuit}\,\boxed{\heartsuit} \rightarrow \underbrace{\boxed{?}\,\boxed{?}}_{x}\ \underbrace{\boxed{?}\,\boxed{?}}_{x}\ \boxed{\clubsuit}\,\boxed{\heartsuit}.$$

By executing the COPY protocol twice, we have

Table 1. Essential truth table for deriving statuses of our protocol.

a^1	a^2	b^1	b^2	$a^1 \wedge b^1$	$a^1 \wedge b^2$	$a^2 \wedge b^1$	$a^2 \wedge b^2$	$\overline{a^1} \wedge b^1$	$\overline{a^1} \wedge b^2$	$\overline{a^2} \wedge b^1$	$\overline{a^2} \wedge b^2$	Prob. trace
0	0	0	0	0	0	0	0	0	0	0	0	$(p_{00}/4, 0, 0, 0)$
0	0	1	1	0	0	0	0	1	1	1	1	$(p_{00}/4, 0, 0, 0)$
1	1	0	0	0	0	0	0	0	0	0	0	$(p_{00}/4, 0, 0, 0)$
1	1	1	1	1	1	1	1	0	0	0	0	$(p_{00}/4, 0, 0, 0)$
0	0	0	1	0	0	0	0	0	1	0	1	$(0, p_{01}/4, 0, 0)$
0	0	1	0	0	0	0	0	1	0	1	0	$(0, p_{01}/4, 0, 0)$
1	1	0	1	0	1	0	1	0	0	0	0	$(0, p_{01}/4, 0, 0)$
1	1	1	0	1	0	1	0	0	0	0	0	$(0, p_{01}/4, 0, 0)$
0	1	0	0	0	0	0	0	0	0	0	0	$(0, 0, p_{10}/4, 0)$
0	1	1	1	0	0	1	1	1	1	0	0	$(0, 0, p_{10}/4, 0)$
1	0	0	0	0	0	0	0	0	0	0	0	$(0, 0, p_{10}/4, 0)$
1	0	1	1	1	1	0	0	0	0	1	1	$(0, 0, p_{10}/4, 0)$
0	1	0	1	0	0	0	1	0	1	0	0	$(0, 0, 0, p_{11}/4)$
0	1	1	0	0	0	1	0	1	0	0	0	$(0, 0, 0, p_{11}/4)$
1	0	0	1	0	1	0	0	0	0	0	1	$(0, 0, 0, p_{11}/4)$
1	0	1	0	1	0	0	0	0	0	1	0	$(0, 0, 0, p_{11}/4)$

$$\boxed{?}\boxed{?}\ \boxed{?}\boxed{?}\ \clubsuit\clubsuit\ \heartsuit\heartsuit \ \rightarrow\ \boxed{?}\boxed{?}\ \boxed{?}\boxed{?}\ \boxed{?}\boxed{?}\ \boxed{?}\boxed{?}\ \clubsuit\heartsuit .$$

(underbraces: b^1, b^2 on left; b^1, b^1, b^2, b^2 on right)

During this first phase, any action (turn, $\{i\}$) reveals at most one bit among b^1 and b^2; hence, similar to the setup phase, any resulting status from an illegal reveal will be opaque. (We omit the details owing to page limitations.)

5.3 Second Phase

In this phase, we use the existing AND protocol [8]:

$$\boxed{?}\boxed{?}\ \boxed{?}\boxed{?}\ \boxed{?}\boxed{?}\ \clubsuit\clubsuit\ \heartsuit\heartsuit \ \rightarrow\ \boxed{?}\boxed{?}\ \boxed{?}\boxed{?}\ \boxed{?}\boxed{?}\ \boxed{?}\boxed{?}\ \clubsuit\heartsuit .$$

(underbraces: x, y, z on left; $x \wedge y$, $x \wedge z$, $\overline{x} \wedge y$, $\overline{x} \wedge z$ on right)

We destroy the commitments to $\overline{x} \wedge y$ and $\overline{x} \wedge z$ by shuffling each of them.

By executing the AND protocol twice, we have

$$\boxed{?}\boxed{?}\ \boxed{?}\boxed{?}\ \boxed{?}\boxed{?}\ \boxed{?}\boxed{?}\ \boxed{?}\boxed{?}\ \boxed{?}\boxed{?}\ \clubsuit\clubsuit\ \heartsuit\heartsuit$$

(underbraces: a^1, b^1, b^2, a^2, b^1, b^2)

$$\rightarrow\ \boxed{?}\boxed{?}\ \boxed{?}\boxed{?}\ \boxed{?}\boxed{?}\ \boxed{?}\boxed{?}\ \clubsuit\clubsuit\clubsuit\ \heartsuit\heartsuit\heartsuit .$$

(underbraces: $a^1 \wedge b^1$, $a^1 \wedge b^2$, $a^2 \wedge b^1$, $a^2 \wedge b^2$)

During this second phase, any action (turn, $\{i\}$) reveals at most one bit among $a^1, a^2, b^1, b^2, a^1 \wedge b^1, a^1 \wedge b^2, a^2 \wedge b^1, a^2 \wedge b^2, \overline{a^1} \wedge b^1, \overline{a^1} \wedge b^2, \overline{a^2} \wedge b^1, \overline{a^2} \wedge b^2$; Table 1 implies that any illegal resulting status will be opaque.

5.4   Third Phase

In this phase, we compute $(a^1 \wedge b^1) \oplus (a^1 \wedge b^2) \oplus (a^2 \wedge b^1) \oplus (a^2 \wedge b^2)$ from the commitments to $a^1 \wedge b^1, a^1 \wedge b^2, a^2 \wedge b^1, a^2 \wedge b^2$. Our "4-bit XOR subprotocol" proceeds as follows.

1. Negate the commitment to $a^1 \wedge b^1$ by $(\mathsf{perm}, (1\,2))$:

2. Rearrange the sequence of the eight cards by $(\mathsf{perm}, (2\,5\,3)(4\,6\,7))$:

3. Apply a random bisection cut [10], denoted by $[\,\cdot\,|\,\cdot\,]$, which is the shuffle action $(\mathsf{shuf}, \{\mathsf{id}, (1\,5)(2\,6)(3\,7)(4\,8)\})$:

4. Apply $(\mathsf{perm}, (2\,3\,5)(4\,7\,6))$, which is the inverse permutation of Step 2:

5. Apply a random cut, namely $(\mathsf{shuf}, \mathsf{RC}_8)$, where RC_8 is defined similarly to RC_5:

6. Reveal all the cards by $(\mathsf{turn}, \{1, 2, 3, 4, 5, 6, 7, 8\})$. Count the commitments[2]:
   - If the number of commitments to 1 is odd, $a \wedge b = 0$.
   - If the number of commitments to 1 is even, $a \wedge b = 1$.

Owing to page limitations, we omit the KWH-tree of our XOR subprotocol, which implies the correctness and secrecy.

6   Conclusion

In this paper, we first described the KWH-tree of the five-card trick and formally defined non-committed protocols. Against the actively revealing card attack, we defined the t-secureness and presented a 1-secure AND protocol.

Acknowledgments. This work was supported by JSPS KAKENHI Grant Numbers JP17K00001 and JP19J21153. We would like to thank the anonymous reviewers for their fruitful comments.

---

[2] We can specify the boundary between commitments by the color of consecutive cards. For example, if we obtain a sequence ♣♣♡♣♡♣♡♡, we can place delimiters in the middle of each of ♣♣ and ♡♡ as ♣|♣♡♣♡♣♡|♡; hence, we have ♣♡|♣♡|♣♡|♡♣.

References

1. Boer, B.: More efficient match-making and satisfiability *the five card trick*. In: Quisquater, J.-J., Vandewalle, J. (eds.) EUROCRYPT 1989. LNCS, vol. 434, pp. 208–217. Springer, Heidelberg (1990). https://doi.org/10.1007/3-540-46885-4_23
2. Ishikawa, R., Chida, E., Mizuki, T.: Efficient card-based protocols for generating a hidden random permutation without fixed points. In: Calude, C.S., Dinneen, M.J. (eds.) UCNC 2015. LNCS, vol. 9252, pp. 215–226. Springer, Cham (2015). https://doi.org/10.1007/978-3-319-21819-9_16
3. Koch, A., Walzer, S.: Foundations for actively secure card-based cryptography. Cryptology ePrint Archive, Report 2017/423 (2017). https://eprint.iacr.org/2017/423
4. Koch, A., Walzer, S., Härtel, K.: Card-based cryptographic protocols using a minimal number of cards. In: Iwata, T., Cheon, J.H. (eds.) ASIACRYPT 2015. LNCS, vol. 9452, pp. 783–807. Springer, Heidelberg (2015). https://doi.org/10.1007/978-3-662-48797-6_32
5. Mizuki, T., Komano, Y.: Analysis of information leakage due to operative errors in card-based protocols. In: Iliopoulos, C., Leong, H.W., Sung, W.-K. (eds.) IWOCA 2018. LNCS, vol. 10979, pp. 250–262. Springer, Cham (2018). https://doi.org/10.1007/978-3-319-94667-2_21
6. Mizuki, T., Kumamoto, M., Sone, H.: The five-card trick can be done with four cards. In: Wang, X., Sako, K. (eds.) ASIACRYPT 2012. LNCS, vol. 7658, pp. 598–606. Springer, Heidelberg (2012). https://doi.org/10.1007/978-3-642-34961-4_36
7. Mizuki, T., Shizuya, H.: A formalization of card-based cryptographic protocols via abstract machine. Int. J. Inf. Secur. **13**(1), 15–23 (2014). https://doi.org/10.1007/s10207-013-0219-4
8. Mizuki, T., Shizuya, H.: Practical card-based cryptography. In: Ferro, A., Luccio, F., Widmayer, P. (eds.) Fun with Algorithms. Lecture Notes in Computer Science, vol. 8496, pp. 313–324. Springer, Cham (2014). https://doi.org/10.1007/978-3-319-07890-8_27
9. Mizuki, T., Shizuya, H.: Computational model of card-based cryptographic protocols and its applications. IEICE Trans. Fundam. Electron. Commun. Comput. Sci. **100**(1), 3–11 (2017). https://doi.org/10.1587/transfun.E100.A.3
10. Mizuki, T., Sone, H.: Six-card secure AND and four-card secure XOR. In: Deng, X., Hopcroft, J.E., Xue, J. (eds.) FAW 2009. LNCS, vol. 5598, pp. 358–369. Springer, Heidelberg (2009). https://doi.org/10.1007/978-3-642-02270-8_36
11. Niemi, V., Renvall, A.: Secure multiparty computations without computers. Theor. Comput. Sci. **191**(1–2), 173–183 (1998). https://doi.org/10.1016/S0304-3975(97)00107-2
12. Shamir, A.: How to share a secret. In: Ashenhurst, R.L. (ed.) Communications of the ACM, vol. 22, pp. 612–613. ACM, New York (1979). https://doi.org/10.1145/359168.359176
13. Ueda, I., Nishimura, A., Hayashi, Y., Mizuki, T., Sone, H.: How to implement a random bisection cut. In: Martín-Vide, C., Mizuki, T., Vega-Rodríguez, M.A. (eds.) TPNC 2016. LNCS, vol. 10071, pp. 58–69. Springer, Cham (2016). https://doi.org/10.1007/978-3-319-49001-4_5

Evolutionary Computation

Optimizing Convolutional Neural Networks for Embedded Systems by Means of Neuroevolution

Filip Badan and Lukas Sekanina[(✉)][iD]

Faculty of Information Technology IT4Innovations Centre of Excellence,
Brno University of Technology, Božetěchova 2, 612 66 Brno, Czech Republic
badan.filip@gmail.com, sekanina@fit.vutbr.cz

Abstract. Automated design methods for convolutional neural networks (CNNs) have recently been developed in order to increase the design productivity. We propose a neuroevolution method capable of evolving and optimizing CNNs with respect to the classification error and CNN complexity (expressed as the number of tunable CNN parameters), in which the inference phase can partly be executed using fixed point operations to further reduce power consumption. Experimental results are obtained with TinyDNN framework and presented using two common image classification benchmark problems – MNIST and CIFAR-10.

Keywords: Evolutionary Algorithm · Convolutional neural network · Neuroevolution · Embedded Systems · Energy Efficiency

1 Introduction

Deep neural networks (DNNs) currently show an outstanding performance in challenging problems of image, speech and natural language processing as well as in many other applications of machine learning. The design of high-quality DNNs is a hard task even for experienced designers because the state of the art DNNs have large and complex structures with millions of tunable parameters [4,11]. Automated DNN design approaches, often referred to as the *Neural Architecture Search* (NAS), that have recently been developed, provide networks comparable with DNNs created by human designers.

This paper deals with automated design and optimization of *convolutional neural networks* (CNN), a subclass of DNNs primarily utilized for image classification. Our objective is to design and optimize not only with respect to the classification error, but also with respect to hardware resources needed when the final (trained) CNN is implemented in an embedded system with limited resources. As energy-efficient machine learning is a highly desired technology, various *approximate implementations* of CNNs have been introduced [2,7]. Contrasted to the existing neuroevolutionary approaches trying to minimize the classification error as much as possible and assuming that CNN is executed using

© Springer Nature Switzerland AG 2019
C. Martín-Vide et al. (Eds.): TPNC 2019, LNCS 11934, pp. 109–121, 2019.
https://doi.org/10.1007/978-3-030-34500-6_7

floating point (FP) operations on a Graphical Processing Unit (GPU) [1,3], our target is a highly optimized CNN whose major parts are executed with reduced precision in fixed point (FX) arithmetic operations.

We propose EA4CNN (Evolutionary Algorithms for Convolutional Neural Networks) – a neuroevolution platform capable of evolving and optimizing CNNs with respect to the classification error and model complexity (expressed as the number of tunable CNN parameters), in which the inference phase can partly be executed using FX operations. One of our goals is to demonstrate that the proposed method is capable of reducing the number of parameters of an already trained CNN and, at the same time, providing good tradeoffs between the classification error and CNN complexity. Experimental results are obtained with TinyDNN framewrok [6] and presented using two common benchmark problems – the classification of MNIST and CIFAR-10 data sets.

2   Related Work

Image classification conducted by CNNs is the state of the approach in the image processing domain. CNNs usually contain from four to tens layers of different types [11]. *Convolutional layers* are capable of extracting useful features from the input data. In these layers, each neuron is connected to a subset of inputs with the same spatial dimensions as the tunable kernels. The convolution is computed as $y = b + \sum_i \sum_j \sum_k (\mathbf{x}_{i,j,k} \cdot \mathbf{w}_{i,j,k})$, where $\mathbf{x}$ is the input subset, $\mathbf{w}$ is the convolution kernel and b is a scalar bias. *Pooling layers* combine, e.g. by means of averaging, a set of input values into a small number of output values to reduce the network complexity. *Fully connected* (FC) layers are composed of artificial neurons; each of them sums weighted input signals (coming from a previous layer) and produces a single output. Convolutional layers and fully connected layers are typically followed by non-linear *activation functions* such as $\tanh(\cdot)$ or rectified linear units (ReLU). The structure of the network is defined by hyperparameters (e.g., the number of layers, filters etc.) and this structure also determines the number of tunable parameters (weights and neuron biases). Modern CNNs also utilize normalization layers, residual connections, dropout layers etc. (see [4,11]).

In the *training phase*, the objective is to optimize the CNN parameters in order to minimize a given *error metric*. The training is a time-consuming iterative procedure which is typically implemented with the standard FP number representation. A trained CNN is then used, for example, for classification, in which an input image (a set of pixels) is classified to one of several classes. This (feed-forward) procedure is called *inference* and only this procedure is typically implemented in low power hardware CNN accelerators [11].

In order to automatically design the architecture (hyperparameters) and the parameters of CNNs, machine learning as well as evolutionary approaches have been proposed. Evolutionary design of neural networks (the so-called *neuroevolution*) that was introduced three decades ago [9], is now being extended for CNN design [5]. As both CNN training and evolutionary optimization are very computationally expensive methods, the key problem of the current neuroevolution research is to reduce computational requirements and provide competitive CNNs with respect to the human-created CNNs. Most papers are focused on single-objective automated design methods, where the main goal is to minimize the classification error of CNN running on a GPU [5,8,10]. Recent works have been focused on multi-objective approaches in which the error is optimized together with the computation requirements [1,3], but again, for GPU-based platforms. Evolved CNNs are now competitive with human-created CNNs for some challenging data sets; for example, some evolved CNNs achieve a 95% accuracy on CIFAR-10 data set. Note that a CNN with more than 1 million parameters is required in order to reach this accuracy and its training can take days on a GPU cluster [8].

Another research direction is focused on energy efficient (hardware) implementations of CNNs – with the aim of deploying advanced machine learning methods to low power systems such as mobile devices and IoT nodes. The most popular approach is to introduce approximate computing techniques to CNNs and benefit from the fact that the applications utilizing CNNs are highly error resilient (i.e., a huge reduction in energy consumption can be obtained for an acceptable loss in accuracy) [7]. Approximate implementations of CNNs are based on various techniques such as innovative hardware architectures of CNN accelerators, simplified data representation, pruning of less significant neurons, approximate arithmetic operations, approximate memory access, weight compression and "in memory" computing [2,7,11]. For example, employing the FX operations has many advantages such as reduced (i) power consumption per arithmetic operation, (ii) memory capacity needed to store the weights and (iii) processor-memory data transfer time.

To best of our knowledge, there has been no research on fully automated design of approximate CNNs by means of neuroevolution. As this is a very computationally expensive approach, we will focus this initial study on automated approximation of middle-size CNNs. Our method is based on simplifying the CNN architecture and reducing the precision of arithmetic operations.

3   CNN Design and Optimization with Neuroevolution

The proposed EA4CNN framework exploits an evolutionary algorithm (EA) and TinyDNN library for the design and optimization of CNN-based image classifiers. TinyDNN was chosen because it can easily be modified with respect to the requirements of EA. TinyDNN can, however, be replaced by another suitable CNN library because EA4CNN provides a general interface between EA and CNN implementations. EA4CNN is able to optimize and approximate an existing CNN, but it can also evolve a new CNN from scratch. CNN parameters as well as hyperparameters are optimized together.

3.1   Evolutionary Algorithm

Algorithm 1 presents the EA developed for the design and optimization of CNNs. The EA is initialized with existing or randomly generated CNNs (line 1 in

Algorithm 1) and runs for G_{max} generations (line 3). It employs a two-member tournament selection (line 6) to determine the parents that later undergo crossover (line 7; with probability p_c; see Sect. 3.3 for details) and mutation (line 8; with probability p_m, see Sect. 3.3). All offspring are continuously stored to the Q set (line 9) and undergo a training process implemented in TinyDNN (line 11).

Every new population is composed of the individuals selected from the sets of parents (P) and offspring (Q). The replacement algorithm (line 14) uses a simple speciation mechanism based on the CNN age (Sect. 3.3). To prevent the overfitting, the data set is divided into three parts – training set D_{train}, test set D_{test} and validation set D_{val}. During the evolution, candidate individuals are trained using D_{train} (line 11), but their fitness score is determined using D_{eval} (lines 2 and 13). At the end of the evolution process, the best solution is evaluated on the validation set D_{val} and this result is reported.

Algorithm 1. Neuroevolution

1: P = Create Initial Population; // randomly or using existing CNN
2: Evaluate(P, D_{test}) using TinyDNN; i = 0;
3: **while** ($i < G_{max}$) **do**
4:     $Q = \emptyset$;   // a set of offspring
5:     **while** ($|P| \neq |Q|$) **do**
6:         (a, b) = Tournament Selection (P);
7:         (a', b') = Crossover(a, b, p_{cross});
8:         a'' = Mutation(a', p_{mut}); b'' = Mutation(b', p_{mut});
9:         $Q = Q \cup \{a''\} \cup \{b''\}$;
10:     **end while**
11:     Run TinyDNN's Training Algorithm for all NNs in Q with D_{train};
12:     Update the Age counter for all NNs.
13:     Evaluate(Q, D_{test}) using TinyDNN;
14:     P = Replacement With Speciation (P, Q);
15:     $i = i + 1$;
16: **end while**

3.2   CNN Encoding

A candidate CNN is represented in the chromosome as a variable-length list of layers with a header containing the chromosome identifier, the age and the learning rate. Two types of layers can occur in the chromosome: (1) *Convolutional layer* with hyperparameters: kernel size, number of filters, stride size and padding. (2) *Pooling layer* with hyperparameters: stride size, subsampling type and subsampling size.

Each convolutional layer is (obligatorily) followed by a batch normalization and ReLU activation. The last (obligatory) layers of each CNN are a convolutional flattening layer and a fully connected layer, followed by a softmax activation to obtain a classifier. These layers are not represented in the chromosome as shown in the example of genotype-phenotype mapping in Fig. 1.

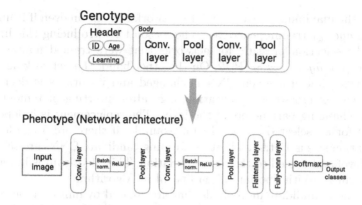

Fig. 1. Example of the genotype-phenotype mapping, where some parts of CNN (such as the flattening, fully connected and softmax layers) are not directly represented in the genotype.

3.3 Genetic Operators

The mutation operator is applied with the probability p_m per individual. One of the following mutation options (MO) is chosen with a predefined probability:

1. MO1: Weight reset – all weights of a given layer are randomly generated.
2. MO2: Add a new layer – a randomly generated layer (with randomly generated hyperparameters) is inserted on a randomly chosen position in CNN.
3. MO3: Remove layer – one layer is removed from a randomly chosen position.
4. MO4: Modify layer – some parameters of a randomly selected layer are randomly modified.
5. MO5: Modify hyperparameters of the fully connected layer – the number of connections in the last fully connected layer is increased or decreased.
6. MO6: Modify the learning rate (randomly).

We use a simple one-point crossover operator on each pair of parents obtained with the tournament selection. If a CNN layer is modified by a genetic operator, EA4CNN automatically ensures its correct connection to the previous/next layer. For example, superfluous weights are cut off or missing weights are added and randomly initialized.

3.4 Training and Evaluation of Candidate CNNs

As some candidate CNNs exist for many generations while others exist only for a short time, these long-lived CNNs have more opportunities for a good training (line 11 in Algorithm 1). It turns out that candidate CNNs do not have, in principle, the same chance during the selection and replacement process. Hence, inspired in [9], we introduced a speciation mechanism based on the *network age*. A species is defined by all individuals having the same age. The age is increased with every new training process a given candidate CNN undergoes. We define

age_{max} as the maximum age a candidate network can obtain even if it undergoes more than age_{max} training exercises. The reason for introducing this limit is to increase the selection pressure for networks that were trained many times. A typical setup of age_{max} is $\sim |P|/2$. On the other hand, the network age is reset to the initial value if a given CNN is changed and its fitness is decreased as a consequence of crossover or mutation, e.g., after inserting or removing some layer(s) or changing parameters of the layer. The replacement is independently performed for all selected age levels; for example, if there are 5 age levels and the population size is 15 then 3 best-performing candidate CNNs are selected for each age level and copied to the new population. This algorithm is implemented by 'Replacement With Speciation' on line 14 in Algorithm 1.

For the new candidate individuals that are created by mutation or crossover, the principles of *weight inheritance* are applied [8]. All the weights that can be reused in the offspring are copied from the parent(s) to the offspring. If needed, superfluous weights are cut off or missing weights are added and randomly initialized. Before each training phase is executed, D_{train} is randomly shuffled [4].

3.5   Fitness Function

The fitness function is based on the CNN accuracy (a is the number correctly classified inputs divided by all inputs from the test set D_{test}) and the CNN relative size (s_{rel} is the number of parameters divided by the number of parameters of the best CNN of the initial population):

$$f = \begin{cases} a * (k * \frac{1}{\log(s_{rel}+1)} + 1) & \text{if } a \geq a_{min} \\ 0 & \text{otherwise,} \end{cases} \tag{1}$$

where k is a coefficient reflecting the impact of CNN size on the final fitness score and a_{min} is the minimal acceptable accuracy. It is important to introduce a_{min} as less complex CNNs providing unacceptable (low) classification accuracy would dominate the entire population.

3.6   Data Type and CNN Size Optimization

Almost all major CNN design frameworks operate over (32 bit) FP numbers and their computation is optimized for arithmetic FP operations and accelerated using GPUs. In order to enable FX operations (in particular, FX multiplications conducted during the inference phase in convolutional and fully connected layers), we modified relevant parts of TinyDNN source code. When a multiplication has to be executed in these layers, the FP operands are converted to a given FX number format, the multiplication is performed in FX and the product is converted back to FP. While this process emulates the error introduced by FX representation in a low cost hardware, all the remaining CNN steps can be implemented with the (highly optimized) FP operations. Unfortunately, this implementation slows down the CNN simulations approx. 8 times in our case.

When a CNN which should (partly) operate in the FX representation is evolved, we apply the aforementioned procedure in the fitness function (line 13 in Algorithm 1); however, the training is completely conducted in FP.

In our study, a (signed) FX number is implemented using 16 bits, in which 8 bits are fractional. If a 32 bit FP multiplication is replaced with a 16 bit FX multiplication, energy consumption of this operation is reduced approx. $c_1 = 2.4$ times (for 65 nm technology [2]). Let E_{mult} denote the energy consumed by all multiplications performed during one inference phase carried out in a CNN embedded accelerator (E_{mult} is approx. 20 % – 40 % of the total energy required by the accelerator [11]). If the number of parameters of CNN is reduced from par_{orig} to par_{red} by EA4CNN and 16 bit FX instead of 32 bit FP multipliers are employed, E_{mult} is reduced approx. $c_1 \times par_{orig}/par_{red}$ times because each parameter is associated with at least one multiplication in CNN.

4   Experimental Setup

EA4CNN is implemented in C++. We utilized the parallel training of CNNs supported in TinyDNN (by means of OpenMP and SSE instructions). Experiments were executed on a computer node containing two Intel Xeon E5-2680v3 processors @ 2.5 GHz, 128 GB RAM and 24 threads. As the entire neuroevolution process is very time consuming (an average run in which 750 candidate CNNs are evaluated takes almost 72 h for CIFAR-10), we typically generated only 50 populations of 15 individuals and performed only five independent runs for a particular setup. Hence, most EA parameters and CNN (hyper)parameters were set up on the basis of preliminary results from several test runs.

EA4CNN was evaluated using MNIST (10 digit classes) and CIFAR-10 (10 image classes) classification problems. MNIST consists of 28×28 pixel grayscale images of handwritten digits and includes 60 000 training images and 10 000 test images. In CIFAR-10, the numbers of training and test images are 50 000 and 10 000, respectively, and the size of images is 32×32 pixels. For our purposes, these data sets were divided into three parts in such a way that there are 75 % vectors in D_{train}, 10 % vectors in D_{test} and and 15 % in D_{val}.

The basic setup of EA parameters is as follows: $G_{max} = 20-50$, $|P| = 8-15$, $p_{cross} = 0.35$, $p_{mut} = 0.7$, $age_{max} = |P|/2$, $k = 0.5$, $a_{min} = 0.80$ for MNIST and 0.60 for CIFAR-10. Mutation operators MO1 – MO6 are used with the probabilities 0.41, 0.07, 0.03, 0.29, 0.10, and 0.10, respectively.

Table 1 summarizes the initial CNN hyperparameters for both data sets. Randomly generated networks of the initial populations contain from 1 to 8 layers in which all weights are randomly initialized to the close to zero values. TinyDNN utilizes the stochastic gradient descent learning method.

5   Results

5.1   Basic Evaluation Of EA4CNN

In the first experiment, we compared the randomly-initialized EA with a random search of CNNs (RS-CNN). EA used the setup presented in Sect. 4, but

Table 1. The initial setting of CNN hyperparameters in EA4CNN. The hyperparameters given in the first part of the table can be modified during the evolution.

Parameter/Data set	MNIST	CIFAR-10
Learning rate	0.1	0.1
Initial number of neurons in FC layers	50	70
Max. filters in a newly added layer	12	20
Max. pooling layer size	4	4
Batch size	32	32
Epochs for training	1	1

$G_{max} = 20$, $|P| = 8$ for MNIST and $|P| = 12$ for CIFAR-10. RS-CNN starts with $|P|$ randomly generated CNNs and performs their training for G_{max} epochs to ensure the same number of training exercises as in EA in which only one epoch of training is conducted for each candidate CNN in each generation. The average accuracy out of 5 independent runs of both algorithms is given in Fig. 2. Because MNIST classification is currently considered as a simple problem for NNs (the best reported accuracy is 99.79% [11]), even randomly generated CNN architectures provide (after their training) almost perfect classification accuracy. The average number of parameters of resulting CNNs is 200k for RS-CNN, but only 58k for EA which indicates that EA can optimize not only accuracy but also the CNN complexity (resulting CNNs have only 1–2 convolutional layers). While EA is only slightly better than RS-CNN for MNIST, the difference in the average accuracy on CIFAR-10 is relatively high (5.7% for 5 runs) which indicates that EA can also effectively increase the CNN size to improve the accuracy.

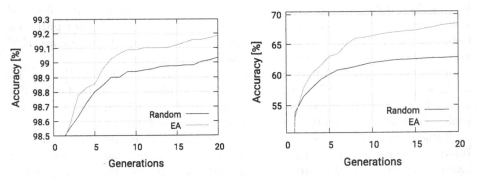

Fig. 2. The average accuracy obtained from five EA and five RS-CNN runs for MNIST (left) and CIFAR-10 (right) data sets.

In the second experiment, we investigated the impact of genetic operators on the progress of evolution of CNNs. Let EA1 denote Algorithm 1 in which neither crossover nor mutation are used. EA1, in fact, does not introduce any new CNN structures, but optimizes how CNNs (randomly generated in the initial population) are selected for training by means of TinyDNN. Note that D_{train} is randomly shuffled before each training. Higher-scored CNNs can thus undergo more training exercises and improve their fitness score. Let EA2 and EA3 denote EA1 with mutation ($p_{mut} = 0.80$; no crossover) and EA1 with mutation ($p_{mut} = 0.50$) and crossover ($p_{cross} = 0.35$). The other parameters remained as given in Sect. 4. The average classification accuracy out of 5 independent runs of EA1, EA2 and EA3 is given in Fig. 3 (left). Because of limited space only results on CIFAR-10 are reported. One can observe that performance of EA1 is roughly similar with RS-CNN. Incorporating the mutation operator (EA2) and crossover (EA3) leads to a higher classification accuracy of resulting CNNs.

Finally, Fig. 3 (right) illustrates the impact of employing the speciation mechanism on the accuracy during the CNN evolution. If the speciation "is not used" vs. "is used", the classification accuracy of resulting five CNNs is between 59.93% – 72.96% vs. 62.02% – 73.05%; the average accuracy is 66.93% vs. 68.46%; the average depth of the network is 3.6 vs. 4.6 layers and the average number of parameters is 114k vs. 173k. We can conclude that the EA benefits from the proposed speciation mechanism.

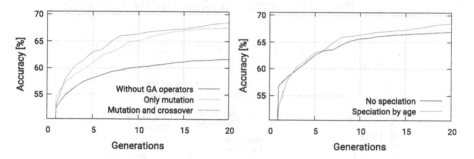

Fig. 3. Left: The average classification accuracy if EA uses selection only (EA1); selection and mutation (EA2); selection, mutation and crossover (EA3). Right: The average accuracy for EA3 with and without speciation (on CIFAR-10).

5.2 Evolution of Approximate CNNs

The experiments reported in this section have started with a *baseline CNN* shown in Fig. 4 (top) which contains 360,264 parameters, operates in FP and provides 75.8% accuracy on CIFAR-10 (trained with TinyDNN). We decided to approximate this middle-size CNN as less complex CNNs are our target and our computational resources are limited.

Figure 5 shows the fitness score, classification accuracy and complexity of CNNs obtained from a single run of the proposed EA which was seeded with the baseline CNN. The EA parameters are set according to Sect. 4, but $k = 1$ to

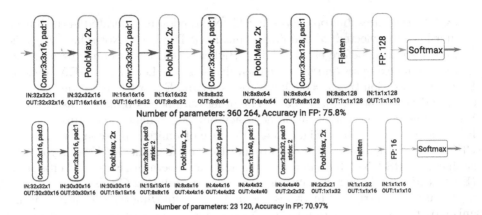

Number of parameters: 360 264, Accuracy in FP: 75.8%

Number of parameters: 23 120, Accuracy in FP: 70.97%

Fig. 4. Hyperparameters and architecture of the baseline CNN (top) and one of the CNNs optimized with EA4CNN (bottom) for CIFAR-10 data set.

find good tradeoffs between the accuracy and the number of CNN parameters; $G_{max} = 50$, and $|P| = 15$. Note that the accuracy shown in the plot is the test accuracy on D_{test}. The resulting CNN is presented in Fig. 4 (bottom).

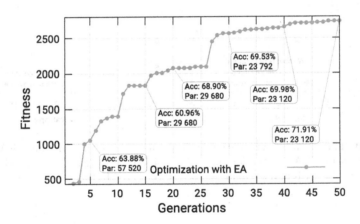

Fig. 5. An example run of the evolutionary CNN approximation process on CIFAR-10 data set.

Table 2 summarizes the best tradeoffs obtained from multiple EA runs. CNN*-FP and CNN*-FX denote CNNs performing the multiplication operations in FP and FX representation, respectively. Because of limited computing resources, we could only execute 20 generations to evolve CNNs utilizing the FX representation, which negatively influenced the quality of CNN*-FX networks. For example, a similar classification accuracy ($\sim 67.5\%$) was obtained by CNN2-FP and CNN1-FX, but CNN1-FX needs 2.9× more parameters and hence it is less energy efficient despite the usage of FX multiplications. Reduction in the energy (E_{mult}) needed for multiplication (calculated according to Sect. 3.6, $c_1 = 2.4$) is clearly traded off for the loss in accuracy. EA4CNN allowed us to obtain this reduction by simplifying the CNN structure (fewer parameters) or/and employing FX operations. A more significant contribution of the FX representation is expected if EA4CNN could prolong the optimization and thus further reduce the number of parameters in CNN*-FX networks.

Table 2 also presents some CNNs that are available in the NAS literature. CNNs achieving a 90% and higher classification accuracy on CIFAR-10 contain more than one million parameters [8] and their design takes days on a GPU, which is unreachable with our setup. The impact of employing the FX representation was reported for a human-created CNN (based on AlexNET [4]) which exhibits 81.22 %, 79.77 % and 77.99 % accuracy in FP, 16 bit FX and 8 bit FX, respectively. The 16 bit and 8 bit FX implementations reduce the energy requirements approx. 2.5 and 6.8 times, respectively. Contrasted to our approach, these FX designs only implemented the original FP implementation with reduced precision in FX, i.e. without optimizing the CNN architecture.

Table 2. Examples of CNNs and their parameters obtained from the evolutionary approximation conducted with EA4CNN and from literature (for CIFAR-10).

CNN	Parameters	Accuracy	Layers	E_{mult} reduction
Evolved with EA4CNN				
Baseline CNN (FP)	360,264	75.80 %	7	1.0
CNN1-FP	8 480	64.33 %	9	42.9×
CNN2-FP	12 784	67.50 %	7	28.1×
CNN3-FP	15 728	68.92 %	8	22.9×
CNN4-FP	23 120	70.97 %	9	15.6×
CNN5-FP	0.17 M	72.96 %	6	2.1×
CNN1-FX (16 bit)	36 720	67.66 %	11	23.6×
CNN2-FX (16 bit)	30 672	66.52 %	8	28.2×
CNN3-FX (16 bit)	19 632	65.63 %	7	44.0×
From literature				
[10] (FP) default scenario	1.68 M	94.02 %	–	–
[10] (FP) small data set (5k)	0.83 M	76.53 %	–	–
[8] (FP)	5.40 M	94.60 %	–	–
ALEX [2] (FP)	~10 M	81.22 %	–	1.0
ALEX [2] (FX, 16 bit)	~10 M	79.77 %	–	~2.5×
ALEX [2] (FX, 8 bit)	~10 M	77.99 %	–	~6.8×

6   Conclusions

The proposed EA4CNN platform can automatically evolve a CNN (with 29k parameters) showing almost the state-of-the-art accuracy (99.36 %) for the MNIST task. Evolved CNNs for CIFAR-10 are far from the state-of-the-art, but it was expected because we used only the basic CNN techniques (no data augmentation, residual connections, dropout layers etc.) and very limited computing resources. However, we demonstrated that EA4CNN, if seeded with a trained CNN, can find interesting tradeoffs between the accuracy and implementation cost.

Our future work will focus on improving the search quality by incorporating advanced CNN techniques and employing more computing resources. We will also explore more options for optimizing the CNN cost in order to develop a fully automated holistic CNN approximation method.

Acknowledgments. This work was supported by the Ministry of Education, Youth and Sports, under the INTER-COST project LTC 18053, NPU II project IT4Innovations excellence in science LQ1602 and by Large Infrastructures for Research, Experimental Development and Innovations project "IT4Innovations National Supercomputing Center – LM2015070".

References

1. Dong, J.-D., Cheng, A.-C., Juan, D.-C., Wei, W., Sun, M.: DPP-Net: device-aware progressive search for pareto-optimal neural architectures. In: Ferrari, V., Hebert, M., Sminchisescu, C., Weiss, Y. (eds.) ECCV 2018. LNCS, vol. 11215, pp. 540–555. Springer, Cham (2018). https://doi.org/10.1007/978-3-030-01252-6_32
2. Hashemi, S., Anthony, N., Tann, H., Bahar, R.I., Reda, S.: Understanding the impact of precision quantization on the accuracy and energy of neural networks. In: DATE, pp. 1478–1483. EDAA (2017)
3. Hsu, C., et al.: MONAS: multi-objective neural architecture search using reinforcement learning. CoRR abs/1806.10332 (2018). http://arxiv.org/abs/1806.10332
4. Krizhevsky, A., Sutskever, I., Hinton, G.E.: Imagenet classification with deep convolutional neural networks. In: Pereira, F., Burges, C.J.C., Bottou, L., Weinberger, K.Q. (eds.) Advances in Neural Information Processing Systems 25, pp. 1097–1105. Curran Associates, Inc. (2012)
5. Miikkulainen, R., et al.: Evolving deep neural networks. CoRR abs/1703.00548 (2017). http://arxiv.org/abs/1703.00548
6. Nomi, T.: TinyDNN. https://github.com/tiny-dnn/tiny-dnn (2016)
7. Panda, P., et al.: Invited - cross-layer approximations for neuromorphic computing: from devices to circuits and systems. In: 53rd Design Automation Conference, pp. 1–6. IEEE (2016). https://doi.org/10.1145/2897937.2905009
8. Real, E., et al.: Large-scale evolution of image classifiers. arXiv e-prints arXiv:1703.01041 (2017)
9. Stanley, K.O., Miikkulainen, R.: Evolving neural networks through augmenting topologies. Evol. Comput. **10**(2), 99–127 (2002)

10. Suganuma, M., Shirakawa, S., Nagao, T.: A genetic programming approach to designing convolutional neural network architectures. In: Proceedings of the Genetic and Evolutionary Computation Conference, GECCO 2017, pp. 497–504. ACM (2017)
11. Sze, V., Chen, Y., Yang, T., Emer, J.S.: Efficient processing of deep neural networks: a tutorial and survey. Proc. IEEE **105**(12), 2295–2329 (2017)

Migration Threshold Tuning in the Deterministic Dendritic Cell Algorithm

Julie Greensmith[✉][iD]

School of Computer Science, University of Nottingham, Nottingham NG8 1BB, UK
julie.greensmith@nottingham.ac.uk
https://www.nottingham.ac.uk/computerscience/people/julie.greensmith

Abstract. In this paper we explore the sensitivity of the migration threshold parameter in the Deterministic Dendritic Cell Algorithm (dDCA), one of the four main types of Artificial Immune System. This is with a view to the future construction of a DCA augmented with Deep Learning. Learning mechanisms are absent in the original DCA although tuneable parameters are identified which have the potential to be learned over time. Proposed in this paper is the necessary first step towards placing the dDCA within the context of Deep Learning by understanding the maximum migration threshold parameter. Tuning the maximum migration threshold determines the results of the signal processing within the algorithm, and here we explore a range of values. We use the previously explored Ping Scan Dataset to evaluate the influence of this key parameter. Results indicate a close relationship between the maximum migration threshold and the signal values of given datasets. We propose in future to ascertain an optimisation function which would learn the maximum migration threshold during run time. This work represents a necessary step towards producing a DCA which automatically interfaces with any given anomaly detection dataset.

Keywords: Artificial immune systems · Dendritic cell algorithm · Parameter tuning

1 Introduction

The Dendritic Cell Algorithm (DCA) is an Artificial Immune System (AIS) based on the function and behaviour of the dendritic cells of the human immune system. It is driven by a concept termed the danger theory, which postulates that the human immune system has the ability to discriminate between 'safe' and 'dangerous' contexts [17], informally known as 'danger signals'. The danger theory is in opposition to the classical self-nonself theory of discrimination of antigen proteins via their structure and origin. In the danger theory, and indeed in the DCA, antigen is classified through correlation of context with danger signals and not via examination of the structure of the antigen proteins. The

C. Martín-Vide et al. (Eds.): TPNC 2019, LNCS 11934, pp. 122–133, 2019.
https://doi.org/10.1007/978-3-030-34500-6_8

DCA is inspired by this model, as are other similar danger based algorithms [15, 19]. Details of the function of the DCA are given in Sect. 2.

This paper is motivated by a comparison study performed by Lau & Lee in 2018 [16], where a direct comparison between the DCA and an artificial neural network (ANN) is performed. This is an innovative application of the DCA, applied as a monitor for human behaviour in carrying out tasks in a VR/AR CUBE setup. The study's results indicate that the DCA can produce a similar good performance on this task. They also indicate that the DCA has a distinct advantage over ANNs when lengthy training periods are required. ANNs have enjoyed a resurgence in popularity in the guise of 'Deep Learning'. This extends on the traditional ANN through adding an optimisation function (frequently gradient descent) to the signal inputs, multiple nodes in multiple layers and a discrimination technique such as softmax to aggregate classification. The implication is that Deep Learning based on ANNs can now tackle 'Big Data' in a computationally feasible manner. Ease of implementation facilitated through TensorFlow and Keras have further increased the popularity beyond the machine learning community. Widespread application of this technique, and the automation of the selection of inputs has heightened the learning capacity of these techniques, now popular in image processing in particular. Given the direct comparison in Lau and Lee [16], we postulate that if the DCA can be directly compared to an ANN, there must be properties of the DCA which make transforming the algorithm into a Deep Learning framework possible at least in principle.

The DCA dispenses with a lengthy training period in favour of expert learning to map input streams. However, multiple authors have attempted to automatically map inputs to the algorithm, as reviewed in Chelly and Elouedi [2].. This already suggests a step towards incorporating a dynamic learning component to this algorithm akin to the first stage in deep learning. However, there are numerous "back-end parameters" in the DCA which have not been subjected to the same automation processes. In this paper we identify a particular parameter which is ideally suited to parameter tuning. Furthermore, Elisa et al. [4] apply k-means clustering to the output of the algorithm to refine the discrimination features of the algorithm. A significant improvement is shown in this re-imagined DCA architecture when applied to a standardised intrusion detection dataset, highlighting the importance of the state-change based discrimination performed by the algorithm, indicating the importance of the "back-end parameters". We focus on examining the assignment of the migration threshold across the agents in the DCAs population, to highlight the importance of this parameter's influence on classification accuracy. This is the most basic experiment possible to investigate learning within this algorithm, while maintaining the DCA's key advantage of dispensing with the requirement for a lengthy training period.

The main contribution of this paper is to assess the impact of tuning the maximum migration threshold parameter on the algorithm's classification accuracy. Section 2.1 describes the major features of the algorithm and formal analysis of the algorithm is reviewed in Sect. 2.2. A rationale for exploring the sensitivity of

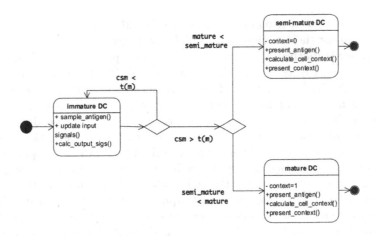

Fig. 1. Schematic representation of the processing by a single population member, demonstrating the migration process, from [5]

the maximum migration threshold parameter is given in Sect. 3. A preliminary experiment including learning the migration threshold parameter is shown in Sect. 4 comparing a range of values. We conclude the paper by suggesting how this modification can be extended to further enhance the DCA towards a Deep Learning DCA framework. For a comprehensive review of the DCA see [2], and the original DCA is described in detail in [5].

2   The Dendritic Cell Algorithm

2.1   Algorithm Overview

As an algorithm, the DCA was first presented in 2005 [6] as an anomaly detector in the style of a population based algorithm. Individual DCs in a population are transformed from an immature state to either 'mature' or 'semi-mature', depending upon the type of 'signal' they have encountered throughout their defined lifespan. Expert knowledge couples data streams to the DC population through a rough categorisation of the streams into 'safe' or 'danger'. The stream data is processed by individual DCs though a simple weighted sum equation. The output of this weighted sum increments internal values, either the 'mature' or 'semi-mature' indicator The data collection window for each DC is determined by a lifespan limit, termed in the literature as 'migration threshold' [8]. Upon migration a DC is classed as either 'mature' or 'semi-mature' via the application of a linear threshold or simply labelling the cell based on which of the mature or semi-mature variables is the larger value, demonstrated in Fig. 1.Classification cannot be performed with the DCA without an orthogonal data stream termed 'antigen' - this is a representation of the item to be classified.

Each member of the set of antigen in a dataset is termed an 'antigen type', of which will have multiple instances. This decoupling of the data allows for data correlation within the DCA. The first real-world test for the DCA involved experiments similar to this though monitoring an individual host information and not a network and system calls [7]. Each system call per process is captured in this dataset, and the process ID associated with each system call forms the antigen types in this dataset. This same dataset is used to experiment with the maximum migration threshold in this paper.

In the population each DC agent samples signals from the signal stream and antigen from the antigen stream within a dynamic lifespan. The sampling duration of a DC is controlled by its migration threshold, assigned upon creation of the immature DC. An internal variable of an immature DC, termed in the literature as 'csm' [9], is incremented in proportion to the strength of signal experienced by the DC. Upon the 'csm' variable having a greater value than the assigned migration threshold, the DC is removed from the sampling pool and presented for analysis. The secondary analysis phase of the algorithm counts for each antigen type the percentage of DCs which are mature versus semi-mature. This ratio returns a value between 0–1 for each antigen type, with values closer to 1 indicating an anomaly, and this is referred to as the 'mean context antigen value' or MCAV. Once all data is sampled a final value for each antigen type is calculated, a linear threshold is applied. A range of values for this threshold can be used to create ROC curves out of the DCA output.

2.2 Theoretical Research and Formal Specification

The prototype version of the DCA was first presented by Greensmith et al. in 2005 [6], with the full version published in 2006 [8]. While implementable details were attempted, the algorithm's function and behaviour were obfuscated by the complex agent based framework used to implement the DCA and the over twenty potentially tuneable parameters. Two approaches were taken to 'demystify' this algorithm and to increase its applicability. The first approach was to reduce the number of tuneable parameters to two in the Deterministic DCA [10] **dDCA**, leaving population size and range of migration threshold across the population. Dynamic antigen buffers, sigmoidal functions for weighted sum inputs, and MCAV was replaced with a real valued metric, K_α.

The dDCA as a simplified algorithm has proven popular for implementation and assisted in some of the earliest theoretical research for the DCA [13]. Aside from the simplification of the algorithm, a key motivator for the development of the dDCA was to provide a 'stripped down' version of the algorithm in order to build in new components, to add in stochastic elements individually. This has not happened to any great extent, though the dDCA has become a studied and applied algorithm e.g. [14] in its own rite as detailed in the review in [2]. Further theoretical analysis of the DCA is performed in Oates et al. [18], Stibor et al. [20] and Gu et al. [12], which analysed the DCA as a set of linear classifiers, without analysing the impact of the antigen stream.

The second attempt to clarify the algorithm is motivated by the inconsistencies in DCA implementations. Ambiguity surrounding signal mapping, the use on inappropriate datasets and direct comparison with unsuitable supervised learning techniques motivated Greensmith and Gale in 2017 [11]. A formal specification of the dDCA with Haskell is presented. Haskell is a purely functional language, where the specification becomes the implementation, therefore if the specification is verified as correct, then the implementation is also correct. This research shows that the input to the DCA is stream data, and not necessarily 'feature vectors' and that the 'antigen stream' must be de-coupled from the signal streams in order for the algorithm to be effective. This is the version of the dDCA used in experiments in Sect. 4 using a verified dDCA. If the learning process for "back-end" tuning is possible, the Haskell specification will be extended to ensure correct future implementation of this component.

3   Cell Migration Control in the DCA

It came as a surprise to reviewers past that there is no explicit learning process, optimisation or local search operator in the DCA. The assumption in the literature is that an AIS must behave like any other evolutionary algorithm. It is thought that it must converge upon a solution like the clonal selection or at least engage in a training process akin to supervised learning techniques in AIS including negative selection [1]. However, the DCA does not have such facility, the deterministic DCA even more so as it dispenses with reliance on any random elements included in the original variant.

The obvious approach is to replace with the requirement to use expert knowledge to decide how signals from the signal stream are mapped to the categories of safe and danger as indeed has been widely performed in the DCA literature, as reviewed in [2], including the use of fuzzy systems, rough set theory and PCA. Secondarily is the optimisations of the weights in the signal processing equation which encompasses a training phase for the DCA, as performed by Elisa et al. [3] though the use of a genetic algorithm. This is in contrast to the work presented in [16] which determined that the lack of lengthy training period of the algorithm was indeed how the DCA has an advantage over ANNs.

There are other aspects of the DCA which can be augmented with some form of learning capability outside of the paradigm of requiring a training period. Two tuneable parameters with optimisation potential are **population size** and the assignment of the **maximum migration threshold** of the DC population. The maximum migration threshold is tested for its sensitivity in this paper through performing a preliminary investigation in the link between the parameter and the algorithm's performance. Optimisation of this parameter during the algorithm's runtime may be able to enhance its performance, though this must be done in an incremental manner.

The migration threshold is important in the DCA as it determines the exact set of signal and antigen instances processed within an individual DC throughout the run-time duration of the algorithm. It controls the length of time a DC remains in the sampling pool before being presented for analysis. A migration threshold is assigned to each DC upon the initialisation of the algorithm. In the dDCA, each DC is given a specific value of migration threshold which is calculated in proportion to an overall maximum migration threshold, set as

Table 1. Example of migration threshold assignment for a population of 5 DCs with a maximum migration threshold Max_{mt} of 10

Cell ID	DC_mt
1	2
2	4
3	6
4	8
5	10

a user-definable parameter as $DC_{mt} = f(Max_{mt}/NumCells)$. For example if there are 5 DCs in the sampling pool and a maximum migration threshold of 10 is assigned the DCs migration thresholds are assigned as a simple modulus function as shown in Table 1.

The migration threshold is applied to a parameter termed 'csm'[1] is incremented through summation of the danger and safe signals collected at each signal sampling iteration. Once the value of 'csm' exceeds that of the DC_{mt}, the cell is removed from the sampling pool and presents data for the analysis phase. At this point, the DC is destroyed, and a new DC is created with an identical DC_{mt} and repopulated the sampling pool. This process is specified formally in [11].

We commence the investigation into parameter tuning in the dDCA by firstly ascertaining the sensitivity of the algorithm to variation in the migration threshold of the individual cells, controlled by tuning the master maximum migration threshold parameter. The dDCA is useful for this task as it allows for a high degree of reproducibility and traceability of data within the algorithm. An initial specific set of parameter values are chosen with a view to exploring optimisation techniques in future research.

4   Experiments on Migration Thresholds

4.1   Ping Scan Dataset

Ten datasets are created, originally for [8] and used for the sensitivity analysis in [7], based on performing a series of ICMP Ping Scans on a medium scale university network. This data is designed specifically to assess the parameters of the DCA, and not necessarily to capture all of the nuances of network intrusion detection. Given the experiments relate to a DCA parameter, this justifies the use of this dataset in this case. The generated data captured the processes involved

---

[1] This is based on the biological model of the up-regulation of the CCR7 receptor in natural DCs in response to binding to intracellular molecules of both cell damage and of healthy tissues. This up-regulation attracts the DC away from the potential site of infection and results in its trafficking to the lymph node where is ceases to sample signals and antigen.

Table 2. Summary of **danger signal** data across 10 ping scan datasets

Dataset	Mean	Stdev	Median	Sum
S1	7.85	15.96	0.40	243.20
S2	4.81	10.45	0.00	317.60
S3	21.28	27.16	2.00	1425.60
S4	27.53	42.57	0.40	1073.60
S5	29.09	41.19	0.00	1134.40
S6	28.55	42.88	0.00	1056.40
S7	30.03	42.72	2.60	1141.20
S8	24.93	37.36	1.20	1072.00
S9	26.36	42.28	0.00	1107.20
S10	26.83	41.95	0.40	1046.40
Mean	**22.73**	**34.45**	**0.70**	**961.76**

Table 3. Summary of **safe signal** data across 10 ping scan datasets

Dataset	Mean	Stdev	Median	Sum
S1	54.19	41.72	60.00	1680.00
S2	65.10	42.20	86.67	4296.67
S3	50.30	48.48	80.00	3370.00
S4	36.75	45.80	0.00	1433.33
S5	58.46	43.98	70.00	2280.00
S6	51.35	45.53	50.00	1900.00
S7	43.68	47.73	10.00	1660.00
S8	38.14	48.27	0.00	1640.00
S9	57.62	48.43	90.00	2420.00
S10	34.87	41.98	30.00	1360.00
Mean	**49.05**	**45.41**	**47.67**	**2204.00**

during the scan to form the antigen and measured the network attribute of packets per second sent from the machine instigating the scan. The danger signal is the number of packets per second sent, normalised into a range of 0–100. The safe signal is the inverse rate of change of number of packets per second sent also normalised in the range of 0–100. Summary statistics of the signal data for the ten datasets (S1-S10) are shown in Tables 2, 3 and Table 4, including the duration of the monitored session in Table 4.

As part of this data capture exercise, antigen data is also captured. While over 25 processes were active during the scan duration, four 'processes of interest' were identified as making over 100 system calls for the duration of each scan. These are the bash process which is the terminal from which the scan is instigated; the

Table 4. Signal maximums across all datasets, including normalisation of signal total per dataset duration

Dataset	Danger (D)	Safe (S)	Sum ($D + S$)	Duration	Normalised sigtotal/ duration
S1	243.20	1680.00	1923.20	30.81	62.42
S2	317.60	4296.67	4614.27	66.08	69.82
S3	1425.60	3370.00	4795.60	66.96	71.62
S4	1073.60	1433.33	2506.93	38.08	65.84
S5	1134.40	2280.00	3414.40	38.14	89.52
S6	1056.40	1900.00	2956.40	36.62	80.74
S7	1141.20	1660.00	2801.20	37.53	74.64
S8	1072.00	1640.00	2712.00	42.34	64.06
S9	1107.20	2420.00	3527.20	41.14	85.74
S10	1046.40	1360.00	2406.40	38.50	62.50
Mean	**961.76**	**2204.00**	**3165.76**	**43.62**	**72.57**

nmap process used to instigate the scan; the pts pseudo-terminal slave process which is a helper process for the nmap process; and sshd process which was used to log into the linux terminal from which the data was collected. We expect in the results for the experiments to indicate the nmap and pts processes as anomalous and the sshd and bash processes to be classified as normal, as indicated in the results in [7]. In previous experiments where the anomaly score is given as the *mean context antigen value - MCAV*, a coarse threshold of 0.5 is added to discriminate between the normal and anomalous processes as in [7].

4.2   Experiments

A control experiment is performed with the dDCA using the standard parameters for population size of 100 and the Max_{mt} set at 100. All other settings are as detailed in [10] and [11]. The results for each dataset are shown in Table 5.

Five parameters are chosen on a logarithmic scale to examine the link between the dataset and Max_{mt} set at 1, 10, 100, 1000 and 10000. Given the ranges of the data, this covers the smallest window possible ensuring that the cells will migrate each iteration. The maximum value of 10000 exceeds the total signal amount for each dataset, ensuring that each cell will only migrate once. For the sake of completeness, we also test the average signal sum across all 10 datasets which is 3165. We also test a normalised version of this value which takes into account the duration of each dataset, resulting in a Max_{mt} value of 73. Results of these experiments are shown in Table 6, as mean values per process of interest and the related standard deviation. A more detailed presentation of individual results per process is given in Fig. 2. We expect correct classification to produce values of below 0.5 for bash and sshd, and above 0.5 for nmap and pts.

Table 5. Control experiment using previously published parameters: population size = 100; $Max_{mt} = 100$

Dataset	Bash	Nmap	Pts	Sshd
S1	0.00	1.00	0.62	0.08
S2	0.03	0.92	0.56	0.00
S3	0.03	0.93	0.85	0.00
S4	0.37	0.87	0.90	0.09
S5	0.05	0.79	0.86	0.04
S6	0.76	0.68	0.87	0.05
S7	0.53	0.97	0.93	0.14
S8	1.00	1.00	1.00	0.29
S9	0.05	0.87	0.86	0.04
S10	0.93	1.00	0.88	0.00
Mean	**0.38**	**0.90**	**0.83**	**0.07**

Table 6. Results of parameter variation of Maximum Migration Threshold, including mean across all 10 datasets, and accompanying standard deviation. The value of 3165 represents the mean signal per session, and 73 is the mean signal per session normalised by the number of signal instances.

Max migration	Bash mean	Bash stdev	Nmap mean	Nmap stdev	Pts mean	Pts stdev	Sshd mean	Sshd stdev
1	0.44	0.44	0.90	0.10	0.84	0.14	0.08	0.09
10	0.44	0.44	0.90	0.10	0.84	0.14	0.08	0.09
100	0.25	0.37	0.87	0.11	0.75	0.23	0.03	0.06
1000	0.17	0.20	0.64	0.25	0.50	0.23	0.03	0.03
10000	0.03	0.03	0.07	0.04	0.06	0.03	0.00	0.010
3165	0.08	0.08	0.27	0.12	0.21	0.10	0.02	0.03
73	0.44	0.43	0.90	0.10	0.84	0.14	0.08	0.09

4.3   Discussion

The results clearly show that the maximum migration threshold parameter is important for the dDCA, producing marked changes in classification perfor-mance. The result that identical $MCAV$s are obtained for all values under 100 was initially surprising, and assumed to be a fault in the experimental test har-ness. Thorough investigation of this phenomena was performed as a result, and we are confident that this is a genuine observation and not due to a bug in the dDCA code or in the test harness. Upon analysis, we see that for each sig-nal instance a combined value of 100 is present. This means that for instance, for cells with a migration threshold of less than 100, all cells in the popula-tion migrate, making parameter variability in this range immaterial. This is a

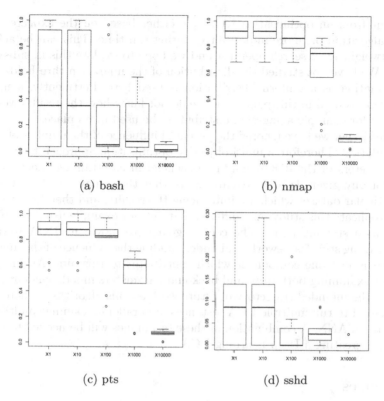

(a) bash   (b) nmap

(c) pts   (d) sshd

Fig. 2. Boxplots of the four processes of interest, showing the MCAV for each of the parameter settings per process

useful observation for future guidance on setting this parameter. As the parameter increased above 1000, there is a deterioration in the discrimination of the anomalous processes, though changes in the discrimination of the normal processes were not significant. This is most pronounced with the value of 10000 in which no migration occurs until all signal instances are processed, as shown in Fig. 2. These results indicate that this parameter and the migration thresholds of individual DCs within the population does warrant further investigation and the application of an optimisation method.

4.4   Conclusions

The contribution of this paper is that it shows the sensitivity of the migration threshold parameter in the dDCA and on a wider range of data than in previous experiments with the dDCA. Deterioration of classification is shown with excessively large migration thresholds, and lower limits related to the current system signal values. Therefore this represents a small but important step towards implementing a learning mechanism in the DCA independent of an initial training phase. The results suggest that the maximum migration threshold is likely to benefit from an optimisation technique either based on the expected input for the algorithm or, more importantly, during run time. This can be achieved via lightweight local search operator and we hope to explore this in subsequent studies. We have not studied the distribution of the migration thresholds across the population as a uniform distribution is used here. Pertinently, a uniform distribution is used in this paper, and we do not know how the results would be affected if for example a gaussian distribution be used in its place.

In this paper we have ignored the potential influence of the number of cells in the population. Therefore a multi-objective optimisation approach to tune both key parameters of the dDCA may be beneficial in ascertaining their optimum values for any given dataset. We are aware that there may also be nuances of this particular dataset which are influencing the results, and therefore we would seek to replicate this study on a different dataset, for example using the KDD99 dataset as a starting point. The central goal is to move the DCA towards a Deep Learning style framework, and understanding the influence of the migration threshold is just one component which contributes to this aim. An integrated approach examining both front and back-end parameters in a dependent fashion would be the intended trajectory of future work on this algorithm. There is also the potential to run multiple DCA instances in parallel in a similar multilayered fashion to an ANN. A combination of these techniques will be needed to achieve the aim of creating a Deep Learning DCA.

References

1. de Castro, L., Timmis, J.: Artificial Immune Systems: A New Computational Approach. Springer, London (2002)
2. Chelly, Z., Elouedi, Z.: A survey of the dendritic cell algorithm. Knowl. Inf. Syst. **48**(3), 505–535 (2016). https://doi.org/10.1007/s10115-015-0891-y
3. Elisa, N., Yang, L., Naik, N.: Dendritic cell algorithm with optimised parameters using genetic algorithm. In: 2018 IEEE Congress on Evolutionary Computation, CEC 2018, Rio de Janeiro, Brazil, 8–13 July 2018, pp. 1–8 (2018). https://doi.org/10.1109/CEC.2018.8477932
4. Elisa, N., Yang, L., Qu, Y., Chao, F.: A revised dendritic cell algorithm using k-means clustering. In: 20th IEEE International Conference on High Performance Computing and Communications; 16th IEEE International Conference on Smart City; 4th IEEE International Conference on Data Science and Systems, HPCC/SmartCity/DSS 2018, Exeter, United Kingdom, 28–30 June 2018, pp. 1547–1554 (2018)
5. Greensmith, J.: The Dendritic cell algorithm. Ph.D. thesis, School of Computer Science, University Of Nottingham (2007)
6. Greensmith, J., Aickelin, U., Cayzer, S.: Introducing dendritic cells as a novel immune-inspired algorithm for anomaly detection. In: Jacob, C., Pilat, M.L., Bentley, P.J., Timmis, J.I. (eds.) ICARIS 2005. LNCS, vol. 3627, pp. 153–167. Springer, Heidelberg (2005). https://doi.org/10.1007/11536444_12
7. Greensmith, J., Aickelin, U., Tedesco, G.: Information fusion for anomaly detection with the DCA. Inf. Fusion **11**(1), 21–34 (2010)

8. Greensmith, J., Aickelin, U., Twycross, J.: Articulation and clarification of the dendritic cell algorithm. In: Bersini, H., Carneiro, J. (eds.) ICARIS 2006. LNCS, vol. 4163, pp. 404–417. Springer, Heidelberg (2006). https://doi.org/10.1007/11823940_31

9. Greensmith, J., Twycross, J., Aickelin, U.: Dendritic cells for anomaly detection. In: Proceedings of the Congress on Evolutionary Computation (CEC), pp. 664–671 (2006)

10. Greensmith, J., Aickelin, U.: The deterministic dendritic cell algorithm. In: Bentley, P.J., Lee, D., Jung, S. (eds.) ICARIS 2008. LNCS, vol. 5132, pp. 291–302. Springer, Heidelberg (2008). https://doi.org/10.1007/978-3-540-85072-4_26

11. Greensmith, J., Gale, M.B.: IEEE: the functional dendritic cell algorithm: a formal specification with Haskell. In: 2017 IEEE Congress on Evolutionary Computation, CEC 2017, Donostia, San Sebastián, Spain, 5–8 June 2017, pp. 1787–1794. IEEE (2017)

12. Gu, F., Feyereisl, J., Oates, R., Reps, J., Greensmith, J., Aickelin, U.: Quiet in class: classification, noise and the dendritic cell algorithm. In: Liò, P., Nicosia, G., Stibor, T. (eds.) ICARIS 2011. LNCS, vol. 6825, pp. 173–186. Springer, Heidelberg (2011). https://doi.org/10.1007/978-3-642-22371-6_17

13. Gu, F., Greensmith, J., Aickelin, U.: Theoretical formulation and analysis of the deterministic dendritic cell algorithm. Biosystems 111(2), 127–135 (2013)

14. Igbe, O., Darwish, I., Saadawi, T.: Deterministic dendritic cell algorithm application to smart grid cyber-attack detection. In: 2017 IEEE 4th International Conference on Cyber Security and Cloud Computing (CSCloud). IEEE, New York (2017)

15. Kim, J., Bentley, P., Wallenta, C., Ahmed, M., Hailes, S.: Danger is ubiquitous: detecting malicious activities in sensor networks using the dendritic cell algorithm. In: Bersini, H., Carneiro, J. (eds.) ICARIS 2006. LNCS, vol. 4163, pp. 390–403. Springer, Heidelberg (2006). https://doi.org/10.1007/11823940_30

16. Lau, H.Y.K., Lee, N.M.Y.: Danger theory or trained neural network - a comparative study for behavioural detection. In: Joint 10th International Conference on Soft Computing and Intelligent Systems (SCIS) and 19th International Symposium on Advanced Intelligent Systems (ISIS), Toyama, Japan, 5–8 December, pp. 867–874 (2018). https://doi.org/10.1109/SCIS-ISIS.2018.00143

17. Matzinger, P.: Tolerance, danger and the extended family. Annu. Rev. Immunol. 12, 991–1045 (1994)

18. Oates, R., Kendall, G., Garibaldi, J.M.: Frequency analysis for dendritic cell population tuning: Decimating the dendritic cell. Evolutionary Intelligence: Special Issue on Artificial Immune Systems (2008)

19. Sarafijanović, S., Le Boudec, J.-Y.: An artificial immune system for misbehavior detection in mobile ad-hoc networks with virtual thymus, clustering, danger signal, and memory detectors. In: Nicosia, G., Cutello, V., Bentley, P.J., Timmis, J. (eds.) ICARIS 2004. LNCS, vol. 3239, pp. 342–356. Springer, Heidelberg (2004). https://doi.org/10.1007/978-3-540-30220-9_28

20. Stibor, T., Oates, R., Kendall, G., Garibaldi, J.M.: Geometrical insights into the dendritic cell algorithm. In: Proceedings of the 11th Annual Conference on Genetic and Evolutionary Computation, pp. 1275–1282. ACM (2009)

Improving Resource Allocation in MOEA/D with Decision-Space Diversity Metrics

Yuri Lavinas[1(✉)], Claus Aranha[1], and Marcelo Ladeira[2]

[1] University of Tsukuba, Tsukuba, Japan
lavinas.yuri.xp@alumni.tsukuba.ac.jp, caranha@cs.tsukuba.ac.jp
[2] University of Brasilia, Brasília, Brazil
mladeira@unb.br

Abstract. One of the main algorithms for solving Multi-Objective Optimization Problems is the Multi-Objective Evolutionary Algorithm Based on Decomposition (MOEA/D). It is characterized by decomposing the multiple objectives into a large number of single-objective subproblems, and then solving these subproblems in parallel. Usually, these subproblems are considered equivalent, but there are works that indicate that some subproblems can be more difficult than others, and that spending more computational resources in these subproblems can improve the performance of MOEA/D. One open question about this strategy of "Resource Allocation" is: what should be the criteria for allocating more computational effort on one problem or another? In this work we investigate this question. We study four different ways to prioritize subproblems: Randomly, Relative Improvement, Diversity in Decision Space (proposed in this work), and inverted Diversity in Decision Space (also proposed in this work). We compare the performance of MOEA/D using these four different "priority functions" on the DTLZ and UF benchmarks. We evaluate the resulting IGD, proportion of non-dominated solutions, and visually analyse the resulting resource allocation and Pareto Front. The result of our experiments is that the priority function using diversity in decision space improved the MOEA/D, achieving better IGD values and higher proportion of non-dominated solutions.

Keywords: Multi-Objective Optimization · Resource Allocation · Priority Functions

1 Introduction

Multi-objective Optimization Problems (MOP) are minimization[1] problems characterized by multiple, conflicting objective functions. It arises in real world applications that require a compromise among multiple objectives. The set of optimal trade off solutions in the decision space is the *Pareto Set (PS)*, and

---

[1] or maximization

© Springer Nature Switzerland AG 2019
C. Martín-Vide et al. (Eds.): TPNC 2019, LNCS 11934, pp. 134–146, 2019.
https://doi.org/10.1007/978-3-030-34500-6_9

the image of this set in the objective space is the *Pareto Front (PF)*. Finding a good approximation of the Pareto Front is a hard problem for which multiple Evolutionary Algorithms have been proposed [10,12,17].

The Multi-Objective Evolutionary Algorithm Based on Decomposition, (MOEA/D) [13] is an effective algorithm for solving MOPs. The key idea of the MOEA/D is to decompose the multi-objective optimization problem into a set of single objective subproblems. All subproblems are then solved in parallel.

Standard MOEA/D handles all subproblems uniformly. However, it has been observed that some subproblems are harder than others, and take more effort to converge to an optimal solution [16]. Therefore, MOEA/D may sometimes waste computational effort by trying to improve solutions that are not very promising [1]. This can be a critical issue in large-scale MOP problems that require costly simulations on supercomputers to evaluate each candidate solution [8].

To address this issue, *Resource Allocation* (RA) techniques have been proposed. They allocate different amounts of computational effort to different subproblems, based on an estimation of the relative importance of each subproblem [7,14,16]. The estimation of subproblem importance is done by *Priority Functions*, and one of the most popular approaches for this is the *Relative Improvement* (R.I.), which calculates a subproblem's priority by how much its incumbent solution has improved in recent iterations.

In this work, we study new Priority Functions to improve the quality of Resource Allocation. In particular, we propose a new Priority Function based on the diversity of subproblems and their solutions on decision space. In other words, how much the incumbent solution is different from its parent solution indicates whether the algorithm should focus on it or not. We propose two Priority Functions: Decision-Space Diversity (DS), which gives higher priority to solutions that are dissimilar from their parents, and Inverted Decision-Space Diversity (iDS), which gives higher priority to solutions that are similar to their parents. This work extends our previous short paper [9] by including the iDS and investigating the experimental results in much more depth.

In our experiments, we analyze how much each priority function managed to improve the MOEA/D. The results show that DS largely improved the performance of MOEA/D, leading to better Inverted Generational Distance (IGD) and higher percentage of non-dominated solutions on benchmark functions. On the other hand, the iDS did not perform so well. A surprising result is that assigning random priority also improves MOEA/D performance, although not to the degree of DS. Based on these results we suggest an improvement of the MOEA/D-DE base line, using DS for Resource Allocation (MOEA/D-SRA - Simple Resource Allocation).

2   Background

Priority functions are used in Resource Allocation (RA) to determine the preferences between subproblems [4]. These functions take information about the progress of the algorithm's search, and guide the distribution of computational resources among subproblems over iterations [2].

Algorithm 1. MOEA/D-SRA (Simple Resource Allocation)

1: Initialize the weight vectors λ_i, the neighborhood B_i, the priority value u_i every
   subproblem $i = 1, ..., N$.
2: **while** *Termination criteria* **do**
3:     **for** i = 1 to N **do**   ▷ Number of subproblems
4:         **if** *rand()* $< u_i$ **then**
5:             Generate an offspring y for subproblem i.
6:             Update the population by y.
7:         **if** Number of subproblems updated ≤ 3 **then**
8:             (Update all subproblems, reset all u_i to 1)
9:     Evaluate the population, and update all u_i using a Priority Function.

We divide the works concerned with RA in two groups. The first group
uses Relative Improvement (R.I.) as priority function and includes MOEA/D-
GRA [16], MOEA/D-DRA [14] and the Two-Level Stable Matching-Based Selection in MOEA/D [11]. The second group is based on the use of an external archive
and includes EAG-MOEA/D [2] and MOEA/D-CRA [7].

Zhou and Zhang claim that MOEA/D-GRA is an extension of MOEA/D-
DRA and MOEA/D-AMS [5,16]. They reason that MOEA/D-GRA uses a
similar Priority Function as MOEA/D-DRA and MOEA/D-AMS and that
MOEA/D-GRA simulates MOEA/D-DRA or MOEA/D-AMS by changing a single parameter. This Priority Function is the R.I. Priority Function. This function
defines the priority of each subproblem of the current iteration t based on how
much the incumbent solution of that subproblem has improved over the last ΔT
iterations. The idea behind R.I. is that a subproblem that has improved recently
should have higher priority for RA.

These studies show that using Priority Functions for RA can help MOEA/D
performance. However, each of these works focuses on improvements on the
algorithm rather than on the Resource Allocation method itself. For example,
Zhang et al.'s work [14] improves MOEA/D-DRA by using a 10-tournament
selection. Therefore, the influence of the choice of Priority Functions on RA is
still unclear.

In this context, our goal is to improve the performance of MOEA/D based on
the choice of Priority Function. To achieve this, we isolate the Priority Function
as our only change to the standard algorithm and we propose two new Priority
Functions based on decision space diversity (DS and iDS). Our idea is that
MOEA/D will benefit from a focus on diversity, since it is a critical issue to the
search process.

3 MOEA/D-SRA - MOEA/D with Priority Functions

We use the basic framework described in Algorithm 1. This algorithm is based
on MOEA/D-GRA [16], however, unlike that work, we only add Resource Allocation to MOEA/D-DE, with no other changes. Our proposed algorithm has a

---

Algorithm 2. Priority Function: Decision Space Diversity (DS)

1: Input: X^t decision vectors of solutions; X^{t-1}, decision vectors from the previous solutions; N, the population size.
2: **for** i=1 to N **do**
3:     $u[i] = ||X_i^t - X_i^{t-1}||$
4: $u = $ scale (u) ▷ between 0 and 1
5: **return** u

Algorithm 3. Priority Function: Inverted Decision Space Diversity (iDS)

1: Input: X^t decision vectors of solutions; X^{t-1}, decision vectors from the previous solutions; N, the population size.
2: **for** i=1 to N **do**
3:     $u[i] = ||X_i^t - X_i^{t-1}||$
4: $u = 1-$scale (u) ▷ between 0 and 1
5: **return** u

Algorithm 4. Priority Function: Relative Improvement

1: Input: Y^t, objective function values from the incumbent solutions; $Y^{t-\Delta T}$, objective function values from incumbent solution of iteration $t-\Delta T$, u from the previous ΔT iteration;
2: **for** i=1 to N **do**
3:     $u[i] = \frac{Y^t[i]-Y^{t-1}[i]}{Y^t[i]}$
4: **if** $max(u) = 0$ **then**
5:     $\forall u[i]; u[i] = 1$
6: **else**
7:     $u = u \ / \ (\max(u) + 1.0 \times 10^{-50})$
8: **return** u

Algorithm 5. Priority Function: Random

1: Input: N, the population size.
2: **for** i=1 to N **do**
3:     u[i] = value sampled uniformly from the [0,1) interval
4: **return** u

---

simple code structure and represents well the class of variants of MOEA/D with Resource Allocation without a population archive. In consequence, we can study any proposed Priority Function and integrate them to the MOEA/D framework.

Algorithm 1 differentiates from MOEA/D-DE [14] only on lines 4 and 7–9. Line 9 assigns a priority value u_i between 0 and 1 to each subproblem i, based on a priority function. Line 4 performs the Resource Allocation, by selecting whether each subproblem (and its incumbent solution) is to be updated on that iteraction. Each subproblem has probability equal to u_i of being selected for update on line 4, so subproblems with higher priority values are updated more often over the run of the algorithm.

At the start of the algorithm, all subproblems have the same priority $u_i = 1$. Also, if the number of subproblems selected for update at line 4 is less than 3 at any iteration, we reset all the priority values u_i to 1 and update all subproblems in that iteration on lines 7–8. Finally, note that even though some of the incumbent solutions are not updated under this algorithm, they may still be replaced by neighboring solutions that are updated, as in the standard MOEA/D-DE.

The choice of Priority Function allow us to easily design MOEA/D variants that allocate more resources on any desired characteristics of the population and the search, such as diversity or convergence. In this work, we consider three Priority Functions: R.I., DS and iDS. There are two main differences between R.I. and the proposed Priority Functions. First, R.I. uses information from the objective space of solutions while DS and iDS use information from the decision space of solutions. Second, R.I. has to maintain information about the objective values of all solutions in all past ΔT iterations, while DS and iDS only use information from the current iteration and the one before it. For R.I., we set the value of ΔT to 20, as in the work of Zhou and Zhang [16].

3.1   Decision Space Distance: DS and iDS Priority Functions

To consider diversity on the decision space, we measure the difference of a current solution and its parent using the (2-)Norm. Given this difference we define the metrics: *Decision Space Distance* (DS) and the *inverted Decision Space Distance* (iDS).

The DS Priority Function directly uses this distance. Algorithm 2 details the calculation. First we calculate the distance between an incumbent solution and its parent solution, and then we scale the distance to the $(0,1]$ interval, based on the entire solution set.

The idea behind DS is that by considering diversity as the Priority Function more resources are given to solutions that are different to their parents, forcing MOEA/D to focus on less explored areas, and leading to higher exploration of the decision space.

In the opposite fashion, the iDS gives more resources to solutions that are similar to their parents, forcing them to improve more. iDS is the inverse of DS, prioritizing solutions that DS does not prioritize. Algorithm 3 details the implementation: like DS, the distance between incumbent solution and parent solution is calculated, and then scaled. However, the priority is based on the complement of this scaled value.

3.2   Relative Improvement Priority Function

The Relative Improvement (R.I.) Priority Function allocates resources to subproblem based on an estimation of problem difficulty. Subproblems where the fitness of the incumbent solution has improved further over the last ΔT iterations receive higher priority under this function. Algorithm 4 details the implementation. For more information about this Priority Function, see the works of Zhou, Zhang and Nasir [11, 14, 16].

3.3   Random Priority Functions

As a baseline for comparison we also define a Random Priority Function. This function samples the priority value u_i from an uniform distribution. This should, on average, allocate the same amount of resources for all subproblems over the optimization process. Algorithm 5 gives the details on its implementation.

4   Experimental Results and Discussion

To examine the effects of Resource Allocation (RA) under different Priority Functions on MOEA/D, we perform a comparative experiment on benchmark functions. In this experiment, we use MOEA/D-DE implemented by the MOEADr package [3], modified to include RA as described in the previous section.

We compare MOEA/D-SRA, Algorithm 1, with five different RA strategies: four RA using DS, i-DS, Random and Relative Improvement Priority Functions; and MOEA/D-DE with no RA. In the following figures and tables, these strategies are referred, respectively, as: DS, i-DS, Random, R.I. and MOEA/D-DE.

For comparison we use two function sets: the DTLZ function set [6], with 100 dimensions and $k =$ dimensions $-$ number of objectives $+1$, where the number of objectives is 2; and the UF function set [15], with 100 dimensions.

4.1   Experimental Parameters and Evaluation

We use the conventional MOEA/D-DE parameters [10] for each RA strategy: update size $nr = 2$, neighborhood size $T = 20$, and the neighborhood search probability $\delta_p = 0.9$. The DE mutation operator value is $F = 0.5$. The Polynomial mutation operator values are $\eta_m = 20$, $p_m = 0.03333333$ and the lower and upper bounds are respectively $(-2, 2)$. The decomposition function is Simple-Lattice Design (SLD), the scalar aggregation function is Weighted Sum (WS), the update strategy is the Restricted Update Strategy and we performed a simple linear scaling of the objectives to $[0, 1]$. For every strategy/function pair we perform 21 repetitions with 30000 function evaluations and population size $N = 350$.

We compare the results of the different strategies based on their Inverted Generational Distance (IGD) metrics. Lower values of the IGD indicate better approximations. We also evaluate the proportion of non-dominated solutions.

The difference in IGD among the different techniques is analyzed using the Pairwise Wilcoxon Rank Sum Tests (paired on all functions examined) with confidence $\alpha = 0.05$ and with the Hommel adjustment method for multiple comparisons. For reproducibility purposes, all the code, data and experimental scripts are available online[1].

---

[1] https://github.com/yclavinas/MOEADr/tree/tpnc_2019.

Table 1. IGD medians ans standard deviation (in parenthesis) for every function and technique. The number in parenthesis is the standard deviation. The best value for each function is indicated in Bold.

IGD	MOEA/D-DE	DS	i-DS	Random	R.I.
UF1	0.425 (0.042)	**0.146 (0.013)**	0.326 (0.022)	0.250 (0.032)	0.223 (0.030)
UF2	0.130 (0.009)	0.104 (0.012)	0.104 (0.009)	0.103 (0.010)	**0.093 (0.008)**
UF3	0.301 (0.006)	**0.274 (0.010)**	0.283 (0.006)	0.278 (0.009)	0.281 (0.008)
UF4	0.112 (0.003)	0.108 (0.002)	0.111 (0.003)	0.109 (0.003)	**0.107 (0.003)**
UF5	2.163 (0.060)	**1.333 (0.106)**	1.923 (0.093)	1.591 (0.086)	1.551 (0.103)
UF6	0.408 (0.054)	**0.177 (0.042)**	0.332 (0.049)	0.250 (0.039)	0.236 (0.033)
UF7	0.392 (0.067)	**0.141 (0.015)**	0.332 (0.034)	0.231 (0.039)	0.208 (0.034)
UF8	0.380 (0.028)	**0.261 (0.010)**	0.303 (0.014)	0.278 (0.013)	0.282 (0.013)
UF9	0.521 (0.014)	**0.440 (0.0154)**	0.476 (0.015)	0.475 (0.013)	0.474 (0.015)
UF10	4.105 (0.153)	**2.97 (0.216)**	3.788 (0.179)	3.24 (0.189)	3.094 (0.273)
DTLZ1	411.5 (157.1)	387.8 (95.08)	564.4 (112.1)	301.7 (123.0)	**257.8 (99.73)**
DTLZ2	0.309 (0.027)	**0.140 (0.019)**	0.218 (0.035)	0.187 (0.022)	0.179 (0.017)
DTLZ3	1409 (300.2)	1006 (318.0)	1440 (346.1)	801.6 (225.3)	**245.4 (380.5)**
DTLZ4	0.404 (0.071)	**0.131 (0.034)**	0.263 (0.050)	0.206 (0.029)	0.230 (0.102)
DTLZ5	0.326 (0.027)	**0.148 (0.020)**	0.224 (0.034)	0.186 (0.020)	0.179 (0.019)
DTLZ6	29.23 (2.814)	**0.096 (0.777)**	23.29 (1.267)	16.68 (2.663)	16.32 (2.586)
DTLZ7	3.213 (0.353)	**0.287 (0.222)**	2.229 (0.244)	1.719 (0.213)	0.783 (0.208)

4.2   Analysis of IGD Results

Tables 1 and 2 show that the methods using RA, specially the DS Priority Function, perform better than not using Resource Allocation. Methods with RA always show better IGD values, and higher proportion of non-dominated solutions. The Pairwise Wilcoxon test results in Table 3 indicate significant differences in IGD favoring the use of Resource Allocation over MOEA/D-DE without RA, no matter the Priority Function. We can see examples of the achieved Pareto Fronts on Fig. 1a and b.

Among the Priority functions, the DS achieves best IGD values in 13 out of 17 functions (see Table 1). While R.I. achieved better results on some functions, overall the DS showed itself more appropriate, as our statistical analysis (paired over all tested function), showed that the DS was superior to each of the other methods (See Table 3).

One surprising result is that the statistical test did not show a difference between the R.I. priority function and the Random priority function. While the Random priority function was initially designed as an "easy" baseline, this result indicates that holding part of the population every iteration under MOEA/D might have a positive effect, regardless of Priority Function. It also indicates that there is still space for finding better Priority Functions than those currently listed in the literature. Another interesting result is that iDS did not perform nearly

Table 2. Proportion of non-dominated: median values and standard deviation (in parenthesis) of non-dominated solutions on UF and DTLZ benchmarks.

Proportion	MOEA/D-DE	DS	i-DS	Random	R.I.
UF1	24% (03%)	**90% (08%)**	28% (04%)	52% (06%)	41% (13%)
UF2	28% 03%)	**92% (06%)**	44% (05%)	77% (06%)	63% (15%)
UF3	16% (03%)	**76% (09%)**	34% (05%)	52% (08%)	29% (09%)
UF4	59% (04%)	**97% (11%)**	63% (06%)	86% (03%)	76% (08%)
UF5	15% (02%)	**97% (04%)**	30% (04%)	64% (07%)	57% (13%)
UF6	22% (04%)	**90% (08%)**	28% (04%)	50% (05%)	39% (16%)
UF7	27% (04%)	**91% (07%)**	38% (05%)	58% (07%)	54% (10%)
UF8	48% (05%)	**97% (03%)**	69% (06%)	87% (05%)	95% (10%)
UF9	38% (04%)	**98% (04%)**	61% (05%)	89% (05%)	89% (06%)
UF10	38% (05%)	**98% (03%)**	61% (08%)	88% (06%)	90% (07%)
DTLZ1	09% (02%)	**98% (07%)**	13% (04%)	50% (16%)	41% (18%)
DTLZ2	15% (02%)	**92% (08%)**	31% (05%)	68% (08%)	70% (19%)
DTLZ3	02% (0.9%)	**95% (11%)**	05% (02%)	29% (13%)	15% (15%)
DTLZ4	06% (02%)	**94% (17%)**	18% (05%)	43% (10%)	58% (21%)
DTLZ5	15% (02%)	**92% (08%)**	31% (05%)	68% (08%)	70% (19%)
DTLZ6	05% (03%)	**99% (27%)**	07% (02%)	15% (11%)	28% (13%)
DTLZ7	16% (05%)	**85% (11%)**	21% (06%)	32% (10%)	45% (22%)

Table 3. Statistical analysis of the IGD difference between methods, paired on the benchmark functions, using the Pairwise Wilcoxon Rank Sum test. "←" indicates superiority of the row method, while "↑" indicates superiority of the column method. "≃" indicates no statistical difference.

	DS	iDS	R.I.	Random	MOEA/D-DE
DS	–	1.3e−12 ←	1.1e−06 ←	5.9e−08 ←	< 2e−16 ←
iDS	1.3e−12 ↑	–	0.00078 ↑	0.00172 ↑	9.0e−05 ←
R.I	1.1e−06 ↑	0.00078 ←	–	0.41140 ≃	1.0e−08 ←
Random	5.9e−08 ↑	0.00172 ←	0.41140 ≃	–	1.0e−08 ←
MOEA/D-DE	< 2e−16 ↑	9.0e−05 ↑	1.0e−08 ↑	1.0e−08 ↑	–

as well as DS, R.I. or Random, although it still performed better than not using Resource Allocation at all.

4.3 Analysis of the Proportion of Non-dominated Solutions

Looking at the proportion of non-dominated solutions (Table 2), we see that DS obtains the highest value on all functions for both benchmark sets, often with a very clear lead.

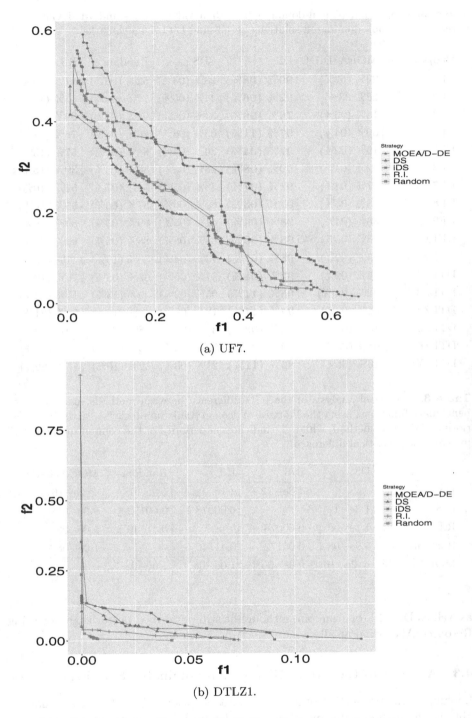

(a) UF7.

(b) DTLZ1.

Fig. 1. Median Pareto Front of all methods on two functions.

This reflects the idea behind the creation of the DS Priority Function: by focusing more resources on solutions that are different from its parents, DS is able to achieve a more diverse set of solutions. On the other hand, R.I. focus on improving the fitness values of individual solutions means it is not surprising that it did not perform so well in terms of non-dominated solutions.

4.4   Discussion on Resource Allocation

Figures 2a, b, c, d illustrates the differences in Resource Allocation for the four Priority Functions. They show how many times each subproblem (horizontal axis) was updated (vertical axis) over the course of the optimization for each priority function on the UF7 function. We can see that DS allocated a higher amount of resources to subproblems 95 to 120, while iDS and R.I. slightly favored the first and last few subproblems. Random allocated the resources uniformly.

From these figures, we can clearly see that the DS is able to choose and focus on certain regions of the problem, while other priority functions are much more

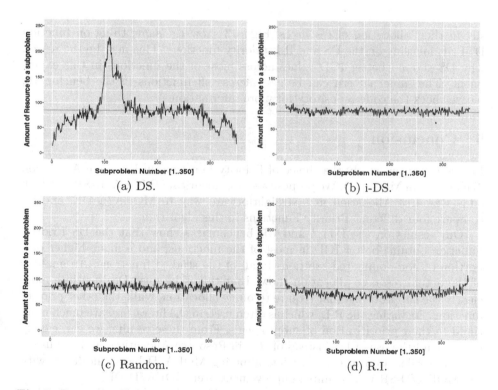

Fig. 2. Resource allocation on the UF7 function. The horizontal axis indicates the subproblems, while the vertical axis indicate the number of updates accumulated over the optimization. Higher values on the vertical axis indicate higher priority for that subproblem. The horizontal red line indicates the default number of updates (with no Resource Allocation).

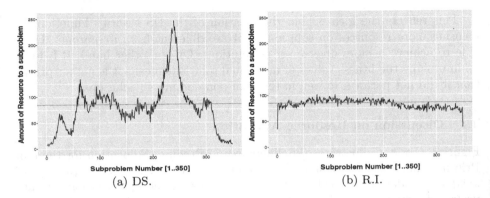

(a) DS.   (b) R.I.

Fig. 3. Resource Allocation on the DTLZ1 function. The horizontal axis indicates the subproblems, while the vertical axis indicate the number of updates accumulated over the optimization. Higher values on the vertical axis indicate higher priority for that subproblem. The horizontal red line indicates the default number of updates (with no Resource Allocation).

shy in their allocation of resources. Figure 3 show the same thing on function DTLZ1, focusing on the DS and R.I. priority functions. This may be the reason why DS showed better IGD values across most of the functions in this experiment. The same pattern can be seen across all functions in the benchmark, please check the code repository for more information.

5   Conclusion

In this paper, we study the choice of Priority Function on Resource Allocation Techniques in MOEA/D. We propose a simple algorithm (MOEA/D-SRA) which adds Resource Allocation in a straightforward way to MOEA/D-DE, and we compare four different Priority Functions in this algorithm.

Our results on the DTLZ and UF benchmarks show that the DS Priority Function obtains better IGD in most of the functions, and a much higher proportion of non-dominated solutions in all of the studied functions. An analysis of the actual resource allocation shows that this is because DS identifies more clearly the subproblems that require resource allocation, while the other priority functions, including the R.I., which is often used in the literature, are much more timid in their prioritization of subproblems. From these results, we can clearly recommend the use of DS instead of R.I. in Resource Allocation, and the use of Resource Allocation in general when applying MOEA/D based methods, with the MOEA/D-SRA as a simple improvement over MOEA/D-DE.

One surprising observation was that the Algorithm which assigned random priority values to subproblems performed as well as R.I., and better than not using Resource Allocation at all. This suggests that holding part of the population inactive at every iteration of MOEA/D might have a positive effect unrelated to resource allocation. As future work, we are further investigating this effect, aiming to find out what would be the optimal fraction of the population that should be kept inactive to improve the performance of standard MOEA/D.

References

1. Bezerra, L.C.T., López-Ibáñez, M., Stützle, T.: Comparing decomposition-based and automatically component-wise designed multi-objective evolutionary algorithms. In: Gaspar-Cunha, A., Henggeler Antunes, C., Coello, C.C. (eds.) EMO 2015. LNCS, vol. 9018, pp. 396–410. Springer, Cham (2015). https://doi.org/10.1007/978-3-319-15934-8_27
2. Cai, X., Li, Y., Fan, Z., Zhang, Q.: An external archive guided multiobjective evolutionary algorithm based on decomposition for combinatorial optimization. IEEE Trans. Evol. Comput. **19**(4), 508–523 (2015)
3. Campelo, F., Aranha, C.: MOEADr: Component-wise MOEA/D implementation, R package version 1.2.0 (2018). https://cran.R-project.org/package=MOEADr
4. Chankong, V., Haimes, Y.: Multiobjective Decision Making: Theory and Methodology. North Holland, New York (1983)
5. Chiang, T.C., Lai, Y.P.: MOEA/D-AMS: improving MOEA/D by an adaptive mating selection mechanism. In: 2011 IEEE Congress on Evolutionary Computation (CEC), pp. 1473–1480. IEEE (2011)
6. Deb, K., Thiele, L., Laumanns, M., Zitzler, E.: Scalable test problems for evolutionary multiobjective optimization. In: Abraham, A., Jain, L., Goldberg, R. (eds.) Evolutionary Multiobjective Optimization, pp. 105–145. Springer, London (2005). https://doi.org/10.1007/1-84628-137-7_6
7. Kang, Q., Song, X., Zhou, M., Li, L.: A collaborative resource allocation strategy for decomposition-based multiobjective evolutionary algorithms. IEEE Trans. Syst. Man Cybern. Syst. (2018)
8. Kohira, T., Kemmotsu, H., Akira, O., Tatsukawa, T.: Proposal of benchmark problem based on real-world car structure design optimization. In: Proceedings of the Genetic and Evolutionary Computation Conference Companion, pp. 183–184. ACM (2018)
9. Lavinas, Y., Aranha, C., Sakurai, T.: Using diversity as a priority function for resource allocation on MOEA/D. In: Proceedings of the Genetic and Evolutionary Computation Conference Companion. ACM (2019)
10. Li, H., Zhang, Q.: Multiobjective optimization problems with complicated pareto sets, MOEA/D and NSGA-II. IEEE Trans. Evol. Comput. **13**(2), 284–302 (2009)
11. Nasir, M., Mondal, A.K., Sengupta, S., Das, S., Abraham, A.: An improved multiobjective evolutionary algorithm based on decomposition with fuzzy dominance. In: 2011 IEEE Congress on Evolutionary Computation (CEC), pp. 765–772. IEEE (2011)
12. Trivedi, A., Srinivasan, D., Sanyal, K., Ghosh, A.: A survey of multiobjective evolutionary algorithms based on decomposition. IEEE Trans. Evol. Comput. **21**(3), 440–462 (2017)
13. Zhang, Q., Li, H.: MOEA/D: a multiobjective evolutionary algorithm based on decomposition. IEEE Trans. Evol. Comput. **11**(6), 712–731 (2007)
14. Zhang, Q., Liu, W., Li, H.: The performance of a new version of MOEA/D on CEC09 unconstrained MOP test instances. In: 2009 IEEE Congress on Evolutionary Computation, CEC 2009, pp. 203–208. IEEE (2009)

15. Zhang, Q., Zhou, A., Zhao, S., Suganthan, P.N., Liu, W., Tiwari, S.: Multiobjective optimization test instances for the CEC 2009 special session and competition. University of Essex, Colchester, UK and Nanyang Technological University, Singapore, special session on performance assessment of multi-objective optimization algorithms, Technical report 264 (2008)
16. Zhou, A., Zhang, Q.: Are all the subproblems equally important? Resource allocation in decomposition-based multiobjective evolutionary algorithms. IEEE Trans. Evol. Comput. **20**(1), 52–64 (2016)
17. Zitzler, E., Künzli, S.: Indicator-based selection in multiobjective search. In: Yao, X., et al. (eds.) PPSN 2004. LNCS, vol. 3242, pp. 832–842. Springer, Heidelberg (2004). https://doi.org/10.1007/978-3-540-30217-9_84

An Analysis of Evolutionary Algorithms for Multiobjective Optimization of Structure and Learning of Fuzzy Cognitive Maps Based on Multidimensional Medical Data

Alexander Yastrebov[iD], Łukasz Kubuś[iD], and Katarzyna Poczeta[(✉)][iD]

Kielce University of Technology, Kielce, Poland
{a.jastriebow,lkubus,k.piotrowska}@tu.kielce.pl

Abstract. The paper concerns the use of evolutionary algorithms to solve the problem of multiobjective optimization and learning of fuzzy cognitive maps (FCMs) on the basis of multidimensional medical data related to diabetes. The aim of this research study is an automatic construction of a collection of FCM models based on various criteria depending on the structure of the model and forecasting capabilities. The simulation analysis was performed with the use of the developed multiobjective Individually Directional Evolutionary Algorithm. Experiments show that the collection of fuzzy cognitive maps, in which each element is built on the basis of particular patient data, allows us to receive higher forecasting accuracy compared to the standard approach. Moreover, by appropriate aggregation of these collections we can also obtain satisfactory accuracy of forecasts for the new patient.

Keywords: Fuzzy cognitive maps · Multiobjective optimization · Evolutionary algorithms · Multidimensional medical data

1 Introduction

A fuzzy cognitive map (FCM) is a directed graph whose nodes represent concepts important for the analyzed phenomenon, and the connections correspond to the causal relationships between them [11]. The FCM model is a flexible and effective tool for modeling decision support systems [12]. FCMs can been applied to predict time series [8,16,22] or in classification problems [17,18]. Various types of the FCM structure can be applied to solve complex problems. Nested fuzzy cognitive maps [5] or multi-layer FCMs [4,15] were proposed to solve the problem connected with the large number of concepts that are composed of other elements. A multi-relational fuzzy cognitive maps was developed in order to model multi-dimensions and multi-granularities oriented complex systems [18]. Relational FCMs [27], interval-based cognitive maps [1], granular cognitive maps [6], and fuzzy grey cognitive maps [23] can be used to model uncertain systems.

© Springer Nature Switzerland AG 2019
C. Martín-Vide et al. (Eds.): TPNC 2019, LNCS 11934, pp. 147–158, 2019.
https://doi.org/10.1007/978-3-030-34500-6_10

The FCM model can be initialized based on expert knowledge or with the use of machine learning. In the first way, experts choose the most significant concepts and determine the weights of the relationships between them [15]. Learning of fuzzy cognitive maps is a popular and significant field of research. Evolutionary algorithms with the objective function based on data errors are usually used to build the FCM model. The real-coded genetic algorithm was used by Stach et al. [25] to automatically construct fuzzy cognitive maps. The resulted models are denser, less readable and more difficult to analyze then those created by the experts. Some novel learning algorithms have been developed to solve this problem. A sparse real-coded genetic algorithm to learn FCMs was proposed in [26]. This method allows to obtain a formation of maps of a certain predefined density. The authors in [3] used a multiobjective evolutionary algorithm with two objective functions of density and data error to learn fuzzy cognitive maps. Their approach can provide models with different densities for decision makers. In [28], a framework based on compressed sensing and convex optimization method to learn large-scale sparse fuzzy cognitive maps is proposed. The process of FCM learning is decomposed into sparse signal reconstruction problems. The results show that this approach obtains good performance by just learning from a small amount of data. Kolahdoozi et al. [10] proposed a new learning algorithm called the quantum fuzzy cognitive map. It combines the quantum inspired evolutionary algorithm and the particle swarm optimization algorithm for obtaining the ability of static and dynamic analysis.

In [20], we developed an evolutionary algorithm for fuzzy cognitive map learning based on graph theory metrics: the degree of the node, the value of the node and the total influence of the concept. It allows for the automatic selection of significant concepts based on graph theory metrics and determining the relationships between them during learning process. The resulting models are more readable and easier to analyze. In [19], we additionally introduced the FCM bank, in which each element is a suitable map with one output concept. Experiments confirmed that using the bank of fuzzy cognitive maps could improve the learning process compared to the standard approaches. Similar solutions were also analyzed on the example of artificial neural networks [21,29].

This paper is devoted to the synthesis and simulation analysis of fuzzy cognitive maps with the use of evolutionary algorithms. The aim of this research study is an automatic construction of a collection of the optimal in some sense FCM models on the basis of multidimensional historical data. Therefore, various criteria for FCMs construction have been introduced depending on: the number of concepts, the structure of their relationships and learning criteria based on forecasting of historical data. The developed approach was applied to solve the problem of forecasting complex multidimensional medical data related to diabetes [9]. We used data of 20 patients to construct a collection of fuzzy cognitive maps in which each element was built on the basis of particular patient data. Next, aggregation of the FCM models developed for each patient was done and the resulting models were verified with the use of data of the 21-th patient. The comparison was done with the standard approach for learning of the FCM model based on all available data. The whole simulation analysis was performed with the use of the developed multiobjective Individually Directional Evolutionary Algorithm (m-IDEA), enabling solving multiobjective optimization problems with various types of constraints. This algorithm can be used to solve tasks with one criterion and more criteria. The obtained solutions are from the appropriate Pareto-optimal set [2]. As a result of this analysis, we can conclude that the collection of fuzzy cognitive maps allows us to receive more accurate forecasts of multidimensional data related to diabetes compared to the standard approach. Moreover, by appropriate aggregation of these collections we can also obtain satisfactory accuracy of forecasts for the new patient.

Section 2 presents the problem of multiobjective optimization of structure and learning of fuzzy cognitive maps. Section 3 contains a description of the developed multiobjective Individually Directional Evolutionary Algorithm. Section 4 describes multidimensional medical data on diabetes and presents the results of simulation analysis. The last section contains conclusions and directions for further research.

2 Problem of Multiobjective Optimization of Structure and Learning of FCMs

A classical FCM model is described as follows:

$$<X, W> \tag{1}$$

where: $X = [X_1, X_2, ..., X_n]^T$ – the concepts vector, $W = \{w_{ij}\}_{i,j=1}^n$ – general matrix of relationships between concepts X_i, X_j, $i, j = 1, ..., n$.

It should be noted that at the beginning of the analysis, the maximum number of possible concepts n_{max} should be determined, and the relationships between them can be zero or non-zero numbers in the range $[-1, 1]$. Therefore, the idea of FCM structure optimization means that we can reduce the number of concepts and reset specific relationships based on historical data or expert knowledge. The weights of the relationships w_{ij} are determined on the basis of machine learning. The previously developed appropriate evolutionary algorithm [14,20] was used to solve the tasks of FCM structure optimization and determining the weights of the relationships.

For fuzzy cognitive maps, the proper dynamics model can be used to enable dynamic analysis. It is usually described by the following equation:

$$X_i(t+1) = F(X_i(t) + \sum_{j=1, j\neq i}^{n} w_{ji}X_j(t)) \tag{2}$$

where: $X_i(t)$ – the state of the i-th concept at the time t, $t = 0, 1, ..., T$, $i = 1, 2, ..., n$, n – the number of concepts, $w \in [-1, 1]$, $i, j = 1, ..., n$. The stabilizing function $F(x)$ can be chosen in the logistic form, which means that $X_i(t) \in [0, 1]$.

2.1   Optimization of Structure of the FCM Model

According to the above information, we introduced the optimization criteria for choosing the most significant concepts and relationships between them in the following form [20]:

– the degree of the node [4]:

$$J_i^1(w) = deg_i = \frac{\sum\limits_{j=1,j\neq i}^{n} \theta(w_{ij})}{n-1} \rightarrow max_{w\in W_0} \tag{3}$$

where: $\theta(w_{ij}) = \begin{cases} 1 \,, & w_{i,j} \neq 0 \\ 0 \,, & w_{i,j} = 0 \end{cases}, i = 1, ..., n.$

– the total value of the node [4]:

$$J_i^2(w) = val_i = \frac{\sum\limits_{j=1,j\neq i}^{n} |w_{ij}| + \sum\limits_{j=1,j\neq i}^{n} |w_{ji}|}{\sum\limits_{j=1}^{n} \sum\limits_{k=1,k\neq j}^{n} |w_{jk}|} \rightarrow max_{w\in W_0} \tag{4}$$

where: $i = 1, ..., n.$

These criteria are based on graph theory metrics and were analyzed in [20]. Set W_0 in (3)–(4) means the following constraints on w_{ij}:

$$W_0 = \{|w_{ij}| \leq 1\} \tag{5}$$

where: $i, j = 1, ..., n.$

2.2   Multiobjective Learning

Multiobjective machine learning of fuzzy cognitive maps based on historical data can be implemented on the basis of the following criterion:

$$J_j^3(w) = \frac{1}{T} \sum_{i=1}^{n} |Z_{i_j}(t) - X_{i_j}(t)|^\mu -> min_{w\in W_0} \tag{6}$$

where: $\mu = 1, 2$, $j = 1, ..., K$, K – the number of output concepts, $K \leq n$, $W_0 \subseteq \mathbb{R}_{n\times n}$ – set of constraints on w_{ij} type (5), $Z_{i_j}(t)$ – normalized historical data.

Criteria $J_j^3(w)$ $(j = 1, ..., K)$ relate to the output (decision) concepts (from the total number of possible concepts) defining the forecasting capabilities of the FCM model type (1)–(2) based on historical data (measurements). The general problem representing some summary of the formulas presented in Sects. 2.1 and 2.2 is described below.

2.3   General Multiobjective Problem of Optimization and Learning

The multiobjective problem for optimization of structure and learning of fuzzy cognitive maps can be described as follows:

$$
\begin{cases}
J_i^1(w) \to max_{w \in W_0} \\
J_i^2(w) \to max_{w \in W_0} \\
J_j^3(w) \to min_{w \in W_0}
\end{cases}
\tag{7}
$$

where: $i = 1, ..., n$, $j = 1, ..., K$, K – the number of criteria (output concepts). This problem is based on historical data.

2.4   The FCM Model as a Solution to the Problem (7)

In this research, we turn problem (7) on the equivalent multiobjective optimization problem [2] by converting criteria $J_i^1(w)$, $J_i^2(w)$, $(i = 1, ..., n)$ to constraints on w_{ij} $(i, j = 1, ..., n)$.

The resulting equivalent problem of multiobjective (in some sense) optimization is described as follows:

$$
\begin{cases}
J_j^3(w) \to min_{w \in W} \\
W = W_0 \cap W_1 \cap W_2
\end{cases}
\tag{8}
$$

where: $j = 1, ..., K$,

$$
\begin{aligned}
W_1 &= \{J_i^1(w) \geq a_1 \\
W_2 &= \{J_i^2(w) \geq a_2
\end{aligned}
\tag{9}
$$

where: $i = 1, ..., n$, $a_l > 0$ $(l = 1, 2)$ – parameters, in particular, they can satisfy the condition: $a_1 = a_2 = a$. The problem of multiobjective optimization (8)–(9) is the aim of this simulation analysis.

Synthesis and analysis of the FCM models developed on the basis of the proposed approach for multiobjective optimization of structure and learning is realized in the following steps:

1. Finding the Pareto-optimal solution of the problem (8)–(9) with the use of the developed multiobjective Individually Directional Evolutionary Algorithm described in the next section.
2. Converting criterion (8) to a weighted form [2]:

$$
J(w) = \sum_{j=1}^{K} \lambda_j J_j^3(w)
\tag{10}
$$

where: $0 \leq \lambda_j \leq 1$, $\sum_{j=1}^{K} \lambda_j = 1$, λ_j – parameters, K – the number of criteria.

3. Selecting $\lambda_{j^*} = 1$, $\lambda_j = 0$, $j \neq j^*$, $j = 1, ..., K$ which is equivalent for the selection of the main criterion $J_{j^*}^3(w)$, and the others are moved to the constraints (9) in the form:

$$J_j^3(w) \leq t_j \tag{11}$$

where: $j = 1, ..., K$, $j \neq j*$, t_j – a parameter.

4. Analysis of the collection of FCM models received for each realization of multidimensional data and their aggregation.

Remark 1. Since $J_j^3(w) \leq 1$ $(j = 1, ..., K)$, we can choose $t_j = 1$ and inequalities (11) will be met. So we can leave them in constraints (9).

Remark 2. If we choose for j^* each of $j \in \{1, ..., K\}$ then we have K optimization tasks, and the resulting structure can be called a bank of fuzzy cognitive maps [19].

The aim of this research study is to analyze the application of the developed approach for multiobjective optimization of structure and learning of the FCM model based on multidimensional historical data.

2.5   Multidimensional Historical Data

The general matrix of multidimensional historical data can be described as follows:

$$Y(t) = \{Y^l(t)\} \tag{12}$$

where: $t = 1, ..., T$, T – the number of historical data (measurements) for each realization of multidimensional data, $l = 1, ..., L$, L – the number of realizations (dimensions, e.g. patients).

$$Y^l(t) = [Y_1^l(t), ..., Y_k^l(t)]^T \tag{13}$$

$$X^l(t) = [X_1^l(t), ..., X_k^l(t)]^T \tag{14}$$

where: $l = 1, ...L$, $X^l(t) = \{X_i^l(t)\}$ – matrix of values of the concepts of the l-th FCM model, $l = 1, ..., L$, L – the number of the FCM models, $Y^l(t) = \{Y_i^l(t)\}$ – matrix of historical data for the l-th realization, $l = 1, ..., L$, L – the number of realizations of historical data, $t = 1, ..., T$ – discrete time.

In contrast to the classic FCMs, we adopted the following form:

$$X_i^l(t+1) = F(X_i^l(t) + \sum_{j=1, j \neq i}^{n} w_{ji}^l X_j^l(t)) \tag{15}$$

where: $W^l = \{w_{j,i}^l\}$ – the matrix of the relationships between concepts $X_j^l(t)$ and $X_i^l(t)$, $l = 1, ..., L$, L – the number of the FCM models, $F(x)$ – sigmoid stability function.

Figure 1 presents the block diagram for the analyzed approach. The aim of this approach is to construct the collection of L fuzzy cognitive maps with the use of the m-IDEA algorithm. Aggregation of this collection is a union of the FCM models developed for each single dimension (subset) of data and combines their concepts and relationships.

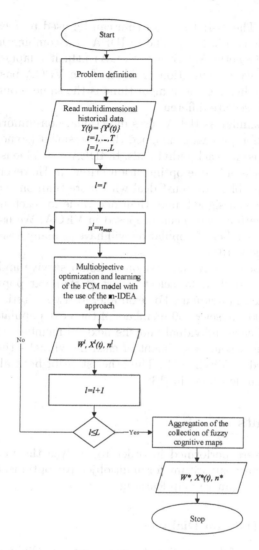

Fig. 1. Block diagram for the developed approach

3   Multiobjective Individually Directional Evolutionary Algorithm (m-IDEA) for Structure Optimization and Learning of FCMs

Individually Directional Evolutionary Algorithm (IDEA) [13] is an evolutionary algorithm. The major rule of IDEA is to monitor and direct the evolution of population to explore promising areas in the search space. Multiobjective Individually Directional Evolutionary Algorithm is an extension of IDEA. The IDEA allows to solve classical optimization problem (where exists only one optimization criteria). The m-IDEA algorithm can be used to solve multiobjective optimization problems ($K > 1$). The m-IDEA is a combination of IDEA and Vector Evaluated Genetic Algorithm (VEGA) [24], it adapts the methods for solving multiobjective optimization problems from VEGA based on the IDEA scheme. The base scheme of both algorithms is the same – only the evaluation and selection processes are different.

The m-IDEA (similar as IDEA) uses directional non-uniform mutation [13]. The aim of evaluation process is assigned the assessment (some value describing how good solution is) for each individuals. In IDEA one value is assigned to each individuals - we have only one optimization criterion. However, for multiobjective optimization problem we must deal with more than one criterion. The one way of deal with it is assigned more than one value for each individuals as the assessment. The method have been proposed in VEGA. We used these method in m-IDEA – each member of population will have as many assigned assessments as there optimization criteria.

In selection process, only the best ones should survive and create the next population [7]. In m-IDEA, we select k-part of the next population based on k-assessment of each individuals. For example, for two criteria and size of population equal to 100, we select 50 members of the next population based on the first assessment of each individual and the next 50 members of the next population based on the second assessment of each individual - these methods also have been proposed in VEGA [24]. The other steps of both algorithms are the same and have been described in [13].

4   Experiments

The simulations were performed in order to analyze the performance of the proposed evolutionary algorithm for multiobjective optimization of structure and learning fuzzy cognitive map learning.

4.1   Historical Data on Diabetes

The dataset consists of data of 70 diabetes patients [9]. Diabetes patient records were obtained from an automatic electronic recording device and paper records. The data contain the informations about diabetes patients, e.g.: date, insulin doses, blood glucose measurements during the day, meal ingestion, exercise activity. The total number of possible concepts is equal 26 ($n_{max} = 26$). We selected 3 concepts as the output of the system: pre-breakfast blood glucose measurement, pre-lunch blood glucose measurement and pre-supper blood glucose measurement ($K = 3$). The number of records for each patient varies and ranges between 8 and 219. Due to the very small number of measurements and incomplete informations in some patients, we selected data of 20 patients to the analysis of the developed approach ($L = 20$). The measurements for each patients were divided into 2 subsets: learning data (67%) and testing data (33%). Additionally we used the data of the 21-th patient to verify and compare the forecasting capabilities of the resulting FCM models. The data were normalized to the range $[0, 1]$ with the use of standard min-max normalization.

4.2   Results

The following learning parameters were used in presented simulations: the population size equal 75, the maximum number of generations equal 100, mutation probability: 0.05, $a_1 = 0.3$, $a_2 = 0.1$, $L = 20$, $K = 3$, $n_{max} = 26$. The parameters were chosen experimentally based on the minimization of the values of forecasting accuracy. The aim of simulations is forecasting of pre-breakfast blood glucose measurement, pre-lunch blood glucose measurement and pre-supper blood glucose measurement for the next 6 days based on current patient measurements. Learning error (LE) and testing error (TE) were calculated respectively for learning and testing data in accordance with criterion (6) for $\mu = 1$.

Various methods of structure optimization and learning of fuzzy cognitive maps were compared. For each experiment, three approaches were compared: standard optimization based on scalar criterion type (10) for $\lambda_1 = \lambda_2 = \lambda_3 = \frac{1}{3}$ (FCM), multiobjective optimization with the use of VEGA algorithm (VEGA) and optimization based on a bank of fuzzy cognitive maps (BANK). For each approach, three methods of structure optimization were used: random selection of concepts and relationships during learning process (RND), selection based on the total degree of the node (3) (DCS) and selection based on the total value of the node (4) (TV).

The analyzed approach is based on constructing of the collection of fuzzy cognitive maps based on data of 20 patients. For each patient, a separate FCM model (or the bank of three FCM models) was built with the use of the m-IDEA algorithm. The results were compared with the standard approach of constructing one FCM model (or one bank of three FCM models) with the use of data for all 20 patients (STD). Table 1 shows the average results of experiments: the number of concepts (NoC) and forecasting errors LE, TE. The highlighted values in bold show the smallest values of learning and testing errors.

Next, we propose to aggregate the obtained collection by proper averaging of fuzzy cognitive maps. Three various methods of aggregation were compared: combining all concepts and relationships (A1), combining only those concepts that appeared in the collection of models more than 5 times (A2), selecting the best FCM model (with the lower values of learning and testing errors) from the collection (A3). Table 2 shows the results of the comparison.

Based on the results, we can conclude that the collection of FCM models (especially a collection of banks of fuzzy cognitive maps) allows us to receive the smallest values of learning and testing errors for the analyzed 20 patients. The FCM models in collections also have fewer concepts, making it easier to determine which concepts most affect the level of blood glucose for a particular patient. The aggregate models obtained a similar level of forecasting accuracy as the models learned immediately on the basis of data of all 20 patients.

Additionally, we used data of the 21-th patient to verify the analyzed approaches. Table 3 presents the average results of testing the aggregate FCM

Table 1. Average results obtained for the collection of FCM models and for the standard approach

		Collection			STD		
		NoC	LE	TE	NoC	LE	TE
FCM	RND	8	0.0938	0.0945	9	0.1143	0.1067
	DCS	11	0.0938	0.0943	26	0.1141	0.1104
	TV	11	0.0940	0.0950	26	0.1160	0.1131
VEGA	RND	8	0.0974	0.0939	14	0.1152	0.1106
	DCS	11	0.0975	0.0952	26	0.1183	0.1130
	TV	11	0.0976	0.0944	26	0.1183	0.1130
BANK	RND	10	**0.0879**	**0.0913**	19	0.1108	0.1034
	DCS	11	**0.0891**	**0.0933**	26	0.1118	0.1060
	TV	11	**0.0893**	**0.0929**	26	0.1115	0.1078

Table 2. Average results obtained for the aggregate FCM models A1, A2, A3

		A1			A2			A3		
		NoC	LE	TE	NoC	LE	TE	NoC	LE	TE
FCM	RND	18	0.1138	0.1055	10	0.1129	0.1037	7	**0.1117**	**0.1030**
	DCS	18	0.1137	0.1052	17	0.1133	**0.1040**	7	**0.1125**	0.1049
	TV	18	0.1149	0.1063	17	0.1144	0.1049	8	**0.1117**	**0.1033**
VEGA	RND	18	0.1169	0.1079	8	0.1140	**0.1047**	7	**0.1134**	0.1056
	DCS	18	0.1155	0.1070	17	0.1151	0.1056	8	**0.1119**	**0.1042**
	TV	18	0.1154	0.1072	17	0.1146	0.1053	7	**0.1118**	**0.1032**
BANK	RND	18	0.1228	0.1143	14	0.1225	0.1120	9	**0.1140**	**0.1060**
	DCS	18	0.1228	0.1141	17	0.1209	0.1104	8	**0.1136**	**0.1055**
	TV	18	0.1224	0.1139	17	**0.1186**	**0.1083**	8	0.1188	0.1112

Table 3. Average results of testing based on the 21-th patient

		A1		A2		A3		STD	
		NoC	TE	NoC	TE	NoC	TE	NoC	TE
FCM	RND	18	0.1572	10	0.1485	7	**0.1467**	9	0.1557
	DCS	18	0.1548	17	0.1523	8	**0.1403**	26	0.1541
	TV	18	0.1586	17	0.1553	8	**0.1444**	26	0.1517
VEGA	RND	18	0.1647	8	0.1490	7	**0.1361**	14	0.1460
	DCS	18	0.1539	17	**0.1508**	8	0.1514	26	0.1573
	TV	18	0.1566	17	0.1527	7	0.1575	26	**0.1462**
BANK	RND	18	0.1785	15	0.1706	9	**0.1437**	19	0.1535
	DCS	18	0.1800	17	0.1747	8	0.1665	26	**0.1439**
	TV	18	0.1800	17	0.1725	8	0.1598	26	**0.1440**

models (A1, A2, A3) and the models obtained for the standard approach (STD). We received similar level of forecasting accuracy for all approaches. The lowest values of testing error were obtained for the approach A3 and STD.

5   Conclusions

This paper is devoted to the analysis of the application of evolutionary algorithms for structure optimization and learning of fuzzy cognitive maps based on complex multidimensional medical data. The simulations were carried out on the basis of data of diabetes patients.

The obtained results show that the collection of fuzzy cognitive maps, in which each element is constructed for data of each patient, allows us to receive the less forecasting errors. Moreover, by proper aggregation of such collections we can also receive satisfactory forecasting accuracy for the new patient.

We plan to analyze the application of the developed approach based on various multidimensional data. We also plan to analyze different ways of grouping data to achieve higher accuracy in predicting new cases/patients.

References

1. Chen, S.M.: Cognitive-map-based decision analysis based on NPN logics. Fuzzy Sets Syst. **71**(2), 153–163 (1995)
2. Chernorutsky, I.G.: Methods of optimization in control theory. Peter, St. Petersburg (2010) (in Russian)
3. Chi, Y., Liu, J.: Learning of fuzzy cognitive maps with varying densities using a multiobjective evolutionary algorithm. IEEE Trans. Fuzzy Syst. **24**(1), 71–81 (2016)
4. Christoforou, A., Andreou, A.S.: A framework for static and dynamic analysis of multi-layer fuzzy cognitive maps. Neurocomputing **232**, 133–145 (2017)
5. Dickerson, J.A., Kosko, B.: Fuzzy virtual worlds as fuzzy cognitive maps. Presence **3**, 173–189 (1994)
6. Falcon, R., Napoles, G., Bello, R., Vanhoof, K.: Granular cognitive maps: a review. Granul. Comput. **4**(3), 451–467 (2019)
7. Fogel, D.B.: Evolutionary Computation: Toward a New Philosophy of Machine Inteligence, 3rd edn. Wiley, Hoboken (2006)
8. Homenda, W., Jastrzebska, A., Pedrycz, W.: Nodes selection criteria for fuzzy cognitive maps designed to model time series. In: Filev, D., et al. (eds.) Intelligent Systems 2014. AISC, vol. 323, pp. 859–870. Springer, Cham (2015). https://doi.org/10.1007/978-3-319-11310-4_75
9. Kahn, M.: UCI Machine Learning Repository, Washington University, St. Louis, MO. http://archive.ics.uci.edu/ml. Accessed 3 Aug 2019
10. Kolahdoozi, M., Amirkhani, A., Shojaeefard, M.H., Abraham, A.: A novel quantum inspired algorithm for sparse fuzzy cognitive maps learning. Appl. Intell. **49**(10), 3652–3667 (2019)
11. Kosko, B.: Fuzzy cognitive maps. Int. J. Man-Mach. Stud. **24**(1), 65–75 (1986)
12. Kreinovich, V., Stylios, C.: Why fuzzy cognitive maps are efficient. Int. J. Comput. Commun. Control **10**(5), 825–833 (2015). Special issue on Fuzzy Sets and Applications

13. Kubuś, Ł.: Individually directional evolutionary algorithm for solving global optimization problems-comparative study. Int. J. Intell. Syst. Appl. (IJISA) **7**(9), 12–19 (2015)
14. Kubuś, Ł., Poczeta, K., Yastrebov, A.: A new learning approach for fuzzy cognitive maps based on system performance indicators. In: 2016 IEEE International Conference on Fuzzy Systems, Vancouver, Canada, pp. 1398–1404 (2016)
15. Mateou, N.H., Andreou, A.S.: Tree-structured multi-layer fuzzy cognitive maps for modelling large scale, complex problems. In: 2005 Proceedings of International Conference on Computational Intelligence for Modelling, Control and Automation and International Conference on Intelligent Agents, Web Technologies and Internet Commerce, pp. 133–141 (2005)
16. Papageorgiou, E.I., Poczeta, K.: A two-stage model for time series prediction based on fuzzy cognitive maps and neural networks. Neurocomputing **232**, 113–121 (2017)
17. Papakostas, G.A., Koulouriotis, D.E., Polydoros, A.S., Tourassis, V.D.: Towards Hebbian learning of fuzzy cognitive maps in pattern classification problems. Expert Syst. Appl. **39**, 10620–10629 (2012)
18. Peng, Z., Wu, L., Chen, Z.: NHL and RCGA based multi-relational fuzzy cognitive map modeling for complex systems. Appl. Sci. **5**(4), 1399–1411 (2015)
19. Poczeta, K., Kubus, L., Yastrebov, A.: Analysis of an evolutionary algorithm for complex fuzzy cognitive map learning based on graph theory metrics and output concepts. BioSystems **179**, 39–47 (2019)
20. Poczeta, K., Kubuś, Ł., Yastrebov, A.: An evolutionary algorithm based on graph theory metrics for fuzzy cognitive maps learning. In: Martín-Vide, C., Neruda, R., Vega-Rodríguez, M.A. (eds.) TPNC 2017. LNCS, vol. 10687, pp. 137–149. Springer, Cham (2017). https://doi.org/10.1007/978-3-319-71069-3_11
21. Rutkowski, L.: Methods and Techniques of Artificial Intelligence (in Polish). Wydawnictwo Naukowe PWN, Warsaw (2005)
22. Salmeron, J.L., Froelich, W.: Dynamic optimization of fuzzy cognitive maps for time series forecasting. Knowl.-Based Syst. **105**, 29–37 (2016)
23. Salmeron, J.L., Papageorgiou, E.I.: Fuzzy grey cognitive maps and nonlinear Hebbian learning in process control. Appl. Intell. **41**, 223–234 (2014)
24. Schaffer, J.: Multiple objective optimization with vector evaluated genetic algorithms. In: Proceedings of the First International Conference on Genetic Algoritihs, pp. 93–100 (1985)
25. Stach, W., Kurgan, L., Pedrycz, W., Reformat, M.: Genetic learning of fuzzy cognitive maps. Fuzzy Sets Syst. **153**(3), 371–401 (2005)
26. Stach, W., Pedrycz, W., Kurgan, L.A.: Learning of fuzzy cognitive maps using density estimate. IEEE Trans. Syst. Man Cybern. Part B **42**(3), 900–912 (2012)
27. Słoń, G.: Application of models of relational fuzzy cognitive maps for prediction of work of complex systems. In: Rutkowski, L., Korytkowski, M., Scherer, R., Tadeusiewicz, R., Zadeh, L.A., Zurada, J.M. (eds.) ICAISC 2014. LNCS (LNAI), vol. 8467, pp. 307–318. Springer, Cham (2014). https://doi.org/10.1007/978-3-319-07173-2_27
28. Wu, K., Liu, J.: Learning large-scale fuzzy cognitive maps based on compressed sensing and application in reconstructing gene regulatory networks. IEEE Trans. Fuzzy Syst. **25**(6), 1546–1560 (2017)
29. Yastrebov, A., Gad, S., SŁoń, S.: Bank of artificial neural networks MLP type in symptom systems of technical diagnostics. Pol. J. Environ. Stud. **17**(2A), 118–123 (2008)

Genetic Algorithms, Swarm Intelligence, and Heuristics

Genetic Algorithm for Optimization of the Replacement Schedules for Major Surface Combatants

Michele Fee[1]([⊠])(iD), Bart van Oers[2], Richard Logtmeijer[2], Jean-Denis Caron[1], and Van Fong[1]

[1] Maritime Operation Research Team, Defence Research and Development Canada, Ottawa, Canada
michele.fee@drdc-rddc.gc.ca
[2] Bureau of Life Cycle Analysis, Defence Material Organization, Utrecht, Netherlands

Abstract. The replacement of aging naval fleets is a multi-faceted problem with many important factors and scheduling constraints, where the development of a sound transition plan relies on leveraging flexibilities. A successful fleet schedule should aim to balance operational requirements, fleet maintenance facility workloads and the availability of ready personnel (operators and maintainers) while conforming to shipbuilding schedules and service life limitations. To evaluate different transition strategies, optimized fleet schedules are generated using a Genetic algorithm with limited-range integer codons. This approach is illustrated with the analysis of five transition scenarios for the replacement of a nine ship frigate class.

Keywords: Optimization · Planning and scheduling · Genetic algorithm · Fleet replacement · Navy

1 Introduction

Many navies around the world are in the process of replacing aging warships. While many models exist to coordinate equipment replacement [4–7,9,13,14], the military setting provides a particular challenge.

Coordinating fleet replacement can be dictated by a variety of factors, not all economic. For example, vehicles may be replaced at the end of their service life, when emissions fail to meet regulated limits, when there is drive to modernize in response to changes in the use case or, of course, when the cost of maintenance becomes prohibitive relative to the profit. Despite this, most models hinge on the ability to accurately evaluate the economic impact of various factors in order to minimize the costs incurred during the transition period [8]. In a military setting, the economic value of a naval fleet is difficult to fully quantify.

During a meeting of the Standing Committee on National Defence, the Commander of the Royal Canadian Navy (RCN) provided clues into evaluating the

© Crown 2019
C. Martín-Vide et al. (Eds.): TPNC 2019, LNCS 11934, pp. 161–172, 2019.
https://doi.org/10.1007/978-3-030-34500-6_11

economic value of a navy. In his address, he mentioned that: "[...] rather than measuring our profits in dollars and cents, we're trying to measure our profits in materiel, technical, personnel, and combat readiness." [1]. In view of this, this paper aims to model the replacement of naval assets with a focus on the impacts of these strategies on naval readiness.

Currently, the RCN is building its future fleet by replacing 12 Halifax-class frigates with 15 surface combatants, and by procuring new Arctic Offshore Patrol Vessels and Joint Support Ships [2]. In these instances, the transition timelines would be informed by shipbuilding schedules, Operation and Maintenance Cycles (OPCYCLEs), Fleet Maintenance Facility (FMF) capacity, crew availability and training requirements, as well as fleet deployment objectives. The interplay of these factors makes this multi-objective optimization problem well suited for use of a genetic algorithm [10]. The idea to investigate such a model was discussed by the authors during a bilateral meeting [12].

This paper describes a model developed to determine optimal fleet replacement schedules. It consists of a genetic algorithm for which integer chromosomes are range-limited by user-defined codons to explore a range of possible strategies. Example applications are presented to illustrate use of the model for a transition from a notional class of 9 frigates to 14 new ships.

2   Important Factors

Four main factors were identified as important considerations when developing a transition strategy. They are discussed in this section.

Crew – Significant fluctuations in the number of ships in a fleet become problematic for navies following a "1-Crew/1-Ship" model (i.e. when the ship is manned and operated by a single crew whether it is in its home port or at sea conducting an operation). While the crew sizes are expected to decrease due to increased automation in the newer ship design, many of the roles aboard require a certain number of training days at sea. A decrease in the number of available ships on which to train impairs the navy's ability to generate the crew needed to man a larger fleet. In this analysis, the total number of ships in service is tracked as a proxy for this crewing consideration.

Fleet Maintenance Facility – FMFs are responsible for carrying out regular maintenance on ships. An optimized schedule should aim to balance the load of these facilities by avoiding periods of no work and high volumes of work as well sudden jumps in workload.

Ship Age – While it is common to expect a service life on the scale of 25–30 years the actual number depends on the maintenance and operation of the ship through its lifespan. In a study of peace-time attrition rates of warships in Five-Eyes nations (Australia, Canada, New Zealand, the United Kingdom and the United States), the average age of frigates was calculated to be 21.5 years [11]. Of the ~1,200 ships considered in this study, only 2% remained in operation for greater than 40 years. As a result, some life extension or early decommissioning in this range are considered feasible in some of the scenarios presented.

High Readiness States – Each ship is operated for a certain number of months per cycle at a higher state of readiness which is required for deployments. Operational objectives often require a given number of ships in a fleet to be at high readiness (HR) at any given time.

3   Model Description

3.1   Problem

In a nutshell, the optimization problem consists of developing an optimal fleet schedule by determining the decommissioning dates of a first class of ships and the commissioning dates of a second class of ships while considering the four factors discussed in Sect. 2.

The operation of a ship through its life-cycle is governed by an OPCYCLE. An example of an OPCYCLE is shown at the top of Fig. 1. It consists of periods where the ship is in maintenance (in red) or in operations, i.e. Normal Readiness (in green) or HR (in blue). Typically, the OPCYCLE is repeated until the ship is decommissioned. The resulting schedules are semi-flexible in that periods of HR may be placed anywhere between maintenance periods to meet operational requirements.

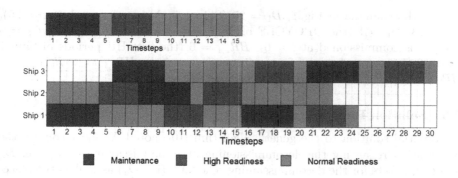

Fig. 1. Simple example to illustrate a solution vector (Color figure online)

This multi-objective optimization problem is non-linear and is well suited for a genetic algorithm, which is versatile and quick at exploring a non-linear solution space. The remainder of this section describes the genetic algorithm.

3.2   Notations

Consider the following notations.

Indices and Sets

- $s \in \mathcal{S}$: the set of S ships.
- $a \in \mathcal{A}$: the set of A ships to decommission, where $\mathcal{A} \subset \mathcal{S}$.
- $b \in \mathcal{B}$: the set of B ships to commission, where $\mathcal{B} \subset \mathcal{S}$.
- $h \in \mathcal{H}$: the set of H inter-maintenance periods considered.
- $t \in \mathcal{T}$: the set of T timestep considered.

In Fig. 1, $S = 3$, $\mathcal{S} = \{1, 2, 3\}$, $A = 2$ (for Ships 1 and 2), $\mathcal{A} = \{1, 2\}$, $B = 1$ (for Ship 3), $\mathcal{B} = \{1\}$, $H = 2$ (one period of HR in-between maintenance periods), $\mathcal{H} = \{1, 2\}$, $T = 30$ and finally, $\mathcal{T} = \{1, 2, \ldots, 30\}$.

Parameters

- $S_{\min}$ and $S_{\max}$: desired minimum and maximum number of ships in the fleet.
- $HR_{\min}$: desired minimum acceptable number of ships in fleet at HR.
- $M_{\min}$ and $M_{\max}$: desired minimum and maximum number of ships in the FMF.
- w_1, w_2, w_3, w_4, w_5 and w_6 : weights for the fitness function components (details later).

Variables

- D_a: decommissioning date of ship a, i.e. time increments since $t = 0$.
- C_b: commissioning date of ship b, i.e. time increments since $t = 0$.
- O_a: offset in the schedule of ship a representing where the OPCYCLE begins.
- $HR_{s,h}$: time between end of last maintenance to beginning of HR period for each ship s and each inter-maintenance period h.

For the example in Fig. 1, $D_1 = 25$ (Ship 1 is decommissioned at $t = 25$), $D_2 = 23$, $O_1 = 1$ (the OPCYCLE of Ship 1 start at $t = 1$), $O_2 = 8$, $C_1 = 6$ (Ship 3 is commissioned at $t = 6$), $HR_{1,1} = 6$ (the first HR periods of Ship 1 starts 6 timesteps after the first maintenance period), $HR_{1,2} = 2$, $HR_{2,1} = 9$, $HR_{2,2} = 2$, $HR_{3,1} = 8$ and $HR_{3,2} = 3$.

3.3   Solution Representation

A potential solution to the genetic algorithm [10], noted X, must contain the information regarding the decommissioning and commissioning dates (i.e. D_a and C_b), offsets for the decommissioning schedules (i.e. O_a) as well as the placement of each HR period within each the inter-maintenance periods (i.e. $HR_{s,h}$). The solution vector X is therefore a simple concatenation of all the variables required to build a schedule. In general terms, it can be expressed mathematically as follows:

$$X = (HR_{1,1}, HR_{1,2}, ..., HR_{S,H}, D_1, D_2, ...D_A, O_1, O_2...O_A, C_1, C_2, ...C_B)$$

As an example, the solution vector X corresponding to the schedule in Fig. 1 is:

$$X = (HR_{1,1}, HR_{1,2}, HR_{2,1}, HR_{2,2}, HR_{3,1}, HR_{3,2}, D_1, D_2, O_1, O_2, C_1)$$
$$= (6, 2, 9, 2, 8, 3, 25, 23, 1, 8, 6)$$

To ensure that the solution is feasible, the values in X are bounded. For example, given the OPCYCLE in the Fig. 1, we know that the $HR_{s,h}$ values have to be within 1 and 9, otherwise the periods when the ships are in operations would not fall in between two maintenance periods. Further tightening the bounds allows for the application of scheduling constraints such as those shown the example application.

3.4   Fitness Function

Genetic algorithms use the framework of evolution to search a solution space for an optimum. It requires a fitness function, which assigns a fitness value to each individual solution. Such fitness value measures the quality of a solution, reflecting how good the solution is. The evaluation is carried out on schedules generated from vector X.

In this problem, the fitness function F of a solution vector X, noted $F(X)$ must measure the quality of a solution with respect to the factors described in Sect. 2, i.e. Crew, FMF, Ship Age and High Readiness States. The factors are seen as *soft* constraints, meaning that they do not have to be all satisfied but they are *desirable*. A series of penalty functions are used, described in the following paragraphs, to handle the constraints where penalties are applied when constraints describing the desired conditions are breached.

High Readiness States: To be operationally relevant, it is important for a navy to have a sufficient number of ships at HR at all times. Let HR_t be the number of ships at HR at timestep t. For instance, in Fig. 1, $HR_1 = 0$ and $HR_5 = 1$. At a given timestep t, having enough ships at HR is defined as $HR_t \geq HR_{min}$. Therefore, we created the following penalty function:

$$HR_{Count} = \sum_{t \in T} \begin{cases} HR_{min} - HR_t & \text{if } HR_t < HR_{min} \\ 0 & \text{otherwise} \end{cases} \tag{1}$$

which computes the number of timesteps where the total number of ships at HR is below HR_{min}.

It is also important to maintain a constant number of ships at HR. This is measured by summing local standard deviations of HR_t. Assuming that we use a rolling window of θ timesteps, this penalty function of the variability of HR is calculated as follows:

$$HR_{Var} = \sum_{t=1}^{T-\theta} \sigma(HR_t, HR_{t+1}, ..., HR_{t+\theta}) \tag{2}$$

Fleet Maintenance Facility: In order to minimize periods of no work and of high volumes at the FMFs, we calculate the number of ships in the maintenance at time t, noted M_t (e.g. in Fig. 1, $M_9 = 2$), and the following penalty function:

$$M_{Count} = \sum_{t \in T} \begin{cases} M_{min} - M_t & \text{if } M_t < M_{min} \\ M_t - M_{max} & \text{if } M_t > M_{max} \\ 0 & \text{otherwise} \end{cases} \tag{3}$$

The value of M_{Count} contains the count of how often the number of ships at the FMFs is outside the desirable range of $[M_{min}, M_{max}]$. Then, in order to have a balanced workload at the FMFs, we also use a rolling window of θ timesteps, to calculate a penalty function, noted M_{Var}, on the variability of the M_t. This is done using Eq. (4).

$$M_{Var} = \sum_{t=1}^{T-\theta} \sigma(M_t, M_{t+1}, \dots, M_{t+\theta}) \tag{4}$$

Crew: As with the previous two factors, we are interested in schedules having a number of ships ranging between S_{min} and S_{max}. To achieve this, the total number of active ships, S_t, is calculated for each t, and a penalty applied that scales with the degree of deviation outside the desireable range, as shown in Eq. (5).

$$S_{sum} = \sum_{t \in \mathcal{T}} \begin{cases} S_{min} - S_t & \text{if } S_t < S_{min} \\ S_t - S_{max} & \text{if } S_t > S_{max} \\ 0 & \text{otherwise} \end{cases} \tag{5}$$

Ship Age: To avoid decommissioning a ship before the end of its expected service life or the need to extend it far beyond this timeframe, a penalty is applied for each month added or removed from the decommissioned ships service life. Within the set $\mathcal{A}$, the increment corresponding to the end of the expected service life for each ship is determined and expressed as SL_a^{exp}. The penalty applied equals to the absolute value of the difference between the expected ship life and actual decommissioning dates as per Eq. (6)

$$\Delta SL_a = \sum_{a \in \mathcal{A}} |D_a - SL_a^{exp}| \tag{6}$$

Finally, we combine the penalty functions in Eqs. (1), (2), (3), (4), (5) and (6) in the following fitness function:

$$F(X) = w_1 S_{sum} + w_2 HR_{Count} + w_3 M_{Count} + w_4 HR_{Var} + w_5 M_{Var} + w_6 \Delta SL_a \tag{7}$$

The weights, $w_1, w_2 ..., w_6$ can be adjusted according to the importance placed on achieving a schedule that meets each of these criteria.

3.5   Implementation

The off-the-shelf genetic algorithm presented above was implemented in R using a function called `GeneticAlg.int` of the `gramEvol.R` package [3]. This function uses limited-range integer as codons allowing for the implementation of scheduling constraints for the commissioning, decommissioning and placement of the HR periods.

4   Example Application

The Aldergrove class is a notional fleet of nine frigates commissioned between 2001 and 2005 by two shipbuilding companies, as shown in Table 1. Upon construction, the in-service life of these ships was estimated at 30 years and so it is reasonable to expect decommissioning to begin in 2031. Due to changes in the shipbuilding policy since the commissioning of the Aldergrove class, only one shipbuilding company will be available to build the new ships. As a result, the ships will be built sequentially with the commissioning date offsets described by ΔC_b below, with the commissioning dates following Eq. (8).

$$\Delta C_b = (24, 24, 20, 20, 16, 16, 12, 12, 12, 12, 12, 12, 12)$$

$$C_b = C_{b-1} + \Delta C_{b-1} \text{ for } 2 \leq b \leq 14 \tag{8}$$

Table 1. Commissioning dates for Aldergrove-class

Ship name	Commissioning date	Shipbuilder	Expected end of service life
Aldergrove	01/01/2001	Northumberland Limited	01/01/2031
Belleville	01/10/2001	Broughton Shipbuilding	01/10/2031
Coquitlam	01/07/2002	Northumberland Limited	01/07/2032
Dorval	05/01/2003	Broughton Shipbuilding	05/01/2033
Elkwater	21/06/2003	Northumberland Limited	21/06/2033
Flin Flon	08/02/2004	Broughton Shipbuilding	08/02/2034
Grandby	31/01/2005	Northumberland Limited	31/01/2035
Hastings	20/06/2005	Broughton Shipbuilding	20/06/2035
Iberville	07/12/2005	Northumberland Limited	07/12/2035

The OPCYCLEs for each class are shown in Fig. 2. The Aldergrove class OPCYCLE has fewer months of availability to reflect the additional maintenance required for a warship reaching the end of its service life.

The five transition scenarios in Table 2 are considered. Each scenario shows the impact of imposing a different set of scheduling constraints to the transition. Cases 1 and 2 bound the problem, representing, respectively, late and early start to commissioning. In each of these, the A cases reflects the outcome if the Aldergrove class was decommissioned after exactly 30 years in service, and the B, that if decommissioning dates are made flexible.

Case 3 explores the middle ground of the first two cases, where the start of commissioning and the decommissioning dates are allowed to vary.

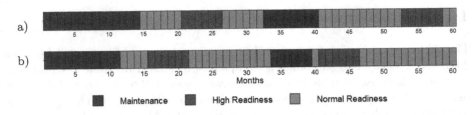

Fig. 2. OPCYCLE for (a) Aldergrove Class and (b) new class. The placement of the six month HR periods are flexible between maintenance periods

Table 2. Transition scenarios

Case	Description	Scheduling constraints	
		Decommissioning dates	Commisioning date [a]
1A	Late commissioning	$D_a = SL_a^{exp}$	$C_1 = SL_1^{exp}$
1B	Late commissioning	–	$C_1 = SL_1^{exp}$
2A	Early commissioning	$D_a = SL_a^{exp}$	$C_{14} = SL_9^{exp}$
2B	Early commissioning	–	$C_{14} = SL_9^{exp}$
3	Optimized commissioning	–	–

[a] Constraint from Eq. (8) also applies to all cases

5 Results

This section presents the results of the genetic algorithm when used to generate optimized solutions for the transition scenario described above. Note that for all the cases described, the algorithm was run using the following parameters: 10 000 iterations, population size of 100, a mutation rate of 0.015, elitism at 10% and single-point cross-over with random points selected. The weights used in the fitness factor are $w_1 = 10$, w_2 to $w_6 = 1$. These were selected since shortages and excess in crew and ships, changes to w_1, were deemed to be of greater importance than the other factors and could result in a reduced ability to meet the other requirements.

The optimized fleet schedules are summarized in the "Castle" plots (so called because their shape is reminescent of crenelations) shown in Figs. 3, 4, 5, 6, and 7. These plots are a quick way of visually identifying M_t, HR_t and S_t. These figures also include graphs which indicate commissioning dates, decommisioning dates and expected end of service life dates as well as distributions for S_t and HR_t.

5.1 Transition

Cases 1 A and 2A. Figures 3 and 4 shows two worst case scenarios for this transition. Should the decommissioning dates of the Aldergrove class be inflex-

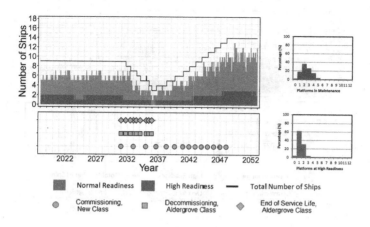

Fig. 3. Results of Case 1A

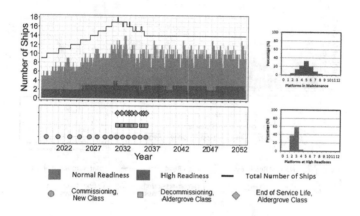

Fig. 4. Results of Case 2A

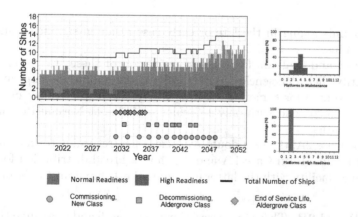

Fig. 5. Results of Case 1B

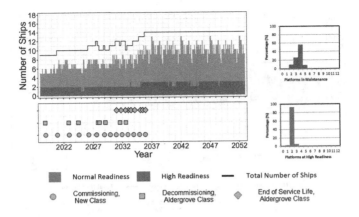

Fig. 6. Results of Case 2B

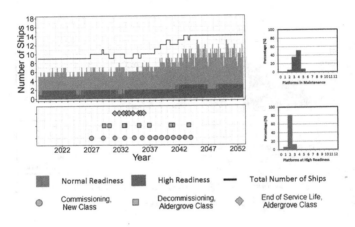

Fig. 7. Results of Case 3

ible, decommissioning in the late or early case result in significant shortage or excess of ships.

Figures 3 and 4 allows for a quick evaluation of these transition strategies and quantify their deficiencies. With Case 1A, the number of ships available at HR drops to zero for 8 months. During this phase of the transition, the navy would have to contend with only 1–2 ships available at Normal Readiness for a block 14 months.

For the Case 2A, the fleet doubles in size before returning to the final steady-state of 14 ships. Both Case 1 A and 2A show a broad distribution for the fleet maintenance facility with the latter exceeding the 4 ship limit 61.8% of the time.

Cases 1B and 2B. These two cases, shown in Figs. 5 and 6, assume the decommissioning date is flexible. Both results in consistent HR availability and fleet

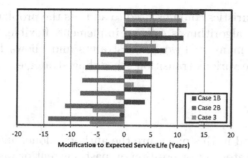

Fig. 8. Necessary modification to service life of the Aldergrove class

maintenance facility load. While the loads still exceed the 4 ship limit, the distributions are less broad and so availability of operational ships is expected to be less variable. These two cases are possible through aggressive life extension (up to +10.7 years) or very early decommissioning (as low as -14.2 years), as shown in Fig. 8. The average age of ship upon decommissioning is 23.9 (1B) and 37.0 (2B) years.

Case 3. Case 3 aims to mitigate the need to greatly change the service life of the ships by finding a middle ground solution. Commissioning of ships begins in 2027, four years before the end of the Aldergrove class expected lifespan. With this schedule, the average ship age upon decommissioning is decreased to 32.2 years. The balancing of the FMF load is nearly achieved, exceeding the 4 ships for 8.3% of the time.

6   Conclusions

This paper described a genetic algorithm used to optimize naval ship fleet schedules according to important factors which have an impact on the ability to generate crew, maintain predictable ship availability, balance FMF load and consistently providing enough ships at high readiness.

To illustrate the model, examples were presented which followed the evaluation of possible transition scheduling strategies in the replacement of a notional nine frigate class. Five scenarios were used to illustrate the impact of scheduling constraints, both to commissioning and decommissioning dates. Using an off-the-shelf genetic algorithm to optimize the fleet schedules provides a best-case scenario for each case that can be used as a basis for comparison. This type of analysis can lead to powerful and convincing evidence to guide decision makers in their best course of action (under the given assumptions).

The analysis showed that, given the flexibility to set the start of commissioning and the decommissioning dates of the incumbent fleet, the genetic algorithm was able to identify a fleet schedule which minimizes changes to the service life of the ships while preserving the characteristics that make for a smooth transition.

While other heuristics could be used to address the problem presented in this paper, the genetic algorithm is easy to implement, flexible, able to accurately take into account many real-world constraints and allows for straightforward metrics to compare various transition scheduling strategies.

7   Disclaimer

The views presented in this paper are the authors' alone, and do not constitute an official policy statement or position on past, current or planned procurement projects at the Netherlands Ministry of Defence or the Canadian Department of National Defence.

References

1. NDDN Committee Meeting 24 Evidence, VAdm Llyod, 27 October 2016. Accessed 29 July 2019
2. Strong, Secure, Engaged: Canada's Defence Policy, Canadian Armed Forces, Government of Canada (2017)
3. Package 'gramEvol'. https://cran.r-project.org/web/packages/gramEvol/gramEvol.pdf. Accessed 26 June 2019
4. Drinkwater, R.W., Hastings, N.A.J.: An economic replacement model. J. Oper. Res. Soc. **18**, 121–138 (1967)
5. Eilon, S., King, J.R., Hutchinson, D.E.: A study in equipment replacement. J. Oper. Res. Soc. **17**, 59–71 (1966)
6. Hartman, J.: A general procedure for incorporating asset utilization decisions into replacement analysis. Eng. Econ. **44**, 217–238 (1999)
7. Hartman, J.C.: Multiple asset replacement analysis under variable utilization and stochastic demand. Eur. J. Oper. Res. **159**, 145–165 (2004)
8. Hartman, J.C., Tan, C.H.: Equipment replacement analysis: a literature review and directions for future research. Eng. Econ. **59**, 136–153 (2014)
9. Hastings, N.A.J.: The repair limit replacement method. J. Oper. Res. Soc. **20**, 337–349 (1969)
10. Holland, J.: Adaptation in Natural and Artificial Systems. MIT Press, Cambridge (1975)
11. Mason, D.: Peace-time attrition expectations for naval fleets. Defence Research and Development Canada (2018)
12. van Oers, B.: An attempt at a model to assess impact of planned maintenance on warship availability. Briefing given during NLD-CAN video conference on fleet-level availability and effectiveness, June 2017
13. Simms, B.W., Lamarre, B.G., Jardine, A.K.S., Boudreau, A.: Optimal buy, operate and sell policies for fleets of vehicles. Eur. J. Oper. Res. **15**, 183–195 (1984)
14. Weissmann, J., Jannini Weissmann, A., Gona, S.: Computerized equipment replacement methodology. J. Transp. Res. Board **1824**, 77–83 (2003)

Adaptive Task Allocation for Planar Construction Using Response Threshold Model

Dalia S. Ibrahim[1]([⊠]) [iD] and Andrew Vardy[2]([⊠]) [iD]

[1] Department of Computer Science, Memorial University of Newfoundland,
St. John's, Canada
dsibrahim@mun.ca
[2] Department of Computer Science,
Department of Electrical and Computer Engineering,
Memorial University of Newfoundland, St. John's, Canada
av@mun.ca
http://www.cs.mun.ca/av/

Abstract. In this paper, a swarm of simulated robots is used to construct an annulus (ring shape) in a distributed behavior approach. We assume robots can do simple arithmetic operations, and sense the projected scalar field, which guides a swarm of robots in their construction task. We are using fixed thresholds in this scalar field to specify the contour of the desired annulus. This work is inspired by insects like termites. Although they have poor vision, they can guide each other and communicate using chemical scents called pheromones, so they are well organized and adapt to environmental changes. To construct the annulus, we need to allocate resources and distribute tasks among the robots. We present three methods to show how co-ordination is done in the swarm. Robots switch between tasks autonomously based on a calculated response function. Simulation experiments are performed to show the differences among these methods. These results show that using local communication among robots outperforms global and no-direct communication in terms of time steps which are required to construct the annulus.

Keywords: Swarm robotics · Response threshold · Planar construction

1 Introduction

Developing self-organized swarm robots as simple agents that can adapt themselves to an unfamiliar environment without any central controller like social insects (ants, bees, and termites) is a complex task [2]. Using swarms in collective construction tasks have exciting and essential applications. They may be used to build a wall around a chemical or radiation leak [3]. Also, they can be used in many automated applications, like sorting recycling or floor cleaning.

© Springer Nature Switzerland AG 2019
C. Martín-Vide et al. (Eds.): TPNC 2019, LNCS 11934, pp. 173–183, 2019.
https://doi.org/10.1007/978-3-030-34500-6_12

Researchers are inspired from the social insects becasue they have limited knowledge and perception of the environment, they communicate between individuals of the same species by producing active chemical substances called pheromones. The author in [5] uses the pheromone idea in swarm robots to construct enclosed shapes like circles, oblongs, and crosses. They used the pheromone as a static template of the desired shape and implemented it by projecting a scalar field with a combination of fixed thresholds to guide the robots to the desired shape's contour. The formation of two-dimensional shapes is called **planar construction**. The author introduces an algorithm called orbital construction (**OC**) in which the swarm of simple robots orbit in a clockwise direction and push pucks inwards and outwards to form a specific shape. Robots consist of two different types: **innies** and **outies**. Firstly, innies work inside the desired shape and pushing pucks outwards. Secondly, outies work outside the shape and pushing the pucks inwards.

These robots have three basic behavior characteristics [5]: Firstly, periphery seeking, in which robots move to the outside of the region occupied by pucks. Secondly, they push these pucks by nudging them inwards. Thirdly, the robots orbit around the environment in a clockwise direction, so their paths are called orbitals. These **orbitals** are defined by the intensity of the projected scalar field.

Figure 1 shows our implementation of **OC** algorithm to form an annulus with a projected scalar field. This algorithm has promising results. Most of the pucks are pushed and placed in the annulus, but there were still some pucks detached from the constructed shape, especially when these pucks were near to environment borders.

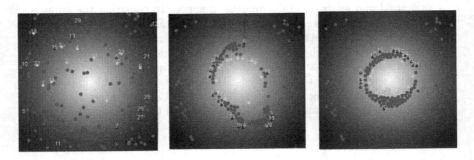

Fig. 1. Sequence of snapshots show our implementation of the OC algorithm at 0, 1000, and 5000 time steps. The simulation is done with 30 robots consisting of 13 innies (yellow) and 17 outies (blue) with 100 red pucks. (Color figure online)

In this work, we introduce the role of **explorers**. The task of an explorer is to scan the environment and push pucks towards the annulus. Outies still take care of the annulus' boundary, and innies work inside the shape to keep it empty by pushing the pucks outwards to the annulus' contour. The main challenges here are knowing which orbital has pucks and the regulation of the division of labor between exploring robots.

This paper is organized as follows: Sect. 2 describes the working environment and how the exponential response threshold is used in a planar construction task. The swarm starts their work in a distributed fashion where there is no centralized controller to guide them, but they have different ways of communicating with each other. These ways are described in Sect. 3. Section 4 presents the simulation and results. Finally, in Sect. 5, the conclusions and future work will be discussed.

2   Using Response Threshold in Orbital Construction

In this paper, we use the exponential response threshold function to help the explorers know if their orbital is empty or occupied. The author in [4], proposed a model based on a response threshold to divide labor in insect societies. Their definition of response threshold is a model of how the insects react to task-associated stimuli. Every worker has its response threshold for every task. This worker will be engaged to perform the task if the task stimuli, s, exceeds its response threshold, θ. Therefore, they are calculating the response function $T_\theta(s)$, which determines if they can do this task or not [1]. After they have engaged in this task, they will have a low task stimulus, so they will switch to another task.

In our work, the response threshold is θ, which is the time taken by a robot to circumnavigate the orbital. This is a function of orbital circumference, C_i, where the subscript i indicates on the orbital number. ω is the robot's constant angular velocity, as shown in Eq. 1.

$$\theta_i = \frac{C_i}{\omega} \tag{1}$$

ΔT is the difference in time between two consecutive actual pushes in the same orbital, as shown in Fig. 2.

Algorithm 1 shows how the $Avg\Delta T$ is calculated. In general, if $Avg\Delta T$ is very small compared with θ, this orbital is occupied with pucks, and the robot should stay on this orbital and keep pushing the pucks to the next orbital. In contrast, if $Avg\Delta T$ is high and equals θ, that means this orbital is empty. To summarize the relationship between the task stimulus and response threshold, we use Eq. 2 and multiply the exponent by -40 to ensure the $F_\theta(Avg\Delta T) \in [0, 1]$

$$F_\theta(Avg\Delta T) = e^{\frac{-40 \cdot Avg\Delta T}{\theta}} \tag{2}$$

3   Proposed Methods

In this section, we present the common configuration for the three proposed methods, and after that, the differences among them are discussed.

The robots N are randomly assigned to one of three categories: innies N_i, outies N_o, and explorers N_e.

$$N = N_i + N_o + N_e \tag{3}$$

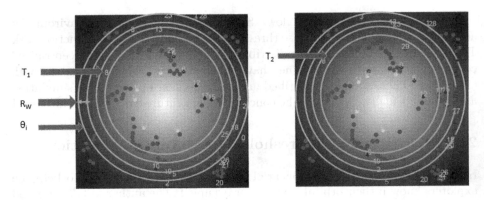

Fig. 2. The left image shows the initial environment configurations; the orbital width R_w, θ_i is the elapsed time to circumnavigate the orbital i, and T_1 is the time in which robot number 8 pushes the red puck. On the right, this image shows next time step in which robot number 8 pushes another puck in the same orbital of T_2. So, the ΔT will be the difference between these two values. Also, this figure shows the three types of robots innies (yellow), outies (blue) and explorers (green). (Color figure online)

Algorithm 1. Measure average time for two consecutive pushes

1: **function** MEASURECONSECUTIVEPUSHES($Last\Delta T, \theta, PrevTime$)
2:     $CurrTime = System.getTime()$
3:     **if** $CurrTime - PrevTime >= \theta$ **then**   ▷ Empty Orbital
4:         $Avg\Delta T = \theta$
5:     **else if** $Robot.Push$ **then**   ▷ Robot pushes a puck now
6:         $Avg\Delta T = \frac{Last\Delta T + (CurrTime - PrevTime)}{2}$
7:     **end if**
8:     $PrevTime = CurrTime$
9:     **return** $Avg\Delta T, PrevTime$
10: **end function**

The robots have sets of sensors. An obstacle sensor (obs_l), which indicate the presence of a wall or another robot in the robot's left region. Three floor sensors ($floor_l$, $floor_c$ and $floor_r$) can measure the light intensity of the projected scalar field. Robots are also equipped with two puck sensors located on the robot's left and right regions ($Pucks_l$ and $Pucks_r$). In addition, there is a lamp that can be switched on or off to indicate if this robot needs help or not and a light sensor ($Light_l$) that detects the existence of lights for the other closest robots on its left. The innies' and outies' movement follows **OC** algorithm in [5] which takes these sensor readings as inputs and produces angular speed. The explorers' movement follows Algorithm 2.

Explorers start their work by choosing a random orbital, because if they start from the environment boundary, after some time, it will be difficult for the robot to push multiple pucks at the same time. During their work, the explorers communicate with each other as described in the following subsections. Finally,

---

Algorithm 2. Orbital Construction for Explorers

1: **function** EXPLORERORBITALCONSTRUCTION($obs_l, floor_l, floor_c, floor_r, pucks_l, pucks_r$)
2:    **if** obs_l **then**
3:        **return** ω_{max} ▷ Robots avoid obstacle by veering to the right
4:    **end if**
5:    **if** $floor_r >= floor_c \wedge floor_c >= floor_l$ **then**   ▷ Robots alignment for clockwise movements
6:        **if** $Explorer \wedge pucks_l$ **then**
7:            **return** $-\omega_{max}$ ▷ Explorers steer outwards to collect remaining pucks
8:        **end if**
9:        **if** $floor_c < \tau$ **then**   ▷ Steering inwards
10:            **return** $0.3\omega_{max}$
11:        **else**   ▷ Steering outwards
12:            **return** $-0.3\omega_{max}$
13:        **end if**
14:    **else if** $floor_c >= floor_r \wedge floor_c >= floor_l$ **then**   ▷ Robots is aligned uphill
15:        **return** $-\omega_{max}$ ▷ Turn left
16:    **else**   ▷ Robots is aligned downhill
17:        **return** ω_{max} ▷ Turn Right
18:    **end if**
19: **end function**

---

when they have entirely scanned all of the environment, the explorers will start to scan the environment again from the beginning in order to not miss any detached pucks and keep searching for any new pucks added to the environment.

Innies will be trapped after some time; that is why their group is very small compared with the other two groups, and their rule is to keep the area inside the desired shape empty. The outies operate outside the shape and keep maintaining the shape's boundary. In case any explorers push pucks towards an annulus, the outies will catch them and push the pucks towards the boundary.

In the following subsections, we present three alternatives for the communication of explorers.

3.1   No-Direct Communication

In this approach, the exploring robots calculate their response function based on Eq. 2. They do not directly communicate. Once the explorer senses its orbital is empty, it switches to the next orbital towards the annulus. When the explorer reaches the annulus' boundary, it goes back to the environment boundary and starts scanning again.

The benefit of this approach is that there is no requirement for direct communication among the swarm.

3.2   Local Communication

In a case where the orbital is fully occupied with pucks, the explorer multicasts this orbital's status to its neighbors by setting its light on to attract other robots to come and help it in this orbital. If any of the others finish working on their orbital, they look for any light on their left side using their left light sensor, see Fig. 3. If they find the light on, they go towards this orbital by decreasing their τ and turn on their lights. After they push these pucks from this orbital, they will switch off the light and go to the next orbital, and so on. The pseudocode is presented as Algorithm 2.

   The advantage of this approach is that the robot searches for help from the very closest neighbors, and they will come directly and help it.

Algorithm 3. Local Communication

1: OrbitalNum = RandomInteger(1 to 6)   ▷ Select random Orbital number
2: $PrevTime = System.getTime()$
3: **while** $OrbitalNum < 7$ **do**
4:     $\tau = 0.1$ OrbitalNum   ▷ Convert to the corresponding scalar field
5:     $ExplorerOrbitalConstruction(obs_l, floor_l, floor_c, floor_r, pucks_l, pucks_r)$
6:     $Radius = \frac{H}{2} - (R_w(\tau_i R_n - 1))$ ▷ H environment height, R_w orbital width and R_n Total number of orbitals
7:     $c_i = 2\pi Radius$ ▷ The circumference for each region
8:     $\theta_i = \frac{c_i}{\omega}$ ▷ The intensity threshold for each orbital
9:     $Avg\Delta T, PrevTime$= MeasureConsecutivePushes($\Delta T, \theta_i, PrevTime$)
10:    $F_\theta(Avg\Delta T) = e^{\frac{-40 Avg\Delta T}{\theta}}$ ▷ Local Response function for each robot
11:    **if** $F_\theta(Avg\Delta T) < 0.1$ **then**   ▷ Orbital is empty
12:        $Robot.Light = "Off"$
13:        $PrevTime = System.getTime()$
14:        **if** $Light_l$ **then**   ▷ Detecting Lighting on robot's left side
15:            $OrbitalNum = OrbitalNum - 1$
16:        **else**
17:            $OrbitalNum = OrbitalNum + 1$
18:        **end if**
19:    **else if** $F_\theta(Avg\Delta T) > 0.7$ **then**   ▷ Highly occupied orbital
20:        $Robot.Light = "On"$
21:    **end if**
22: **end while**
23: OrbitalNum =1   ▷ Robot starts scanning from beginning

3.3   Global Communication

As stated in Sect. 3, the explorer chooses its orbital randomly, calculates its response threshold, and works in this orbital until it is cleaned. While it works, it broadcasts its calculated value and others, who are finished working, listen,

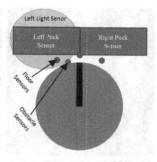

Fig. 3. Explorer's sensors.

calculate global response threshold for all tasks, and choose the orbital with the highest puck capacity and start their work in that orbital.

Every robot has an array initialized with ones, and its size equal to six, which is the number of exploring orbitals. When any robot receives the response threshold values for a specific orbital X, it updates the X orbital's response threshold value in its array based on Eq. 4. The explorer trusts in its calculation more than the received values. Hence, we weight these two thresholds at 70% and 30% respectively, as shown in Eq. 4.

$$ResponseArr[X] = 0.7 ResponseArr[X] + 0.3 RecievedResponseThreshold \quad (4)$$

Random distribution of the robots allows the measuring of the response threshold over the whole environment at the same time. By exchanging this information, the robots determine which orbital is the most occupied.

4 Experiments and Results

This paper addresses the challenge in [5] when trying to construct an annulus with 100 pucks. The author found some pucks near to the border environment were unreached by outies, as shown in Fig. 1. Our proposed methods were performed over ten trials with thirty robots and 100 pucks. The results were generated from a javascript simulator called Waggle [6].

Following the original paper [5], the scalar field has a single point source at the center and is used to split the environment into ten equal orbitals which are uniquely identified by their light intensities $\tau \in [0,1]$. Innies and outies operate on $\tau = 0.75$ and $\tau = 0.7$, respectively, while explorers operate in $\tau \in \{0.1K | K \in \{1,2,3,4,5,6\}\}$ (Fig. 4).

We use the average Euclidean distance between pucks and desired annulus' contour as a performance metric to show how this distance decreases over time steps across these approaches and OC algorithm. The heavy traces in Fig. 5 show the average distance over ten trials for each approach separately. Figure 5a shows the Euclidean distance decreased, but after some time steps it becomes

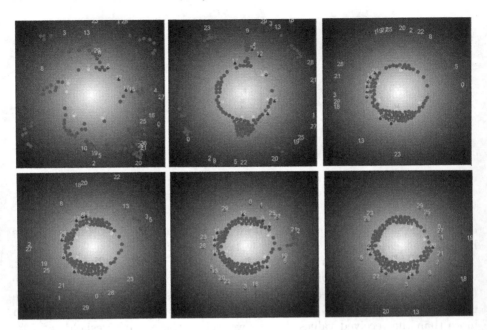

Fig. 4. Screenshots of simulation environment using 100 pucks and thirty robots consisting of five innies (yellow), eight outies (blue) and seventeen explorers (green). The explorers use global communication approach to form the annulus. (Color figure online)

stable, meaning that the outies can not reach the remaining pucks. However, the other three Fig. (5b, c and d) show Euclidean distances of the proposed methods decreased until the reach zero, which means all pucks are pushed and form the annulus.

Figure 6 shows a comparison between OC, global, no-direct, and local communication. The OC algorithm has the worst performance, the average distance is stable after some time steps, and if the pucks are placed far away from the shape, the robots will not be able to push them. In the case of the global communication approach, the highest average distance is at the beginning of the simulation; then it significantly decreased at the end. This is because, in the beginning, all robots distributed randomly to discover the environment and exchange their response threshold values. Once they found the most occupied orbital, their movement may cause two problems: firstly, it may nudge the pucks outwards, especially if some of the explorers are working near to the annulus and the others notify them to go and help in outer orbital. Secondly, robots waste their time in switching between their orbitals and other far away orbitals. On the other hand, near the end of the simulation, most of the pucks have already been pushed toward the desired orbital contour, so the environment is quite clean. In this case, when robots go towards the most occupied orbital, it helps to push these pucks quickly. As a result, the average Euclidean distance is significantly

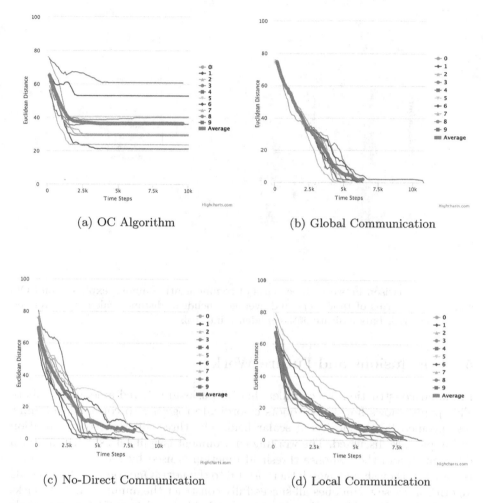

(a) OC Algorithm   (b) Global Communication

(c) No-Direct Communication   (d) Local Communication

Fig. 5. The average distance between pucks and the annulus over ten trials with 100 puck using the OC algorithm and different communicating approaches: no-direct communication and local communication.

decreased. For instance, the global-communication approach has the lowest value for the average Euclidean distance after 7000 steps.

In the case of the no-direct communication approach, it consumes more time to push all pucks because every robot works alone, and they only depend on their local calculations.

On the other hand, local communication takes advantage of sharing environment information between nearby robots and solves the global communications problems by only switching to the very closest orbital. Therefore, local communication outperforms the two communication strategies in terms of execution time, but all can form the annulus correctly.

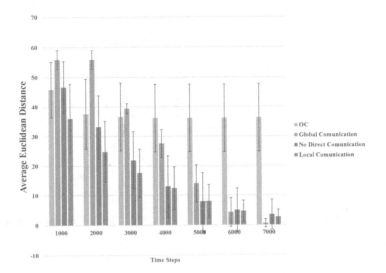

Fig. 6. Comparison between three types of communication among explorers and OC algorithm in terms of time steps and average Euclidean distance calculated over ten trials. The error bars indicate 95% confidence intervals.

5   Conclusions and Future Work

In planar construction, we consider that all pucks are shared among the robots. This paper shows how these robots co-ordinate together to construct an annulus specified by the projected scalar field. The three different communication techniques are discussed. The working environment is split into six orbitals with different τ, and the response threshold function is used by the robots to guide them when they should switch their orbital to the next. One compared to the OC algorithm, these techniques all successfully construct the annulus, and all pucks are attached. We believe the response threshold model is valid for the simple geometric shapes like (ellipses , rectangles and circles). If it is easy to calculate their circumference, we can calculate response threshold functions and apply the same proposed methods. As future work, we will try to build different complex geometric shapes in different environment dimensions. Also, we will investigate hybrid global and local communication approaches to combine their benefits. Finally, we will do practical experiments using a swarm of simple robots.

References

1. Bonabeau, E., Marco, D.D.R.D.F., Dorigo, M., Theraulaz, G., et al.: Swarm Intelligence: From Natural to Artificial Systems, vol. 1. Oxford University Press, Oxford (1999)
2. Castello, E., et al.: Adaptive foraging for simulated and real robotic swarms: the dynamical response threshold approach. Swarm Intell. **10**(1), 1–31 (2016)

3. Stewart, R.L., Russell, R.A.: Building a loose wall structure with a robotic swarm using a spatio-temporal varying template. In: 2004 IEEE/RSJ International Conference on Intelligent Robots and Systems (IROS) (IEEE Cat. No. 04CH37566), vol. 1, pp. 712–716. IEEE (2004)
4. Theraulaz, G., Bonabeau, E., Denuebourg, J.N.: Response threshold reinforcements and division of labour in insect societies. Proc. Roy. Soc. London. Ser. B: Biol. Sci. **265**(1393), 327–332 (1998)
5. Vardy, A.: Orbital construction: swarms of simple robots building enclosures. In: 2018 IEEE 3rd International Workshops on Foundations and Applications of Self* Systems (FAS* W), pp. 147–153. IEEE (2018)
6. Vardy, A.: Waggle: visual programming for swarm robotics (2018). https://github.com/BOTSlab/waggle

Deep Reinforcement Learning
for Multi-satellite Collection Scheduling

Jason T. Lam[1], François Rivest[1,2], and Jean Berger[3(✉)]

[1] School of Computing, Queen's University, Kingston, ON, Canada
[2] Department of Mathematics and Computer Science,
Royal Military College of Canada, Kingston, ON, Canada
[3] Defence Research Development Canada, Valcartier, QC, Canada
jean.berger@drdc-rddc.gc.ca

Abstract. Multi-satellite scheduling often involves generating a fixed number of potential task schedules, evaluating them all, and selecting the path that yields the highest expected rewards. Unfortunately, this approach, however accurate, is nearly impossible to scale up and be applied to large realistic problems due to combinatorial explosion. Furthermore, re-generating solutions each time the tasks change is costly, inefficient and slow. To address these issues, we adapt a deep reinforcement learning solution that automatically learns a policy for multi-satellite scheduling, as well as a representation for the problems. The algorithm learns a heuristic that selects the next best task given the current problem and partial solution, avoiding any search in the creation of the schedule. Although preliminary results in learning a collection satellite scheduling heuristic still fail to outperform baseline domain specific methods, the trained system might be fast enough to potentially generate decisions in near real-time.

Keywords: Planning and scheduling · Deep reinforcement learning · Graph embedding · Multi-satellite collection scheduling

1 Introduction

Earth Observation Satellites (EOS) have been important assets for Intelligence, Surveillance and Reconnaissance applications. With customer requests outnumbering satellite resources, an optimal satellite observation schedule is required to best satisfy customer demands. The multi-satellite collection scheduling problem (m-SatCSP) aims to allocate these requests while optimizing a single or multiple objectives and satisfying operational constraints.

Many attempts have been made to derive a heuristic for m-SatCSP, a known NP-hard problem [8,10]. In previous work, route approximations have been produced via problem reductions; where moderate success has been achieved from transforming m-SatCSP into 0-1 knapsack with limited constraints, mathematical modeling ignoring memory and energy constraints, longest-path problem

© Crown 2019
C. Martín-Vide et al. (Eds.): TPNC 2019, LNCS 11934, pp. 184–196, 2019.
https://doi.org/10.1007/978-3-030-34500-6_13

with time windows, and graph coloring problems [3,15,20]. Unfortunately by ignoring key environmental constraints, the solutions produced by these solvers do not accurately reflect real-world applications (e.g. ignoring clouds or memory and energy constraints). Recently, more naturally inspired computing approach based on genetic algorithms have been used to find quick and satisfactory approximations [2].

Over the last few years, deep artificial neural networks have begun to outperform classical methods in computer vision [9], natural language processing, and games. Inspired from the brain, deep learning aims to add numerous layers of abstraction to learn the representation for a task as well as leveraging the resulting representations to produce a solution. With graphs, it is only recently that researchers have began to apply deep learning to learn heuristics for optimization problems such as the traveling salesman problem [7,13]. In this paper, we extend deep reinforcement learning to solve the m-SatCSP for the first time. It consists in learning an offline policy enabling fast online solution generation for real-time constrained optimization problem.

The paper is structured as follows: In Sect. 2, we formulate the m-SatCSP problem into a directed graph optimization problem with auxiliary information as formulated by Wang et al. [18]. In Sect. 3, we describe and adapt Dai's et al. [7] end-to-end deep graph embedding and reinforcement learning algorithm to automatically learn a deep graph embedding as well as an estimate of the expected future reward for each next available node. Finally, in Sect. 4, we compare the performance of our trained network to a simple heuristic and to Wang et al. [18] results followed by a discussion, before concluding in Sect. 5.

2   Background

To solve m-SatCSP, previous methods developed metaheuristics that applied dynamic programming algorithms on multiple subproblems derived from m-SatCSP [18]; similarly, a hybrid genetic algorithm approach has also demonstrated cost-effective and competitive results [2]. However, as the number of tasks, orbits, and satellites in the problem increase, these approaches become ineffective due to combinatorial explosion. To help mitigate these issues, researchers have begun utilizing deep learning to learn better heuristics in an attempt to reduce the need for a combinatorial search.

One of the areas deep learning aims to address is how to create a representation of graphs in a vector. This idea is similar to the word embeddings used in natural language processing [14]. Graphs are a data structure that model the relationship (i.e. edges) between different actors (i.e. nodes) [6]. In previous approaches, techniques like kernel functions [17] or manually annotated features [11] were used to create these representations; unfortunately, the resulting representations were inflexible, difficult to scale, and provided shallow information.

More recently, deep learning approaches using attention mechanisms and reinforcement learning were used to solve the analogous problem of Vehicle Routing [13]. Nazari et al. leveraged an attention mechanism to help deliver contextual information from preceding time-steps to the current node; similar to the encoder-decoder framework presented by Bhadanau et al. [1]. In our approach the embeddings are contextualized by message passes in a defined neighbourhood and updated simultaneously rather than iteratively. While [13] attempted to use a recurrent unit to provide a set of heuristics to pick the nodes, the approach from [7] focused on building a deep representation that provided an estimate of the future rewards for each available action.

2.1 Problem Formulation

To provide an accurate comparison of our model, we adopted the mathematical model definition from Wang et al. [18]. The problem is typically defined by a set of orbits O from one or more satellites and a set of tasks T of observations to schedule. As in [18], we removed inter-orbit constraints by adding dummy tasks s and t representing the beginning and end of an orbit respectively, where final solutions must contain every dummy node. The objective can be defined as:

$$
\max \sum_{i \in T} \varpi_i \left(1 - \prod_{k \in O} \left(1 - p_i^{(k)} \sum_{\substack{j \in T \cup \{t\} \\ j \neq i}} x_{i,j}^{(k)} \right) \right) \tag{1}
$$

where ϖ_i is the reward associated to task i, $p_i^{(k)}$ is the probability of observing task i in orbit k (accounting for clouds), and $x_{i,j}^{(k)}$ is a binary variable indicating if tasks i and j are both scheduled on orbit k with task j being scheduled next to task i. Equation (1) is such that the expected reward for a task is given by the task reward times one minus the probability of missing it given the current schedule. This optimization is subject to the following constraints from [18]:

$$
\forall k \in O, i \in T, \sum_{\substack{j \in T \cup \{t\} \\ j \neq i}} x_{ij}^{(k)} \leq b_i^{(k)} \tag{2}
$$

$$
\forall k \in O, i \in T, \sum_{\substack{j \in T \cup \{t\} \\ j \neq i}} x_{ij}^{(k)} = \sum_{\substack{j \in T \cup \{s\} \\ j \neq i}} x_{ji}^{(k)} \tag{3}
$$

$$
\forall i, j \in T, k \in O, x_{ij}^{(k)} = 0 \text{ if } we_i^{(k)} + st_{ij}^{(k)} > ws_j^{(k)} \tag{4}
$$

$$
\forall k \in O, \sum_{i \in T} \sum_{\substack{j \in T \cup \{t\} \\ j \neq i}} x_{ij}^k (we_i^{(k)} - ws_i^{(k)}) \, m_k \leq M_k \tag{5}
$$

$$
\forall k \in O, \sum_{i \in T} \sum_{\substack{j \in T \cup \{t\} \\ j \neq i}} x_{ij}^{(k)} (we_i^{(k)} - ws_i^{(k)}) e_k + \sum_{i \in T} \sum_{\substack{j \in T \\ j \neq i}} x_{ij}^{(k)} \rho_{ij}^{(k)} \leq E_k \tag{6}
$$

Table 1. Notation (adapted from Wang et al. [18]).

O	Set of orbits, $O = \{1, \ldots, M\}$
T	Set of tasks, $T = \{1, \ldots, n\}$
i, j	Task index, $i, j \in T \cup \{s, t\}$, in which s and t are dummy tasks
k	Orbit index, $k \in O$
ϖ_i	Profit of task $i, i \in T$
$p_i^{(k)}$	Probability that task i will be successfully observed on orbit $k, i \in T, k \in O$
$x_{ij}^{(k)}$	$x_{ij}^{(k)} = 1$ if task j is schedule right after task i (also scheduled) on orbit k, $x_{ij}^{(k)} = 0$ otherwise, $i, j \in T \cup \{s, t\}, k \in O$
$b_i^{(k)}$	$b_i^{(k)} = 1$ if task i is available for observation on orbit k, otherwise $b_i^{(k)} = 0, i \in T, k \in O$
M_k, E_k	memory capacity and energy capacity on orbit $k, k \in O$
m_k, e_k	memory and energy consumption for each unit of time of observation on orbit $k, k \in O$
$[ws_i^{(k)}, we_i^{(k)}]$	time window of observation of task i on orbit $k, i \in T, k \in O$
$st_{ij}^{(k)}$	setup time between task i and task j on orbit $k, i, j \in T, k \in O$
$\rho_{ij}^{(k)}$	energy consumption for slewing between task i and task j on orbit $k, i, j \in T, k \in O$

where the symbols definition can be found in Table 1. Equation (2) ensures each scheduled task has at most one scheduled successor while Equation (3) ensures that each task has either 0 successor and predecessor (unscheduled) or 1 (scheduled). Equation (4) ensures there is an edge between two tasks only if there is enough setup time while Equations (5)–(6) ensure there is enough memory and energy for the scheduled tasks on each orbit.

2.2 Graph Formulation

We encoded the m-SatCSP problem as a directed graph $G = (V, E)$ that was decomposed into orbits. Each orbit k begins and terminates at a node $s^{(k)}$ and $t^{(k)}$, respectively, with $t^{(k)} = s^{(k+1)}$, except for $s^{(1)}$ and $t^{(M)}$. The nodes on orbit k are the tasks available for observation governed by $b_i^{(k)}$, implementing Equation (2). There exists an edge between two nodes representing tasks i and j on orbit k if and only if there is sufficient transition time as given by Eq. (4). We note that there is an edge from $s^{(k)}$ to all nodes on orbit k as well as an edge from all nodes on orbit k to $t^{(k)}$ without any transitional costs.

Starting from $s^{(1)}$, and forcing the algorithm (or network) to choose a single transition at each node (i.e. setting the appropriate $x_{ij}^{(k)} = 1$), implements Eq. (2). When satellite memory or energy capacities are exhausted, Eqs. (5)–(6), a transition is forced to the current orbit's node t. Starting with $x_{ij}^{(k)} = 0$

$\forall i, j \in T, k \in O$, the selected path from $s^{(1)}$ to $t^{(M)}$ that includes nodes i and j on orbit k (i.e. $x_{ij}^{(k)} = 1$), will receive the following reward:

$$R_{i,j}^{(k)} = \varpi_j p_j^{(k)} \prod_{k' \in \{1,\ldots,k-1\}} \left(1 - p_j^{(k')} \sum_{\substack{i' \in T \cup \{s\} \\ j \neq i}} x_{i',j}^{(k')} \right) \qquad (7)$$

which corresponds to the added expected value of observation task j on orbit k given the existing previous orbits schedule. The partial solution (sequence of nodes) or schedule S is maintained in a list.

3   Model

Dai et al. [7] extended their deep network embedding learning algorithm from [4], `structure2vec`, to a complete reinforcement learning algorithm similar to DeepMind's DQN (Deep Q-Learning Network) [12], the Atari-winning algorithm, to solve graph problems such as the minimum vertex cover, maximum cut, and traveling salesman problem [7]. DQN uses convolution networks, inspired from the visual system, where each unit on a given layer is fed only a few topologically organized units of the previous layer. That is, each unit on a given layer, similar to a neuron in the visual cortex, receives input from neighbouring units of the previous layer. A whole population of units is spread out in 2D to cover the entire previous layer, while maintaining the visual field's spatial organization. Naturally, units in a higher layer possess larger visual field. Given a set of units with the same receptive field, but different weights, each can be thought of as a specialized feature detector (e.g. the first layer contains units activated by edges with different orientations). An advantage of modern computers is that each pool of units can share the same weights, and therefore, look for the same features, across an entire image. This concept can be extended to graphs, where the weight generating features for a node and its edges, can be re-used to interpret the remaining nodes and edges. On top of this architecture, sits the Q-Learning algorithm [19] a variant of the temporal-difference learning algorithm (TD). TD was inspired from animal learning with the hope to make computers learn from each trial. The following section describes the selected algorithm and how we adapt it to the m-SatCSP.

3.1   Deep Graph Embedding and Learning

Given a graph $G = (V, E)$, let $x_v \in \mathbb{R}^d$ be the vector representation of node $v \in V$ and let $w(u, v) \in \mathbb{R}^{d'}$ be the vector representation of the edge between node u and v in E. Let $u_v^{(n)} \in \mathbb{R}^p$ be the nth layer embedding of node v. The embedding for layer $n + 1$ is given by:

$$\mu_v^{(n+1)} = relu \left(\theta_1 x_v + \theta_3 relu \left(\sum_{u \in N(v)} \theta_2 \mu_u^{(n)} + \theta_4 w(u, v) \right) \right) \qquad (8)$$

where $\theta_1 \in \mathbb{R}^{p \times d}, \theta_2, \theta_3 \in \mathbb{R}^{p \times p}$ and $\theta_4 \in \mathbb{R}^{p \times d'}$ are learnable parameters, d is the dimension of the feature vector of a node, d' is the dimension of the feature vector of an edge, p is the dimension of the node's embedding, $N(v)$ is the set of nodes connected to v, $relu$ is the Rectified Linear Unit activation function, and $\mu_v^{(0)} = relu(\theta_1 x_v)$.

Given graph embedding on the top layer N, the system attempts to learn a Q-value, that is, an estimate of the expected sum of future rewards, for a given graph G, partial solution S, and next node v of the form:

$$\widehat{Q}(G, S, v; \Theta) = \theta_5^\top relu\left(\theta_6 \mu_u^{(N)}\right) \tag{9}$$

where $\theta_5 \in \mathbb{R}^2, \theta_6 \in \mathbb{R}^{p \times p}$, and $\Theta = \{\theta_i\}_{i=1}^6$. Note that Eqs. (8)–(9) are from the source code for the TSP problem available at https://github.com/Hanjun-Dai/graph_comb_opt, which differs from those in their corresponding paper [7], as these produce better results on m-SatCSP. Given a graph G, partial solution S and node v, we can update the value of $\widehat{Q}(G, S, v; \Theta)$ toward the reward $r(G, S, v)$ plus the expected value for the partial solution S' under the best possible next action v' as given by:

$$y = r(G, S, v) + \gamma \max_{v'} \widehat{Q}(G, S', v'; \Theta) \tag{10}$$

where $\gamma = 1$ is the usual discount factor, $S' = [S, v]$, and $r(G, S, v)$ comes from Eq. (7). Although the network can provide a value for each node v, only the ones with a valid transition from the last node of the current partial solution S are valid, the other node values are replaced by -Inf.

Starting with randomly initial values for Θ, the network keeps selecting nodes using an ϵ-Greedy policy where the optimal action is selected $1 - \epsilon$ percent of the time, or randomly selected (among the valid nodes) ϵ percent of the time. Each $(G, S, v, r(G, S, v), S', v')$ tuple is put into replay memory for training. The replay memory is filled like a circular buffer and can hold 50,000 tuples.

The replay memory is first filled by scheduling 100 problems using a randomly initialized network (also copied as the target network). Every 10 network updates, 10 more problems are scheduled and placed into the replay memory. Every 100 iterations, the network is evaluated by scheduling the problems of the validation set and is saved. At the end of training, only the version with the best validation score is tested. Finally, every 1000 iterations, the network weights are copied into the target network which is used to compute the target y from Eq. (10) in training. One iteration corresponds to a single step of a gradient descent algorithm (Adam's optimizer with learning rate 0.0001 and momentum 0.9) minimizing Eq. (11) using 32 random samples from the replay memory to improve Θ. The ϵ schedules decays from 1.00 to 0.05 over 300,000 iterations.

$$(y - \widehat{Q}(h(S_n), v_n; \Theta))^2 \tag{11}$$

in which y uses an older version of Θ called the target network. This network is updated with the latest parameter every 100 iterations. The resulting function $\widehat{Q}(h(S_n), v_n; \Theta)$ provides an estimate of the future rewards given the current problem G and partial solution S, for all selectable node v.

Table 2. Node features coding for G and S.

Index	Node feature	Details
0	Bias	Always 1 (if the node is in the embedding)
1	Actionable	1 if the node can be selected from the current node
2	Future	1 if the node is accessible from the current node, but not directly selectable
3	Current	1 if the current node
4	Past	1 if not accessible anymore
5	Energy cost	Energy cost of observing the node
6	Memory cost	Memory cost of observing the node
7	Recurrence	How many times the task will reoccur in the future
8	Number of incoming edges	Number of incoming edges to the node
9	Number of outgoing edges	Number of outgoing edges from the node
10	Dummyness	1 if the node $\in \{s, t\}$
11	Reward	The reward for scheduling the node (Eq. (7))

Table 3. Edge features coding for G and S.

Index	Edge feature	Details
0	Bias	Always 1 (if the node is in the embedding)
1	Actionable tail	Node at the tail can be selected
2	Slewing cost	Energy cost to transition from the node at the tail to the node at the head
3	Dummyness	1 if the head node $\in \{s, t\}$
4	Actionable head	Node at the head can be selected

3.2 Features for Nodes and Edges

We maintained our partial solution S as an ordered list of nodes and train our models using the reward function defined in Eq. (7). The feature vectors x_v for node v and $w(u, v)$ for edge (u, v) are provided in Tables 2 and 3 respectively.

4 Experiments and Results

In this paper we ran 3 experiments. In the first we evaluated whether it was better to train the network on an heterogeneous training set (variable number of tasks) or homogeneous training set (constant number of tasks). In the second experiment, we evaluated if increasing the depth of the network (and therefore, increasing its visual field reducing its myopia) improved the performance (in terms of rewards) of the generated schedules. Finally, we compared the performance to a simple myopic, regret-less heuristic. In every case we also tested the network ability to generalize to problems with a smaller number of tasks, larger number of tasks, and larger number of orbits. Resulting schedules will be compared to those of Wang et al. [18].

4.1   Training and Testing Sets

Wang et al. [18] reports results on 15 test sets of 10 problems each as follows (# orbits - # tasks): 9-10, 9-20, 9-30, 9,40, 9-50, 9-60, 21-10, 21-20, 21-30, 21-120, 21-160, 21-200, 42-120, 42-160, 42-200.

We generated 2 different datasets of 10,000 problems each using our in-house problem generator. The homogeneous set only contains 9-60 problems, while the heterogeneous set contains a mix of {9-10, 9-20, 9-30, 9-40, 9-50, 9-60} problems, each generated independently. Note that in all problems the number of tasks is an upper bound, as each task could have appeared between 0 to 3 times (as in [18]). The memory and energy capacity and consumption were also randomly generated to match the range of values in [18] (memory consumption in [2.0, 4.0], energy consumption in [1.0, 4.0], memory capacity in [120, 160], energy capacity in [180, 240], sampled independently for each orbit). The probability of success of each task is sampled in [.2, 1.0]. Each set was then organized using 10-fold cross-validation, generating 10 homogeneous training and validation sets as well as 10 heterogeneous training and validation sets. This will allow us to train 10 distinct networks for each experiment providing more robust results.

Since test sets in [18] are relatively small, and may come from a slightly different distributions of problems than our training sets, we also generate our own test sets of 100 problems each. We have an homogeneous test set made of 9-60 problems, an heterogeneous test set made of a mix of {9-10, 9-20, 9-30, 9-40, 9-50, 9-60} problems, and two sets with 21 orbits, one with fewer tasks (mix of {21-10, 21-20, 21-30} problems), and one with more tasks (mix of {21-120, 21-160, 21-200} problems), matching the test sets from [18].

4.2   Hardware/Software

All experiments were run on a Dell T7910 having 2x NVidia 1080Ti graphics card, 2 Intel(R) Xeon(R) E5-2650 v3 @ 2.30 GHz CPUs, 32 GB of memory, and a 1 TB SSD hard drive. We used a modified version of Dai's C++/CUDA code from https://github.com/Hanjun-Dai/graph_comb_opt. Each network was limited to 1 graphic card, but some simulations were run concurrently (up to 6 per GPU). Each network was trained for at least 120,000 iterations.

Table 4. Average rewards of our deep neural networks compared to our simple no regret heuristic and to heuristic 4 from [18] on various test sets. The number of orbits is 9, the number of tasks is 60 or selected from MIX = {10,20,30,40,50,60} or Small = {10,20,30}, W = [18]. The average is computed over all test problems, for our networks, we present the average and standard error of the 10 networks average rewards.

Algo. \ Test set	9-60	9-MIX	W 9-MIX	21-Small	W 21-Small
9-60, $N = 5$	46.49 ± 0.25	33.01 ± 0.09	31.40 ± 0.45	28.99 ± 0.05	52.45 ± 0.59
9-MIX, $N = 5$	45.81 ± 0.22	32.95 ± 0.11	32.01 ± 0.61	28.97 ± 0.03	53.81 ± 0.77
9-MIX, $N = 15$	45.80 ± 0.68	32.87 ± 0.25	32.36 ± 0.59	28.95 ± 0.06	54.19 ± 0.83
9-MIX, $N = 25$	45.68 ± 0.62	32.85 ± 0.22	32.73 ± 0.57	28.96 ± 0.05	54.37 ± 0.58
No regret (nodes)	30.82	28.59	31.99	37.82	55.15
Heuristic 4 in [18]	N/A	N/A	38.47	N/A	60.64

Table 5. Average rewards of our deep neural networks compared to our no regret heuristic and to heuristic 4 from [18] on test sets of problems with a larger number of tasks. The number of orbits is 21, the number of tasks is selected from Large = {120,160,200}, W = [18]. The average is computed over all test problems, for our networks, we present the average and standard error of the 10 networks average rewards.

Algorithm	21-Large	W 21-Large
9-60, $N = 5$	117.46 ± 0.58	196.75 ± 17.26
9-MIX, $N = 5$	114.63 ± 0.69	186.88 ± 27.30
9-MIX, $N = 15$	113.73 ± 2.03	173.09 ± 24.98
9-MIX, $N = 25$	108.41 ± 5.67	151.13 ± 30.98
No regret (nodes)	79.59	178.87
Heuristic 4 in [18]	N/A	285.75

4.3   Results

The average expected schedule scores on each test set (as computed from Eq. (1) for each solution) are shown in Tables 4 and 5.

As shown in Table 4, training on a set of 9-60 tasks only (first row) helps by a small margin on a similar test set (first column) and has no significant impact on the performance on a test set made of smaller number of tasks (second column), but performance deteriorates a bit on the test set from [18] (third column), which tends to have fewer tasks opportunities than the problems produced by our generator. Similar results are also true for 21 orbits (last two columns). On the other hand, training on 9-60 problems instead of a mix of smaller ones (9-MIX) improves performances when generalizing to more tasks, as shown in Table 5 (first 2 rows). This may be because the homogeneous set contains more large (60 tasks) problems then the heterogeneous training set. Unfortunately, none of our networks outperformed the heuristics by Wang et al. [18] (last row).

Increasing the depth of the network architecture (N), providing it with a larger field of view, and hopefully making its heuristic less myopic, had basically

Table 6. Average computational time in seconds per problem for our deep neural network compared to heuristic 4 from [18] on our test sets. The number of orbits is either 9 or 21, the number of tasks is selected from MIX = {10,20,30,40,50,60}, Small = {10,20,30}, and Large = {120,160,200}. We present the approximate time to solve one problem. (Time on small problems is less reliable as it is more likely to be affected by other processes.)

Algorithm	9-MIX	21-Small	21-Large
9-MIX, $N = 5$	$\approx$0.1 s	$\approx$0.1s	$\approx$4.7 s
9-MIX, $N = 15$	$\approx$0.1 s	$\approx$0.1s	$\approx$5.0 s
9-MIX, $N = 25$	$\approx$0.3 s	$\approx$0.6s	$\approx$7.2 s

Table 7. Average number of iterations (gradient descent steps) at which the networks reached the best validation score while training.

Algorithm	# of iterations
9-60, $N = 5$	$\approx$12,500
9-MIX, $N = 5$	$\approx$24,000
9-MIX, $N = 15$	$\approx$26,000
9-MIX, $N = 25$	$\approx$63,000

no impact on the results when testing on similar number of tasks, whether on 9 or 21 orbits, as shown in rows 2–4 of Table 4. But it did significantly reduce the network's ability to generalize to a larger number of tasks as shown in rows 2–4 of Table 5. The time to compute a solution also seems to increase linearly with the depth of the network as reported in the last column of Table 6.

We also wanted to verify if deeper network were getting the extra training needed to properly learn more abstract and less myopic heuristics. The average number of iterations (gradient descent steps) to the peak validation set score (point at which the network is saved and used for testing) is reported in Table 7. It can be seen that the number of iterations indeed increases with depth, but those numbers are also extremely small, suggesting that many networks do not cover the whole training set. This lead us to wonder what kind of heuristic the network could learn so quickly, leading to the next section.

4.4   New Heuristic

Since our networks began to overfit very early in training (before seeing the whole training set), we believed it must have been learning a simple heuristic. We posited a straightforward heuristic a network could learn is to sum all the nodes that are still actionable in the future (Table 2, indexes 1–2). This approach would also provide a nice monotonically decreasing estimate of future rewards as nodes are selected, and can also be considered a no-regret policy; trying to make the decision that would keep the highest number of possible options open. To test this, we designed an algorithm to generate satellite schedules by selecting nodes that minimized the number of nodes that become inaccessible (a more advanced version would be similar, but counting rewards). In short, our heuristic would always take the decision that left as many opportunities open as possible, or that represented the least commitment. The results of this heuristic are in Tables 4 and 5 as the "no regret" row. We can see that the score of this simple policy is very similar to the one of our networks on the test sets from [18] (column marked as W). Although usually similar or worse then our network, this heuristic performed better than our networks on the 21-Small test set. Further work along developing a truly no-regret policy could be worthwhile.

4.5 Discussion

Successful results from [5] on TSP required a hand-coded heuristic. While their neural network was used to select the next node, these nodes were always added to the tour such as to minimize the added distance. The importance of this heuristic in the reported performances is unclear. Our networks were trained on m-SatCSP without such heuristic. But, there is a number of research directions that could allow for significant improvements. First, deep reinforcement learning networks have problems with large rewards. It is common to clip rewards to 1, as in Atari DQN [12], or to use gradient clipping. Reward clipping in m-SatCSP could hide important information to the network, but gradient clipping should provide a significant improvement in learning. Another approach would be to evaluate a policy gradient method instead of Q-Learning, which are becoming popular in deep reinforcement learning. One could also combine tree search over a short horizon in training to generate a less myopic and better estimate target value y as in AlphaGo [16]. Other convolution graph network approaches, such as pointer networks [13], shall also be considered. In this method, the network embedding leverages recurrent units that dynamically change how nodes are evaluated as the network builds a partial solution. This can be seen as learning a plan that provides slightly different heuristics depending on the current stage of the scheduling process (earlier orbits versus later orbits). Finally, one could consider building a meta-graph, where, for examples, there could be a different type of edges linking opportunities of the same task together. This could allow the network to learn an embedding that takes into account the future opportunities of a task in evaluating the decision of scheduling its current opportunity.

5 Conclusion

As a preliminary effort, a deep reinforcement learning solution approach has been adapted to solve the multi-satellite scheduling problem for the first time. It consisted of automatically learning a policy for the constrained optimization problem to infer efficient solutions quickly. Our main goal was to effectively provide solutions to combinatorial problems combining offline learning and fast online solution generation.

Future work shall explore recent deep neural network architectures and concepts that shown promise in approximating analogous, combinatorial, optimization problems. Improving on best-known problem representations, training, attention mechanisms, credit assignment, constraint-handling and implementation approaches all represent attractive directions. Investigating more specific classes of CSP to increasingly handle problem complexity may also be a valid research path to further develop a deep neural networks' ability generalize.

References

1. Bahdanau, D., Cho, K., Bengio, Y.: Neural machine translation by jointly learning to align and translate. arXiv preprint arXiv:1409.0473 (2014)
2. Barkaoui, M., Berger, J.: A new hybrid genetic algorithm for the multi-satellite collection scheduling problem. J. Oper. Res. Soc. (To appear)
3. Benoist, T., Rottembourg, B.: Upper bounds for revenue maximization in a satellite scheduling problem. Q. J. Belg. Fr. Ital. Oper. Res. Soc. **2**(3), 235–249 (2004)
4. Dai, H., Dai, B., Song, L.: Discriminative embeddings of latent variable models for structured data. In: International Conference on Machine Learning, pp. 2702–2711 (2016)
5. Dai, H., Khalil, E.B., Zhang, Y., Dilkina, B., Song, L.: Learning combinatorial optimization algorithms over graphs. arXiv preprint arXiv:1704.01665 (2017)
6. Hamilton, W.L., Ying, R., Leskovec, J.: Representation learning on graphs: methods and applications. arXiv preprint arXiv:1709.05584 (2017)
7. Khalil, E., Dai, H., Zhang, Y., Dilkina, B., Song, L.: Learning combinatorial optimization algorithms over graphs. In: Advances in Neural Information Processing Systems, pp. 6348–6358 (2017)
8. Lawler, E.L., Lenstra, J.K., Kan, A.H.R., Shmoys, D.B.: Sequencing and scheduling: algorithms and complexity. Handb. Oper. Res. Manag. Sci. **4**, 445–522 (1993)
9. LeCun, Y., Bengio, Y., Hinton, G.: Deep learning. Nature **521**(7553), 436 (2015)
10. Lenstra, J.K., Kan, A.R., Brucker, P.: Complexity of machine scheduling problems. In: Annals of Discrete Mathematics, vol. 1, pp. 343–362. Elsevier (1977)
11. Liben-Nowell, D., Kleinberg, J.: The link-prediction problem for social networks. J. Am. Soc. Inform. Sci. Technol. **58**(7), 1019–1031 (2007)
12. Mnih, V., et al.: Human-level control through deep reinforcement learning. Nature **518**(7540), 529 (2015)
13. Nazari, M., Oroojlooy, A., Snyder, L., Takac, M.: Reinforcement learning for solving the vehicle routing problem. In: Bengio, S., Wallach, H., Larochelle, H., Grauman, K., Cesa-Bianchi, N., Garnett, R. (eds.) Advances in Neural Information Processing Systems, vol. 31, pp. 9860–9870. Curran Associates, Inc. (2018)
14. Pennington, J., Socher, R., Manning, C.: Glove: global vectors for word representation. In: Proceedings of the 2014 Conference on Empirical Methods in Natural Language Processing (EMNLP), pp. 1532–1543 (2014)
15. Sarkheyli, A., Vaghei, B.G., Bagheri, A.: New tabu search heuristic in scheduling earth observation satellites. In: 2010 2nd International Conference on Software Technology and Engineering, vol. 2, pp. V2–199. IEEE (2010)
16. Silver, D., Huang, A., Maddison, C.J., Guez, A., Sifre, L., Van Den Driessche, G., Schrittwieser, J., Antonoglou, I., Panneershelvam, V., Lanctot, M., et al.: Mastering the game of go with deep neural networks and tree search. Nature **529**(7587), 484 (2016)

17. Vishwanathan, S.V.N., Schraudolph, N.N., Kondor, R., Borgwardt, K.M.: Graph kernels. J. Mach. Learn. Res. **11**(Apr), 1201–1242 (2010)
18. Wang, J., Demeulemeester, E., Qiu, D., Liu, J.: Exact and inexact scheduling algorithms for multiple earth observation satellites under uncertainties of clouds. Available at SSRN 2634934 (2015)
19. Watkins, C.J., Dayan, P.: Q-learning. Mach. Learn. **8**(3–4), 279–292 (1992)
20. Wolfe, W.J., Sorensen, S.E.: Three scheduling algorithms applied to the earth observing systems domain. Manag. Sci. **46**(1), 148–166 (2000)

Evolution of Locomotion Gaits
for Quadrupedal Robots and Reality
Gap Characterization

Usama Mir[1]([✉]), Zainullah Khan[2], Umer Iftikhar Mir[2], Farhat Naseer[2],
and Waleed Shah[2]

[1] Saudi Electronic University, Dammam, Saudi Arabia
u.mir@seu.edu.sa
[2] Engineering and Management Sciences,
Balochistan University of Information Technology, Quetta, Pakistan
zain.9496@gmail.com, umar.i.mir@gmail.com,
farhaty16@gmail.com, willy.jaw47@gmail.com

Abstract. The landscape of isolated areas has been changed due to human intervention to support vehicular transport, however, this is a hectic job, therefore, if our vehicles are morphed to mimic nature, the landscape would not need to be changed. Robots and vehicles inspired from nature are very hard to control because of multiple number of actuators. Manual methods (such as programming individual actuators to form a walking pattern) fall short because of the complexity. Therefore, an automated process that employs artificial intelligence (AI) to evolve locomotion gaits for quadrupedal robots is needed. AI has been used before as well; however, most of the AI implementations are only done in simulation without hardware execution. This article attempts to use genetic algorithms to evolve locomotion gaits that are later implemented on robots both via simulations and real implementation. The simulation is run for 200 generations and the best result is put into effect on a hardware robot. Our results show that the gait is successfully transferred; however, the results are not perfect and suffer from the reality gap. These results also help us conclude that gaits designed for a specific environment have a better chance of transferring than gaits that have been designed without taking into account the surface the robot walks on.

Keywords: Evolutionary robotics · Gait evolution · Genetic algorithm

1 Introduction

Quadrupedal robots, inspired from the morphology of real animals (Bio-inspired), have the ability to traverse uneven terrains better than their wheeled counterparts [1, 2]. The appendages on quadrupedal robots allow them to pass over a region by climbing obstacles, hence providing an efficient capability to perambulate over rough terrains [3]. However, quadrupedal robot morphologies can prove to be quite a challenge to control which, therefore, determines the motivation behind this work [4]. Gait synthesis for such robots can be achieved manually, but this will require a substantial amount of

© Springer Nature Switzerland AG 2019
C. Martín-Vide et al. (Eds.): TPNC 2019, LNCS 11934, pp. 197–207, 2019.
https://doi.org/10.1007/978-3-030-34500-6_14

time since the position of each actuator in the robot is determined manually. Hence, automating the process of gait designing will reduce the time spent by an engineer in designing the gait.

Speaking of which, the gait of bio-inspired robots is actually the sequence with which the actuators in the robot move allowing it to locomote. Multiple combinations of actuator movements can produce locomotion gaits, therefore, determining the right sequence for a robot proves to be a very difficult task if handled by a human. For this purpose, Genetic Algorithms (GAs) can be utilized to handle the multiple actuator movement sequences in an automated way which makes the task of finding the correct gait much easier.

In continuation to above, GAs have been employed in synthesizing gaits for bio-inspired robots on many occasions. For example, in [5], efficient gaits for bipedal robots have been evolved and the neural networks are used to control the robots which is quite a complex task since the solution space is large making the task of finding a suitable gait very difficult. Moreover, the process of gait evolution is not parallelized which slows down the process of gait evolution. Similar kind approach is used in [6] where GA has been used to generate different gaits for snake robots using two layered feedforward fully connected neural networks resulting in improved processing time and reduction in solution space. However, parallelization of gait synthesis remains unaddressed. Some solutions to parallelization can be seen in the form of robot swam behavior evolution in [4] but the issue still persisted in gait evolution for bio-inspired robots. Likewise in [7], gaits for bipedal robots are evolved, yet, these gaits have not been transferred to a setup in the real world, which makes it difficult to draw conclusions about the usability of the gaits on a physical robot. In [8] and [9], gaits are used for a quadruped on a hardware setup producing practical gaits that can be utilized in the real-world, however, the gait evolution process is quite slow. The study by [10] concluded that relying completely on a hardware based gait evolution increases the chances of damaging the electronic parts of the robot which is also highlighted in [11]. Different from the aforementioned approaches, the authors of [12] believe it is completely possible to control robots using fuzzy logic. This study in [12] concludes that fuzzy logic controllers can prove to be effective for small number of generations but as the number of generations increases, neural networks start outperforming fuzzy controllers.

The GAs entirely implemented in simulation often produce movements that cannot be implemented in hardware and hence the results are mostly impractical. Furthermore, the simulations usually run un-parallelized which causes the simulations to run slow. On the other hand, gaits implemented entirely on hardware take a lot of trials and require ample amount of time to produce an acceptable result. The gaits purely evolved in simulation tend to perform really well, however, when transferred to a hardware setup, the robot performs poorly. This disparity in the robot performance is called reality gap and gait evolution suffers from this problem.

Addressing the above untouched concerns, this paper is just a small attempt to use the GA as a novel approach to evolve a gait in a simulation environment by parallelizing the process to reduce the gait synthesis time. The best gait from the parallelized simulation is transferred to a physical robot. However, the simulation is designed specifically for the environment the physical robot will walk in. The results extracted from our approach are quite promising, since they show a perfect match between the real and virtual environments.

The rest of the paper is organized as follows. In the next section, we present a brief overview of GAs. Our methodology and experimental environment are detailed in Sect. 3. Results extracted from software and hardware implementations are provided in Sect. 4. Finally, Sect. 5 concludes our paper.

2 Genetic Algorithm: An Overview

GAs are inspired from simplified model of biological evolution designed to solve a specific problem. An environment is set and potential solutions are evolved. The environment is shaped by the parameters of the problem and encourages the evolution of good solutions.

GAs replicate nature, so in order to ensure the best results that are based on the process of evolution, a population of individuals is generated where each individual has a unique encoding known as the genetic encoding or the "DNA". When a certain behavior dominates in the population it will be allowed to reproduce off-springs portraying the same behavior as the parent, hence the name 'genetic algorithm'.

As stated above, GAs are used to evolve new solutions to problems, however, this property can be used to optimize Artificial Neural Networks (ANNs) also known as the neuro-evolution. In neuro-evolution, a neural network is evolved over time to provide an optimal solution to the stated problem. ANNs are integrated into artificial evolution systems to ensure that the outcome resembles the thought process of a real brain, hence making it useful for evolving gaits for robots.

In our context, an ANN can be used to produce gaits for robots, however, the optimization of the ANN is required in order to produce gaits that progressively improve over time. The GA approach helps us in choosing the optimized ANN. In this regard, the form of GA that we deployed in our scenario (Sect. 3.3) works according to Fig. 1, where a weight matrix is generated randomly and then it is allowed to control a robot. Based on the performance of the robot, our algorithm chooses the best weight matrix and replicates it to make a child population. The weights in the child population matrices are changed slightly causing the population to behave a little different from their parents. This difference in behavior may cause a child in the population to outperform the parent and therefore, the child becomes the new parent.

3   Methodology

We use robot gait synthesis to simulate the robot controller producing acceptable gaits, to be deployed later on a hardware robot. We then measure and compare the distance covered by the robot both via simulation and in reality. The simulator is programmed in C++ and a python script runs the simulator providing it with the weights that will be used by the neural network. There is only a single simulator file, however, the python script runs the simulator 10 times in a single generation, hence parallelizing the simulation process. This parallelization increases the chances of finding an optimal gait and reduces the time spent on simulation. Each simulation consists of an environment with physics applied to it and a quadrupedal robot. The robot is referred to as an individual and all the robots from the 10 parallelized simulations form a population. Each robot is controlled by a fully connected neural network. It is this controller that is evolved in the simulation environment and when the simulation finishes, the best performing robot is selected. This chosen robot is transferred to a hardware robot where the disparity between the real and simulated environments is calculated. Detailed explanation of each step of the methodology is given in our forthcoming subsections.

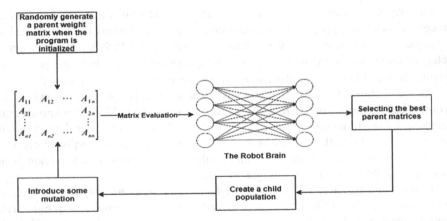

Fig. 1. Block diagram of the genetic algorithm showing how the weight matrices are used to evaluate robot performance.

3.1   Simulation

The gait evolution is performed in a physics simulator called Open Dynamics Engine. Geometric shapes are generated in the simulation environment, a cuboid shape is used for the main body of the robot, and the cylindrical shapes are utilized to make the limbs of the robot. Each limb has two joints, one for the hip and second for the knee. In the end, a total of four limbs and eight joints are created. The parameters in the simulation are set by the user to match the simulation environment to the real one. The details of the robotic structure and the different physics parameters used in the simulation are given in Table 1.

Table 1. Simulation parameters using physics simulator.

Parameter	Symbol	Value
Robot body length	l	0.2 m
Robot body width	w	0.2 m
Robot body height	h	0.05 m
Length of cylinder	cL	0.2 m
Radius of cylinder	cR	0.02 m
Mass of each robot body part in the simulation	m	1 kg
Gravity	g	0.05 $m = s2$
Number of joints	J	8
Number of motors	M	8
Motor impulse	τ	0.15
Simulation world step time	dt	0.05
Total number of timesteps for the simulation	T	1000
ANN recall interval timesteps	Rc	60
ANN inputs	I	9
ANN outputs	O	8
Number of individuals in the population	P	10
Number of generations	G	200

3.2 The Controller

As stated before, our selected controller for the robot is an ANN. ANNs are mathematical models of the biological brain and they are used to imitate the nervous system of biological beings. The "brain" controls the robot in a simple feedforward neural network with hyperbolic tangent activation function. The neural network has nine inputs and eight outputs. The neural network architecture is chosen to be simple so that the search space remains smaller for evolution. The first eight inputs of the neural network are the current joint positions of the robot and the 9th input is a bias neuron [13]. The data is passed through the neural network and the values of the output neurons are generated in the form of new joint positions such as the robot joints are actuated according to the joint positions. The neural network is called once every sixty timesteps to avoid any jerky moment. The proposed neural network is shown in Fig. 2 and the equation below gives the output of the neural network:

$$O_j = \tanh \sum_{i=0}^{I} w_{ij} J_j$$

where O_j is the output value for joint j, w_{ij} represents the weight that connects input neuron i with output neuron j, and J_j is the current joint position of joint j.

3.3 Algorithm for the Optimization of Proposed Neural Network

As mentioned before, we use GA to optimize the neural network. The main steps of our proposed algorithm are shown in Fig. 3. Our algorithm is coded in python and it runs separately from the simulator. At one time, 10 robot controllers are simulated, therefore, the algorithm makes 10 weight matrices, one for each individual robot controller. At first, the controller weights are initialized randomly, then, the GA calls and evaluates the simulator for each individual robot. After a fixed number of timesteps (1000 in our case), the simulation terminates and the algorithm chooses the controller

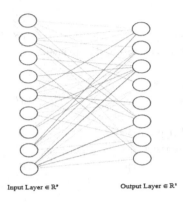

Fig. 2. Proposed neural network used to control the robot.

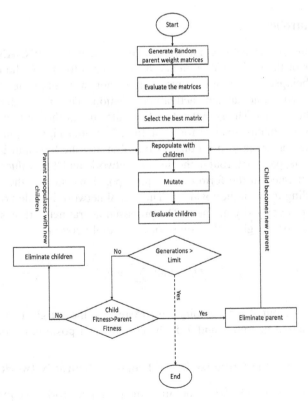

Fig. 3. GA proposed for the optimization of neural network.

with best performance according to the fitness function (explained and shown in our later section). Rest of the controllers are then eliminated. The weights of the best controller are copied into child controllers and a small amount of mutation is introduced into the children. Mutation picks a single value in the weight matrix and changes that for each individual to ensure the children behave different from the parent. The child population is evaluated and if a child performs better than the parent, the child becomes the new parent and reproduces new children, hence the cycle continues for 200 generations.

3.4   Controller Selection Criteria

After the simulation terminates, the robots from the parallelized simulation are all evaluated and the best performing controllers are selected using a mathematical function which is user defined. This function is called the fitness function and provided below:

$$F = \left(\sqrt{x^2 + y^2} \right) \left(\sum_{t=1}^{T} \sum_{j=0}^{J} J_{tj} - J_{(t-1)j} \right) (1 - TS)$$

where x and y are the distances travelled by the robot in the x and y directions, respectively. J_{tj} and $J_{(t-1)}$ represent the position of joint j at time t and $t-1$, respectively. TS is the value of a touch sensor attached to the back of the robot's body such that TS remains one '1' when the robot flips itself over. The equation is divided into two parts. The first part $\sqrt{x^2 + y^2}$ ensures that the robot travelling the farthest distance gets a high fitness value. The second part $\sum_{t=1}^{T} \sum_{j=0}^{J} J_{tj} - J_{(t-1)j}(1 - TS)$ accumulates the difference in the joint movement over the entire period of the simulation, therefore, the robots that do not stay still get high fitness values.

3.5   Hardware

One of our main goals is to transfer the best gaits to a hardware robot. We use the CAD to define our robot's body thereby cutting the robot parts into 5-millimeter-thick plywood. The robot joints are actuated using mg995 high torque servo motors which are connected to a 5 V (20A) power supply in order to provide the high current needed to run the servos. The servos are controlled using an Arduino uno [14].

The home position for all the servos is set to 90° and the joints are moved relative to the home position. The robot is placed on the ground and all the servos are sent to the home position at the start of each gait test. The robot is then allowed to run for the same amount of timesteps as in the simulation until it stops automatically. Our robot is shown in Fig. 4.

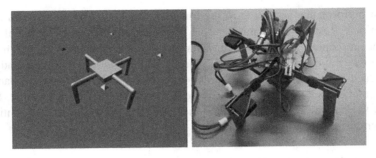

Fig. 4. Quadrupedal robot in the simulation (Left). Hardware quadrupedal robot (Right).

The neural network requires more processing power than the Arduino could provide, therefore, the neural network is run on the computer and the joint positions are then sent to the robot.

3.6   Characterization of the Transferred Gaits

The gaits transferred to the physical robot are visually analyzed to see if they actually match the gaits that were evolved through simulations. A 6-feet-tall and 4-feet-wide cuboid frame is used to analyze the evolved gaits. Our robot is placed inside a frame where an overhead camera is used to monitor its travelling distance. A marker of known length is placed within the cuboid frame and the pixels covered by the marker are used to calculate the robot's travelling distance. We use the distance values measured in simulation and real experiments to compare the differences in fitness level and speed of the robot. A further discussion on this is provided in our forthcoming section.

4   Results and Discussions

In Fig. 5, we first plot the fitness graph of our robot generated through simulations. Clearly, the controller evolves from a low fitness value to a high value. It can also be observed that the fitness of the robot does not change for a few generations like between 50th, 90th, 125th, and 160th generations, because GA is unable to find an offspring that performs better than its parent, hence the parent remains the fittest individual. However, the GA finds a new and better performing solution by continuously mutating the off-springs and the fitness is increased.

In Fig. 6, we provide the values generated by the joint movements of the physical and the simulated robots, respectively. Our results depict a perfect match between the values generated in two different environments showing the efficiency of the proposed algorithm.

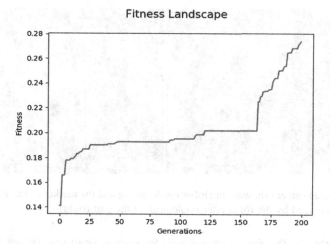

Fig. 5. The fitness landscape over 200 generations.

We choose the best gait from the diagonal joint reverse symmetry configuration and it is implemented on the hardware robot. In Fig. 7, we try to show the distance covered by our robot (on the right) compared to robot's initial position (on the left) using the images captured by the overhead camera. The red tape in the figure is of a known length which is 12.3 cm. The length of the in the picture, in pixels, is directly proportional to the real length of the tape. This direct relationship allows us to calculate the real distance travelled by the robot by analyzing the trajectory of the robot, shown in Fig. 7 (right), and calculating the distance travelled by the robot in pixels.

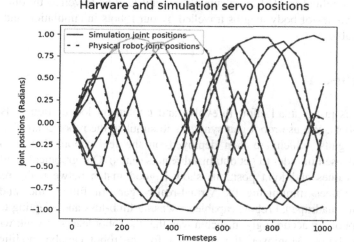

Fig. 6. Joint positions of the robot in simulation and reality over run time.

Fig. 7. Overhead camera showing the robot inside the rig and the marker of known length (left). The distance covered by the robot after implementing the gait (right).

Table 2. The distances travelled by the robot in simulation and reality.

	Simulation	Reality
Body length	60 cm	36.40 cm
Distance travelled	63 cm	46.42 cm
Body lengths travelled	1.05	0.997

Interestingly, the distances covered by the physical and simulated robots are 36.42 cm and 63 cm, respectively. It may seem like there is a lot of difference between the travelled distances, however, robot in physical and simulated environments have different dimensions, therefore, any measurement taken in the SI units will not provide a useful comparison at all. According to [15], the distance travelled by a robot in terms of body lengths is a reliable criterion since it provides results that are comparable between the simulation and the reality. Thus, in our work, we have used the same method highlighted in [15] to calculate the body lengths travelled by our robot. The calculated values of body lengths travelled by our robots in simulation and reality are given in Table 2.

5   Conclusion

Our work is just a small effort to evolve and implement locomotion gaits for quadrupedal robots. We use robot gait synthesis to simulate the robot controller producing acceptable gaits, which are then deployed on the real robot. Genetic algorithmic approach is used in order to get optimized results (gaits). Our graphical results in terms of fitness values and joint positions show a good match between the real and the simulated values minimizing the virtual-reality gap. In future, the study will be extended to quadrupedal robots capable of sensing limb-loss and adapting to their new body morphology accordingly in such a way that the robot learns to walk with reduced number of limbs. Moreover, the controller for the robot can be modified and the optimization method (in particular) needs to be replaced with a more efficient one (ex. gradient descent) ensuring that the robot learns the behavior a user wants it to learn.

References

1. Pfeifer, R., Bongard, J.C.: How the Body Shapes the Way We Think: A New View of Intelligence. MIT Press (2006)
2. Bongard, J.C.: Evolutionary robotics, evolutionary robotics. Commun. ACM **56**, 74–83 (2013)
3. Pongas, D., Mistry, M., Schaal, S.: A robust quadruped walking gait for traversing rough terrain. In: Proceedings - IEEE International Conference on Robotics and Automation, pp. 1474–1479. IEEE, Roma (2007). https://doi.org/10.1109/ROBOT.2007.363192
4. Hauert, S., Zufferey, J.C., Floreano, D.: Reverse-engineering of artificially evolved controllers for swarms of robots. In: 2009 Congress on Evolutionary Computation CEC 2009, pp. 55–61 (2009). https://doi.org/10.1109/CEC.2009.4982930
5. Juang, C.F., Yeh, Y.T.: Multiobjective evolution of biped robot gaits using advanced continuous ant-colony optimized recurrent neural networks. IEEE Trans. Cybern. 1–13 (2017). https://doi.org/10.1109/TCYB.2017.2718037
6. Masood, J., Samad, A., Abbas, Z., Khan, L.: Evolution of locomotion controllers for snake robots. In: 2016 2nd International Conference on Robotics and Artificial Intelligence, ICRAI 2016, pp. 164–169 (2016). https://doi.org/10.1109/ICRAI.2016.7791247
7. Reil, T., Husbands, P.: Evolution of central pattern generators for bipedal walking in a real-time physics environment. IEEE Trans. Evol. Comput. **6**, 159–168 (2002). https://doi.org/10.1109/4235.996015
8. Yosinski, J., Clune, J., Hidalgo, D., Nguyen, S., Zagal, J.C., Lipson, H.: Evolving robot gaits in hardware: the HyperNEAT generative encoding vs. parameter optimization. In: Proceedings of European Conference on Artificial Life, pp. 1–8 (2011)
9. Nygaard, T.F., Torresen, J., Glette, K.: Multi-objective evolution of fast and stable gaits on a physical quadruped robotic platform. In: 2016 IEEE Symposium Series on Computational Intelligence, SSCI 2016 (2017). https://doi.org/10.1109/SSCI.2016.7850167
10. Glette, K., Klaus, G., Zagal, J., Torresen, J.: Evolution of locomotion in a simulated quadruped robot and transferral to reality. In: Proceedings of the Seventeenth International Symposium on Artificial Life and Robotics, pp. 1–4 (2012)
11. Sofge, D.A., Potter, M.A., Bugajska, M.D., Schultz, A.C.: Challenges and opportunities of evolutionary robotics. Robotics (2003)
12. Juang, C.F., Chen, Y.H., Jhan, Y.H.: Wall-following control of a hexapod robot using a data-driven fuzzy controller learned through differential evolution. IEEE Trans. Ind. Electron. **62**, 611–619 (2015). https://doi.org/10.1109/TIE.2014.2319213
13. Phillips, A., Du Plessis, M.: Towards the incorporation of proprioception in evolutionary robotics controllers. In: Proceedings - 3rd International Conference on Robotic Computing IRC 2019. 226–229 (2019). https://doi.org/10.1109/IRC.2019.00041
14. D'Ausilio, A.: Arduino: a low-cost multipurpose lab equipment. Behav. Res. Methods **44**, 305–313 (2012). https://doi.org/10.3758/s13428-011-0163-z
15. Eckert, P., Ijspeert, A.J.: Benchmarking agility for multilegged terrestrial robots. IEEE Trans. Robot. **35**, 529–535 (2019). https://doi.org/10.1109/TRO.2018.2888977

Quantum Computing and Information

Non-abelian Gauge-Invariant Cellular Automata

Pablo Arrighi[1,2], Giuseppe Di Molfetta[1,3], and Nathanaël Eon[1,4(✉)]

[1] Aix-Marseille Univ, Université de Toulon, CNRS, LIS, Marseille, France
nathanael.eon@lis-lab.fr
[2] IXXI, Lyon, France
[3] Departamento de Física Teórica and IFIC, Universidad de Valencia-CSIC,
Dr. Moliner 50, 46100 Burjassot, Spain
[4] École Centrale, Marseille, France

Abstract. Gauge-invariance is a mathematical concept that has profound implications in Physics—as it provides the justification of the fundamental interactions. It was recently adapted to the Cellular Automaton (CA) framework, in a restricted case. In this paper, this treatment is generalized to non-abelian gauge-invariance, including the notions of gauge-equivalent theories and gauge-invariants of configurations.

Keywords: Cellular automata · Gauge-invariance · Quantum information

1 Introduction

In Physics, symmetries are essential concepts used to derive the laws which model nature. Among them, gauge symmetries are central, since they provide the mathematical justification for all four fundamental interactions: the weak and strong forces (short range interactions), electromagnetism [6] and to some extent gravity (long range interactions). In Computer Science, cellular automata (CA) constitute the most established model of computation that accounts for euclidean space. Yet its origins lies in Physics, where they were first used to model hydrodynamics and multi-body dynamics, and are now commonly used to model particles or waves. The study of gauge symmetries in CA is expected to benefit both fields. In order to obtain discrete systems that can simulate physics on the one hand. In order to bring gauge theory to Computer Science, as a tool to study redundancy and fault-tolerant computation for instance, on the other hand.

A study of gauge symmetries in CA has been recently studied, by the same authors, in the particular case of abelian gauge symmetries [3]. Here, we provide a generalization to non-abelian gauge symmetries. In Physics, the generalization from abelian to non-abelian gauge theories was a non-trivial but crucial step, that enabled taking into account a wider range of phenomena.

© Springer Nature Switzerland AG 2019
C. Martín-Vide et al. (Eds.): TPNC 2019, LNCS 11934, pp. 211–221, 2019.
https://doi.org/10.1007/978-3-030-34500-6_15

The paper is organized as follows. Section 2 is a reformulation in a more general framework of the gauge-invariance in CA definitions and procedure given in [3]. It provides the context and notations used in the rest of the paper. In Sect. 3, a complete example of non-abelian gauge-invariant CA is given through the application of the *gauging procedure*. It provides an example of the route one may take in order to obtain a gauge-invariant CA, starting from one that does not implement the symmetry. Section 4 discusses the equivalence of theories and develops the notion of invariant sets. We summarize in Sect. 5 and provide related works perspectives.

2   Gauge-Invariance

Theory to be Gauged. In this paper, *theories* stands for CA. We start from a theory R, which internal state space is Σ and local rule is λ_R. We denote by $\psi_{x,t}$ the state of the cell at position x and time t. ψ_t denotes a configuration which is a function from $\mathbb{Z}$ into Σ that gives a state for each position x. As a running example, we pick possibly the simplest and most nature physics-like reversible CA (RCA): one that has particles moving left and right. More precisely, in this example $\Sigma = \{0, ..., N\}^2$, therefore, we can write $\psi_{x,t} = (\psi_{x,t}^l, \psi_{x,t}^r)$ where the exponents l and r denotes the left and right parts, each being an element of $\{0, ..., N\}$. The local rule λ_R takes the right-incoming left sub-cell (i.e. ψ_{x+1}^l) to the left, and the left-incoming right sub-cell (i.e. ψ_{x-1}^r) to the right:

$$\psi_{x,t+1} = \left(\psi_{x,t+1}^l, \psi_{x,t+1}^r\right) = \lambda_R\left(\psi_{x-1,t}^r, \psi_{x+1,t}^l\right) = \left(\psi_{x+1,t}^l, \psi_{x-1,t}^r\right) \qquad (1)$$

Such a CA is said to be expressed in the block-circuit form which is often referred as the (Margolus-)Partitioned CA in Computer Science vocabulary [8], or Lattice-gas automata in Physics [11]. Figure 1 gives an example of this dynamics for $N = 2$ (where the three colors represent the three possible states), and Fig. 2 introduces the conventions used.

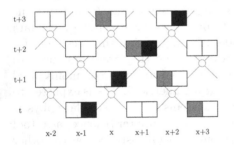

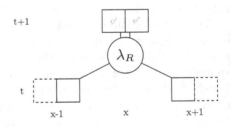

Fig. 1. A spacetime diagram of R.   **Fig. 2.** Conventions. (Color figure online)

This theory R is *to be gauged* because does not yet implement the gauge symmetry, which is a local invariance under a group of operators called *gauge transformations*. The theory R will eventually be extended into a theory T that does implement the symmetry, through a *gauging procedure*.

Gauge Transformations. The gauge symmetry is an invariance of the evolution under a *gauge transformation.* What we call a gauge transformation is based on a monoid Γ of operators acting on the internal state space Σ. A gauge transformation is the application, onto the state of each cell in a configuration, of one of the operators of Γ. More formally, for each cell x is attributed an element γ_x in Γ. Thereby specifying a gauge transformation $\bar{\gamma}$ acting over entire configurations:

$$\bar{\gamma} : \begin{array}{ccc} \Sigma^{\mathbb{Z}} & \to & \Sigma^{\mathbb{Z}} \\ c & \mapsto & \left(x \mapsto \gamma_x(c_x) \right) \end{array}$$

We denote $\bar{\Gamma} \cong \Gamma^{\mathbb{Z}}$ the set of these gauge transformations $\bar{\gamma}$.

Gauge-Invariance. A theory T is said gauge-invariant if its evolution is impervious to gauge-transformations. In other words, applying a gauge transformation $\bar{\gamma}$ followed by the evolution T, *amounts to the same* as applying the evolution R directly. What is meant by *amounts to the same* is that both outputs are the same, up to a gauge-transformation $\bar{\gamma}'$. Given that we want the evolution T to be deterministic, we impose that $\bar{\gamma}'$ be determined from $\bar{\gamma}$ by means of some theory Z. After those consideration, gauge-invariance can be defined as follows which is a reformulation from [3]:

Definition 1 (Gauge-invariance). *A theory T is gauge-invariant if and only if there exists Z a theory such that for all $\bar{\gamma} \in \bar{\Gamma}$*

$$Z(\bar{\gamma}) \circ T = T \circ \bar{\gamma} \tag{2}$$

where the symbol $\circ$ represents the composition.

The gauge-invariance is represented in Fig. 3 where γ_0, γ_1 and γ' are local gauge transformations.

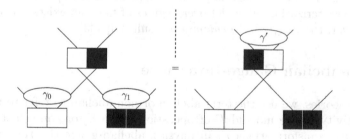

Fig. 3. Illustration of gauge-invariance.

Gauging Procedure. In order to extend the non-gauge-invariant theory R into a gauge-invariant theory T we will apply a gauging procedure, which is strongly inspired from Physics. The procedure begins by introducing new information, namely the gauge field A, at each point in spacetime, and to extend the theory

R into an A-dependant theory R_A that features gauge-invariance. We also need to decide how that gauge field changes under gauge transformations. In order to keep the notations simple, we will write $\bar{\gamma}(A)$ for the gauge transformation of the gauge field A. Even though the gauge field may not transform the same way as the initial configuration, the context shall be enough to lift any ambiguity. Let us make precise what we mean by gauge-invariance, whenever a theory depends on an external field.

Definition 2 (Inhomogeneous gauge-invariance). *A theory* $T_\bullet$ *is said to be* inhomogeneous gauge-invariant *if and only if there exists* Z *a theory such that for all* $\bar{\gamma} \in \bar{\Gamma}$,

$$Z(\bar{\gamma}) \circ T_\bullet = T_{\bar{\gamma}(\bullet)} \circ \bar{\gamma} \tag{3}$$

Typically, this condition puts a strong constraint on the way the gauge transformation must act over the gauge field, i.e. $\bar{\gamma}(A)$. An example is given in Sect. 3.

Having determined such gauge transformation, the final step of the gauging procedure is to give a theory that specifies the dynamics of the gauge field. This theory, joint together with R_A, must give a global theory T that verifies the original gauge-invariance condition (2). Again, an example is given in Sect. 3.

All-in-all, the gauging procedure can be summarized in these four steps which we will use as a basis for the rest of the paper :

1. Start with a theory to be gauged R and a set of gauge transformations $\bar{\Gamma}$.
2. Introduce the gauge field A, transform R into R_A.
3. Define $\bar{\gamma}(A)$ through the requirement that R_A verifies condition (3).
4. Give a theory A in order to define a global gauge-invariant theory T.

The first two steps are free for the user/physicist to choose according to the system to be modelled. The third step however is mostly determined by the gauge-invariance condition. Finally, the degree of freedom in the choice of the dynamics for A – i.e. the last step – may depend on the specific cases and no general characterization of the leftover degrees of freedom exists. In the abelian case however, the *gauge fixing soundness* result helps [3].

3   Non-abelian Gauge-Invariance

In gauge theories, we use the term abelian or non-abelian to refer to the (non-) commutativity of the monoid Γ of operations over Σ, or equivalently to that of the gauge-transformations $\bar{\Gamma}$. In physics, abelian gauge theories give rise to electromagnetism, while non-abelian gauge-theories (Yang-Mills theories in particular) allow for the formulation of the whole standard model—namely the electromagnetic, weak and strong interactions. Whether gravitation is a non-abelian gauge theory is open to interpretation, but it certainly has some flavour of it. By-the-way, non-abelian really means possibly-non-abelian, it still comprises the abelian subcase. In this section, we produce a complete example of a non-abelian gauge-invariant CA by applying the gauging procedure.

Back to the Running Example

Step 1. Recall that our point of departure was the theory R, whose rule λ_R given by Eq. (1) is takes two subcells into two subcells through a bijection. In order to have as simple an example as possible, we choose $N = 2$, thus $\Sigma = \{0, 1, 2\}^2$. Let us choose a monoid Γ that follows the same structure as in [3], i.e. so that the operators $\gamma \in \Gamma$ act identically on both elements of Σ (this choice is traditional in gauge theories, but not a necessity of our definitions). That is, they act by applying the same permutation on both subcells. More formally, let us denote by $S(N)$ the set of permutations over $\{0, ..., N-1\}$, we let:

$$\Gamma = \{s \otimes s \mid s \in S(N)\}.$$

Given some $\gamma = s \otimes s$, the notations $\gamma^l = \gamma^r$ will be short for s.

Step 2. This step is to introduce an external gauge field A and make R into an A-dependent rule R_A. We take the gauge field A to be defined at every half-integer space position (and every time step). This definition is physics-inspired and corresponds to the convention used in [2]. We let A take its values in $S(3)$ the set of permutations over 3 elements. We let R_A be defined by the A-dependent local rule λ_{R_A}, which is spacetime-dependent since A is spacetime-dependent:

$$(\lambda_{R_A})_{x,t} = \lambda_R \circ (A_{x-1/2,t} \otimes A_{x+1/2,t}^{-1})$$

The induced evolution that used to be described by Eq.(1) now becomes:

$$\left(\psi_{x,t+1}^l, \psi_{x,t+1}^r\right) = (\lambda_{R_A})_{x,t}\left(\psi_{x-1,t}^r, \psi_{x+1,t}^l\right) = \left(A_{x+1/2,t}^{-1}\psi_{x+1,t}^l, A_{x-1/2,t}\psi_{x-1,t}^r\right)$$

The local rule λ_{R_A} is represented in Fig. 4.

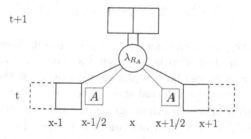

Fig. 4. Introducing the gauge field.

The way R_A depends on the gauge field and the definition of the gauge field itself is motivated through the fact that A can be made to cancel any gauge-transformation done on the input.

Step 3. The gauge transformation of the gauge field A is dictated by the condition (2). Such condition can be developed locally due to the locality of the theory and of the gauge transformation. It gives: there exists Z a theory such that for all $\bar{\gamma} \in \bar{\Gamma}$ and $x \in \mathbb{Z}$

$$Z(\bar{\gamma})_x \circ (\lambda_{R_A})_x = (\lambda_{R_{\bar{\gamma}(A)}})_x \circ (\gamma^r_{x-1} \otimes \gamma^l_{x+1}).$$

Replacing the local rule by its expression gives the following equation:

$$Z(\bar{\gamma})_x \circ \lambda_R \circ (A_{x-1/2} \otimes A^{-1}_{x+1/2})$$
$$= \lambda_R \circ (\bar{\gamma}(A)_{x-1/2} \otimes \bar{\gamma}(A)^{-1}_{x+1/2}) \circ (\gamma^r_{x-1} \otimes \gamma^l_{x+1}).$$

This equation is equivalent to the following system

$$\begin{cases} \bar{\gamma}(A)_{x-1/2} \circ \gamma^l_{x-1} = Z(\bar{\gamma})^l_x \circ A_{x-1/2} \\ \bar{\gamma}(A)^{-1}_{x+1/2} \circ \gamma^r_{x+1} = Z(\bar{\gamma})^r_x \circ A^{-1}_{x+1/2} \end{cases}$$
$$\Leftrightarrow \begin{cases} \bar{\gamma}(A)_{x-1/2} = Z(\bar{\gamma})^l_x \circ A_{x-1/2} \circ (\gamma^l_{x-1})^{-1} \\ \bar{\gamma}(A)_{x+1/2} = \gamma^r_{x+1} \circ A_{x+1/2} \circ (Z(\bar{\gamma})^r_x)^{-1} \end{cases}$$

Such a system gives an information and a constraint. First, the gauge transformation of the gauge field A is given explicitly in terms of that over ψ, which was the main objective. Second, it puts some constraints over Z. In order to satisfy both these equations for any A and $\bar{\gamma}$ given as input, the choice of Z is limited. For instance, Z cannot be a translation to the right, because that would impose for γ to be the same at every position. One solution is to choose $Z(\bar{\gamma}) = \bar{\gamma}$. Such choice, common in physics, was also taken in [2] which gives a quantum CA for one-dimensional QED (quantum electrodynamics).

In the end, the gauge-transformation of the gauge field A reads, for x an half-integer and using $\gamma^r = \gamma^l$:

$$\bar{\gamma}(A)_x = \gamma^l_{x+1/2} \circ A_x \circ (\gamma^l_{x-1/2})^{-1} \tag{4}$$

Step 4. We now have an inhomogeneous gauge-invariant theory R_A, with respect to Γ and $Z = I$. The last step is to provide a theory for the dynamics of the gauge field A, in order to yield a complete gauge-invariant theory T that evolves both ψ and A—i.e. over the internal state space $S(N) \times \Sigma \times S(N)$. The usual way to do this is to propose an inhomogeneous gauge-invariant theory S_ψ, with respect to the same Γ and Z, that acts on A but depend on ψ. Then combining R_A and S_ψ, which are both inhomogeneous gauge-invariant, will give a gauge-invariant theory T with respect to Γ and Z. Let us justify this by writing down the inhomogeneous gauge-invariance condition (3) for R_A and S_ψ: for all $\psi \in \Sigma^{\mathbb{Z}}$, $A \in S(N)$ and $\bar{\gamma} \in \bar{\Gamma}$:

$$R_{\bar{\gamma}(A)} \circ \bar{\gamma}(\psi) = Z(\bar{\gamma}) \circ R_A(\psi)$$
$$S_{\bar{\gamma}(\psi)} \circ \bar{\gamma}(A) = Z(\bar{\gamma}) \circ S_\psi(A)$$

Combining both, we obtain

$$T \circ \bar{\gamma}(\psi, A) = \left(R_{\bar{\gamma}(A)} \circ \bar{\gamma}(\psi), \ S_{\bar{\gamma}(\psi)} \circ \bar{\gamma}(A) \right)$$

$$= \left(Z(\bar{\gamma}) \circ R_A(\psi), \ Z(\bar{\gamma}) \circ S_\psi(A) \right)$$

$$= Z(\bar{\gamma}) \circ T(\psi, A)$$

which is exactly the gauge-invariance condition (2) for T.

In order to find a suitable S_ψ, one therefore has to write the inhomogeneous gauge-invariance condition (3), substituting for Z and γ by their definitions, including $\gamma(A)$ as given by (4). Several possible S_ψ may meet this condition: to the our best knowledge there is no general notion of a minimal S_ψ. However, the running example does exhibit a minimal solution which is the identity. The inhomogeneous gauge-invariance can then be verified easily: for all $x \in \mathbb{Z}$ and $\bar{\gamma} \in \bar{\Gamma}$,

$$Z(\bar{\gamma})_x \circ (\lambda_{S_\psi})_x = (\lambda_{S_{\bar{\gamma}(\psi)}})_x \circ \gamma_x \iff \gamma_x \circ I = I \circ \gamma_x.$$

Combining R_A with $S_\psi = I$, gives a gauge-invariant theory T with local rule λ_T as follows: for any spacetime position x, t,

$$\left(A_{x-1/2}, \psi_x^l, \psi_x^r, A_{x+1/2} \right)_{t+1} = \lambda_T \left(\psi_{x-1}^r, A_{x-1/2}, A_{x+1/2}, \psi_{x+1}^l \right)_t$$

$$= \left(A_{x-1/2}, A_{x+1/2}^{-1} \psi_{x+1}^l, A_{x-1/2} \psi_{x-1}^r, A_{x+1/2} \right)_t$$

where the final time index applies to every element of the list. This framework for this rule is illustrated in Fig. 5 and example is given in Fig. 6.

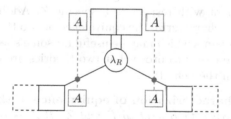

Fig. 5. A complete non-abelian gauge-invariant theory over ψ and A. Whenever a black right-moving (resp. left-moving) wire for ψ crosses a red wire for A, then A (resp. A^{-1}) gets applied upon ψ. (Color figure online)

This fully non-abelian gauge-invariant cellular automaton was built through the simplest possible choices via the gauging procedure. Notice that it is not so trivial however: the introduction of the gauge field A, motivated by the will to restore gauge-invariant, ends up truly enriching the phenomenology of the theory.

Having developed a gauge-invariant theory means having manage to introduce... a redundancy. Thus, there will be other gauge-invariant theories that are equivalent, up to that redundancy. Can we characterize those *equivalent* theories?

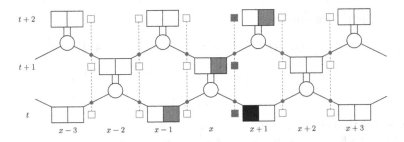

Fig. 6. The complete theory is richer than the initial theory. Here an empty circle for A represent the identity while a full circle represents the permutation of white and black colours (leaving gray untouched). At position $x + 1/2$, the input coming from $x + 1$ is toggled from black to white.

4   Equivalence and Invariant Sets

Given a set of gauge transformations $\bar{\Gamma}$, multiple theories may lead to similar dynamics with respect to $\bar{\Gamma}$:

Definition 3 (Equivalence of two theories). *Let T be a gauge-invariant theory with respect to $\bar{\Gamma}$ and Z. T is simulated by T' if and only if for all configuration c there exists $\bar{\gamma}, \bar{\gamma}' \in \bar{\Gamma}$ such that $(\bar{\gamma}' \circ T)(c) = (T' \circ \bar{\gamma})(c)$. They are equivalent if both simulate each other. We denote the equivalence as $T \equiv T'$.*

Thus $T \equiv T'$ if and only if they give rise to the same dynamics up to a gauge transformation.

T is gauge-invariant with respect to a specific Z. Adding some constraints on Z and Γ, one may characterize the equivalence of two theories using different quantifiers and constraints which may be useful for some specific problems. More specifically, it will be easier to prove that two theories are equivalent using the characterization than the definition.

Proposition 4 (Characterization of equivalence of theories). *Let T be a gauge-invariant theory with respect to $\bar{\Gamma}$ and Z. If Z is reversible and Γ is a group, then T is simulated by T' if and only if*

1. $\forall c, \exists \bar{\gamma} \in \bar{\Gamma}$ *such that* $T(c) = T' \circ \bar{\gamma}(c)$.
2. $\forall c, \forall \bar{\gamma} \in \bar{\Gamma}, \exists \bar{\gamma}' \in \bar{\Gamma}$ *such that* $\bar{\gamma}' \circ T(c) = T' \circ \bar{\gamma}(c)$.

Proof. We shall prove the equivalence through three implications.

- The fact that (3) implies (1) is immediate.
- Suppose (1), then for c a configuration, we have $\bar{\gamma}, \bar{\gamma}' \in \bar{\Gamma}$ such that $(\bar{\gamma}' \circ T)(c) = (T' \circ \bar{\gamma})(c)$. But since $\bar{\Gamma}$ is a group, it implies that $T(c) = (\bar{\gamma}'^{-1} \circ T' \circ \bar{\gamma})(c)$. And since Z is reversible, we obtain $T(c) = (T' \circ Z^{-1}(\bar{\gamma}'^{-1}) \circ \bar{\gamma})(c)$. However, $Z^{-1}(\bar{\gamma}'^{-1}) \circ \bar{\gamma}$ is an element of $\bar{\Gamma}$ therefore we have proven that (1) implies (2).

– Suppose (2), let c be a configuration and take $\bar{\gamma} \in \bar{\Gamma}$ such that $T(c) = (T' \circ \bar{\gamma})(c)$. For any $\bar{\gamma}_1 \in \bar{\Gamma}$ there exists $\bar{\gamma}_3 \in \bar{\Gamma}$ such that $\bar{\gamma} = \bar{\gamma}_3 \circ \bar{\gamma}_1$. Therefore, $T(c) = (Z(\bar{\gamma}_3) \circ T' \circ \bar{\gamma}_1)(c)$ which is equivalent to $(Z(\bar{\gamma}_3)^{-1} \circ T)(c) = (T \circ \bar{\gamma}_1)(c)$. And writing $\bar{\gamma}_2 = Z(\bar{\gamma}_3)^{-1}$ which is in $\bar{\Gamma}$, we conclude that (2) implies (3).

□

Invariant. $\bar{\Gamma}$ defines a set of transformations over the set of configurations. When one configuration can be transformed into another, the two are thought of as physically equivalent. For a gauge-invariant theory T, equivalent configurations with respect to $\bar{\Gamma}$ lead to equivalent configurations after the evolution T. Therefore, one may think that such a theory would be better formulated to act over the set of equivalence classes of configurations instead, i.e. those sets that are left invariant under $\bar{\Gamma}$. Formally, for Σ the internal state space of T, for $\psi \in \Sigma$, let $I_\psi = \{\gamma(\psi) \mid \gamma \in \Gamma\}$. If Γ is a group, which was the case in our running example, then for all ψ and ψ':

$$\exists \gamma \in \Gamma, \, \psi' = \bar{\gamma}(\psi) \iff I_\psi = I_{\psi'}.$$

Then T is indeed equivalent to a theory T' having these invariant sets at its internal state space—or rather the canonical representant elements of these.

However, for an inhomogeneous gauge-invariant theory R_A one needs to be more careful. that is this is true only if the invariant sets are built from (ψ, A) and not just ψ. Indeed, an invariant set built only over ψ and not considering A would be like disregarding the gauge transformation of A and therefore, breaking the inhomogeneous gauge-invariance.

Moreover, to be more subtle, it is not enough to consider the invariant sets for ψ and A separately. Indeed the invariant set for (ψ, A) is generally not the cartesian product of the invariant set of ψ with that of A, because the gauge-transformation acts on both ψ and A synchronously. A simple example is given Fig. 7, which works already when we restrict ourselves to $\Sigma = \{0,1\}^2$ for simplicity, i.e. back in the abelian case. It starts with both sides having the exact same ψ but two different gauge fields related by a gauge-transformation. Here the gauge-transformation applied on A is the identity everywhere except at position x, for which $\gamma^l = \gamma^r$ is the permutation of 0 and 1. This means both sub-figures have the same invariant sets for A because they are linked through a gauge-transformation, and idem for ψ. After a time step however, the invariant sets for ψ are not identical on both sides, because we cannot consider ψ and A separately when looking at the invariant sets. Again this problem does not appear when considering the invariant set for the couple (ψ, A) directly.

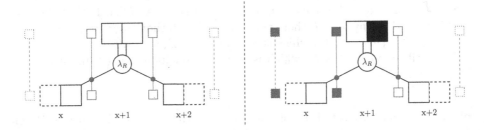

Fig. 7. Both sub-figures initially have the same invariant sets for ψ and A respectively. After a time step, this is not true for ψ: they do not share an invariant set. This figure shows that it is not enough to consider the invariant sets for ψ and A separately

5   Conclusion

Summary. In this paper, we reformulated and generalized the theory of gauge-invariance in CA [3], to cater for non-abelian symmetry groups. The gauging procedure was then made explicit and developed through an example: starting from a non-gauge-invariant theory and a set of gauge transformations, we introduced an external gauge field upon which the theory was made dependent, and extended the gauge transformation to this field, so as to obtain gauge-invariance. Finally the gauge field was 'internalized' by providing a theory for its dynamics, yielding a complete gauge-invariant theory. Now, gauge-invariant theories are redundant almost by definition, and thus several theories may be equivalent to one another up to this redundancy. Equivalence between theories was formalized and characterized. Configuration that are related by a gauge-transformations were gathered into invariant sets, called invariant sets, and CA over these invariant sets were discussed.

Perspectives and Related Works. Since gauge-invariance comes from Physics, the first extension of this model would be a non-abelian gauge-invariant Quantum CA (QCA). An abelian gauge-invariant QCA was already provided in [2], whereas a non-abelian gauge-invariance has been studied in the one-particle sector of QCA, namely quantum walks [1]: this extension is rather promising.

In the field of quantum computation, gauge-invariance is already mentioned for quantum error correction codes [4,5] which can be understood through the redundancy inherent to gauge-invariant theories. The study of gauge-invariance in CA ought to be related, therefore, to questions of error correction for spatially-distributed computation models [9,10].

Finally, gauge-invariance brings another symmetry to field CA, which may be interesting to study for itself, e.g. along the same methods used for color-blind CA [7], where all cells get transformed by the same group element.

References

1. Arnault, P., Di Molfetta, G., Brachet, M., Debbasch, F.: Quantum walks and non-abelian discrete gauge theory. Phys. Rev. A **94**(1), 012335 (2016)
2. Arrighi, P., Bény, C., Farrelly, T.: A quantum cellular automaton for one-dimensional QED. arXiv preprint arXiv:1903.07007 (2019)
3. Arrighi, P., Di Molfetta, G., Eon, N.: A gauge-invariant reversible cellular automaton. In: Baetens, J.M., Kutrib, M. (eds.) AUTOMATA 2018. LNCS, vol. 10875, pp. 1–12. Springer, Cham (2018). https://doi.org/10.1007/978-3-319-92675-9_1
4. Kitaev, A.Y.: Fault-tolerant quantum computation by anyons. Ann. Phys. **303**(1), 2–30 (2003)
5. Nayak, C., Simon, S.H., Stern, A., Freedman, M., Sarma, S.D.: Non-abelian anyons and topological quantum computation. Rev. Mod. Phys. **80**(3), 1083 (2008)
6. Quigg, C.: Gauge Theories of the Strong, Weak, and Electromagnetic Interactions. Princeton University Press, Princeton (2013)
7. Salo, V., Törmä, I.: Color blind cellular automata. In: Kari, J., Kutrib, M., Malcher, A. (eds.) AUTOMATA 2013. LNCS, vol. 8155, pp. 139–154. Springer, Heidelberg (2013). https://doi.org/10.1007/978-3-642-40867-0_10
8. Toffoli, T., Margolus, N.: Cellular Automata Machine - A new Environment for Modelling. MIT Press, Cambridge (1987)
9. Toom, A.: Cellular automata with errors: problems for students of probability. In: Topics in Contemporary Probability and Its Applications, pp. 117–157 (1995)
10. Toom, A., Vasilyev, N., Stavskaya, O., Mityushin, L., Kurdyumov, G., Pirogov, S.: Discrete local Markov systems. Stochastic cellular systems: ergodicity, memory, morphogenesis. In: Dobrushin, R., Kryukov, V., Toom, A. (eds.) Nonlinear Science: Theory and Applications (1990)
11. Wolf-Gladrow, D.A.: Lattice-Gas Cellular Automata and Lattice Boltzmann Models: An Introduction. Springer, Heidelberg (2004)

On Post-processing the Results of Quantum Optimizers

Ajinkya Borle[(✉)][iD] and Josh McCarter[iD]

CSEE Department, University of Maryland Baltimore County,
Baltimore, MD 21250, USA
{aborle1,jmccar1}@umbc.edu

Abstract. The use of quantum computing for applications involving optimization has been regarded as one of the areas it may prove to be advantageous (against classical computation). To further improve the solutions, post-processing techniques are often used on the results of quantum optimization. One such recent approach is the Multi Qubit Correction (MQC) algorithm by Dorband. In this paper, we will discuss and analyze the strengths and weaknesses of this technique. Based on our discussion, we perform an experiment on (i) how pairing heuristics on the input of MQC can affect the results of a quantum optimizer and (ii) a comparison between MQC and the built-in optimization method that D-wave Systems offers. Among our results, we are able to show that the built-in post-processing rarely beats MQC in our tests. We hope that by using the ideas and insights presented in this paper, researchers and developers will be able to make a more informed decision on what kind of post-processing methods to use for their quantum optimization needs.

Keywords: Quantum optimization · Quantum annealing ·
Approximation · Evolutionary algorithm · D-wave · QAOA

1 Introduction

We are entering the era of Noisy Intermediate Scale Quantum (NISQ) devices [23], as of the time of writing this paper. But these devices may not be fault-tolerant to run the traditional quantum algorithms (like Shor's or Grover's Algorithm [9,24]) for doing computation on a useful scale. However, applications such as quantum chemistry [22], sampling [2] and optimization [5,18] among others, are the first to make use of such devices.

It is important to understand that when we talk about NISQ devices, we are also considering quantum annealers such as the D-wave 2000Q to be in that category. This is because, as Preskill points out in his work [23], the quantum annealer is a noisy implementation of adiabatic quantum computing. While there is still controversy about the lack of conclusive evidence of a quantum speedup, research has highlighted areas of promise [2,10,20,21].

For the scope of this work, our domain of interest is quantum optimization. In particular, it is the post-processing that is applied on the results returned by

© Springer Nature Switzerland AG 2019
C. Martín-Vide et al. (Eds.): TPNC 2019, LNCS 11934, pp. 222–233, 2019.
https://doi.org/10.1007/978-3-030-34500-6_16

quantum optimizers. The basic hypothesis is that [4], even if quantum devices cannot reach the global minimum for a hard problem, it can still reach the neighborhood of such a solution. Thus, post-processing the output of quantum solvers (irrespective of the type) can be helpful to find an improved solution at the very least, if not the best one.

Our aim in this paper is to study the Multi Qubit Correction (MQC) [4] and other relevant techniques. Then based on our study, we perform some experiments on it. Section 2 covers the required background information. Section 3 deals with the review of MQC and some of the related post-processing techniques. In Sect. 4, we discuss and theoretically analyze MQC in a more in-depth manner compared to the original work. Based on what we learn in Sect. 4, we perform experiments in Sect. 5 on how the order of inputs given to MQC can affect the final result of the optimization. Finally, we end with concluding remarks in Sect. 6. We would like to mention that a more detailed version of this paper exists on the Arxiv portal (arXiv:1905.13107).

The techniques discussed and proposed in this paper will focus around results from the D-wave quantum annealer. However, they are not limited to the D-wave and can be applied on results of Quantum Approximate Optimization Algorithm (QAOA) [5] and other optimizers.

2   Background

The Ising Model: The Ising Model is a mathematical model originally used in statistical mechanics for ferromagnetism [7]. However, it has applicability beyond statistical mechanics, especially for modeling NP-Hard problems. Quantum Annealers [13] and gate-based optimization approaches like QAOA [5] usually use the Ising Model to encode problems. The two dimensional Ising model, on which the D-wave 2000Q is based, has the following objective function:

$$F(h, J) = \sum_a h_a \sigma_a + \sum_{a<b} J_{ab} \sigma_a \sigma_b \qquad (1)$$

where σ_a is a binary variable which can take either -1 or $+1$, h_a and J_{ab} [3] are the coefficients for the linear and quadratic terms respectively. The σ_a's binary variables are mapped to qubits in a quantum computer. The quantum optimizer's job is to return the set of values for σ_as that would correspond to the smallest value of $F(h, J)$ (or the largest value for QAOA).

Quantum Annealing: The Quantum Annealing process uses quantum mechanics to search the energy landscape of the Ising model to find the ground state configuration of σ_a variables from Eq. (1). The σ_a variables are called as qubits spins in quantum annealing, essentially being quantum bits.

The process begins with the qubits in equal quantum superposition: which means that at this stage, all the potential qubit configurations have an equal probability of being measured. It then attempts to find the lowest energy configuration of the objective function $F(h, J)$ by varying the tunneling field strength (and gradually reducing it to 0), generating the stochastic distribution approximate to $e^{-\beta F(h,J)}$ for a finite β (An ideal annealer would generate $e^{-\beta F(h,J)}$ exactly in $\lim_{\beta \to \infty}$), where β is the inverse temperature parameter [25]. It is not yet clear if the D-wave quantum annealer adheres to the adiabatic principle completely (mostly due to technical constraints and noise). A more detailed description [6] can be found in the book by Tanaka et al. [25].

For our purposes however, we are interested mainly in the results that the quantum annealer provides us. From an accuracy perspective, a quantum annealer is essentially trying to take samples of a Boltzmann distribution (for a finite β) whose energy is the Ising objective function [2]

$$P(\sigma)_\beta \approx \frac{1}{Z_\beta} e^{-\beta F(h,J)} \tag{2}$$

$$\text{where } Z_\beta = exp\Big(-\beta\Big(\sum_{\{\sigma_a\}} \Big[\sum_a h_a \sigma_a + \sum_{a<b} J_{ab}\sigma_a\sigma_b\Big]\Big)\Big) \tag{3}$$

Equation (3), known as the partition function, is the exponentiation of $-\beta$ times the summation of the energies of all possible qubit configurations for the given set of qubits. Eq. (2) tells us that the qubit configuration of the global minimum would have the highest probability to be sampled. Because the quantum annealer is a probabilistic machine, we run it multiple times to get a set of solutions. The run (a configuration of values for the variables in the problems) with the lowest energy is taken as the final result. Alternatively, these runs can be fed into a post-processing method in the hopes of getting a better result.

3   Post-processing Techniques: A Review

3.1   Built-In Optimization Post-Processing

The D-wave developer guide offers an optimization post-processing technique [1] that is based on heuristics to decompose the problem graphs [17] (either the native hardware graph or a logical graph) into several low treewidth graphs. Then each of these subgraphs are solved locally based on belief propagation on junction trees [12] in the hopes of getting a better solution.

It is also important to mention that the D-wave API offers a sampling post-processing technique [1] to create an approximate Boltzmann distribution for a user defined inverse temperature parameter β. However, since the focus of this work is enhancing quantum optimization, we are not going into the details of such a technique.

3.2   Multi Qubit Correction (MQC)

In 2018, the Multi Qubit Correction (MQC) technique by Dorband [4] was proposed as a simple,fast and effective technique to improve upon the results of an Ising problem optimizer (focused on, but not limited to the D-wave quantum

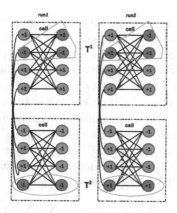

Fig. 1. Example of Tunnels across two runs. We can see tunnels T^1 and T^2 formed in the above configurations for the corresponding qubit values that don't agree (in red). For the problem graph in the example, we take two cells from the chimera graph arranged vertically. (Color figure online)

Algorithm 1. Multi Qubit Correction (MQC)

1: **procedure** MAIN(R, G) ▷ R is the set of results, G is the graph
2:     **while** $|R| \neq 1$ **do**
3:         $R' \leftarrow \{\emptyset\}$, Pair runs from R in put in set P
4:         **for** each run pair (r, s) in P **do**
5:             $R' \leftarrow R' \cup$ MQC(r, s, G)
6:         $R \leftarrow R'$
7:     **return** R
8: **procedure** MQC$(run1, run2, G)$
9:     Initialize $ans\_run \leftarrow \{\emptyset\}$
10:    Create an index set S for qubits that have the same value across $run1$ and $run2$
11:    Create an index set D for qubits that disagree in value across $run1$ and $run2$
12:    $ans\_run \leftarrow ans\_run \cup \{r_i : r_i \in run1 \vee r_i \in run2, i \in S\}$
13:    Find connected components in D to create subsets $T^1, T^2 ... T^k$
14:    $i \leftarrow 1$
15:    **while** $i \leq k$ **do**
16:        Compare energy contribution of T^i w.r.t run1 and run2 by Eqn 4
17:        Select configuration of T^i that has lower energy and add in ans_run
18:        $i \leftarrow i + 1$
19:    **return** ans_run

---

annealers). This work bears some similarities to the work done by Houdayer in 2002 [11]. The difference is that MQC is designed to work with the results of another optimizer and doesn't depend on temperature parameters whereas Houdayer's technique is designed as a full fledged optimization technique that depends on temperature parameters. Also, the MQC can be seen as a greedy descent technique [19] while Houdayer's work is a Monte Carlo algorithm.

The technique works by pairing runs $run1$ and $run2$. It then makes a set of indices of qubits D that have different values across the two runs and a set S for those that have the same values. Then within the set D, we find all T^i subsets of qubits (also known as tunnels) that are transitively connected to each other, i.e within a given tunnel any two qubits are connected by paths and which is not connected to any qubit in the other tunnels. In other words, $D = \{T^1, T^2, ...T^k\}$ where k is the total number of connected components. Figure 1 shows an example of tunnels being formed for a pair of runs. In other words, we find all the connected components in D. No qubit from a subset T^i is connected to a qubit in T^j ($i \neq j$). Once that is done, we look at the relative energy each T^i contributes to the global energy. This is done by

$$I_{run1}^i(h, J) = \sum_{a \in T^i} h_a \sigma_a^{(run1)} + \sum_{a \in T^i} \sum_{b \in S} J_{ab} \sigma_a^{(run1)} \sigma_b \tag{4}$$

Eq. (4) is the energy contribution by the tunnel T^i for the configuration of $run1$. A Similar equation can be created for the energy contribution of $run2$ for the same tunnel. We then select the configuration (from the two paired runs) that contributes the lowest of the two. This is done for each tunnel.

The N runs obtained from the quantum optimizer are paired for applying MQC. The result of step above are $N/2$ new 'runs' that go through the same procedure. In this manner, N runs are reduced down to 1 run.

3.3   Other Post-processing Techniques

Sample Persistence: In 2016, Karimi and Rosenberg proposed a technique to improve the results received from a quantum annealer [14]. It involves fixing the qubits whose values stay the same across the various runs (within a threshold) when retrieved from the quantum annealer, and then run a subset of the original problem (for qubits that are not fixed). This would require us to modify the subset of the problem.

The idea behind this approach is the conjecture that it is easier to solve a smaller subset of the problem with a greater chance of success than it is to solve the complete problem in one go. It also assumes that the qubits that show the same configuration across multiple runs are more likely to be the correct values for the global minimum solution and thus, they are fixed. More details about their work can be found in their papers [14,15].

Ochoa et al.'s Technique: Recently, we came to know of the work done by Ochoa et al. [19] for improving the sampling done by a quantum annealer. The aim of this approach is to arrive at lower energy samples (or runs) (compared to the set of samples/runs that it begins with) during its polynomial time sampling procedure. In contrast, the MQC procedure follows a greedy descent type of approach. A comparison between these two would be an interesting future work.

4 Analysis and Discussion of MQC

4.1 On the Time Complexity of MQC

Although it is not guaranteed that MQC would reach the global minimum, it is still important to consider the amount of time the entire post-processing would require. In the work by Dorband [4], it was stated that N runs can be aggregated to 1 run in $O(\text{ceil}(\log N))$ aggregation steps. While this is true, its not the complete time complexity, for which we must analyze the computation within each run.

Let q be the total number of qubits in the problem. Let D_{max} be the largest set of differing qubits that would be encountered when the N runs are being aggregated into 1 run. Each pair would require

1. A linear search to see whether the qubits match or differ: q or $|V|$, since V is the set of all the vertices in our graph (this can either be the logical problem graph or the hardware graph like the chimera),
2. A connected component analysis using DFS to find the transitive connectivity: $O(|V_{Dmax}| + |E_{Dmax}|)$. We can simplify this to $O(|V| + |E|)$ since they are bounded by the total number of vertices and edges.
3. A check of each tunnel T^i for the relative energy it contributes: $O(|V_{T^i}| + |E_{T^i}^{out}|)$ (energy associated with Eq. (4)) $E_{T^i}^{out}$ is the edge set that connects qubits in T^i with qubits in the S set. We do this for k tunnels. This too simplifies to $O(|V| + |E|)$.

Thus each step takes about $O(|V| + |E|)$ operations. The cost per pair is $\sim O(|V| + |E|)$. The total number of pairs to process go down by half in each step: $N/2 + N/4 + N/8... + 1$, In big O notation, $O(N/2 + N/4 + N/8... + 1) \sim O(N)$. Thus, the total cost of reducing N runs down to 1 run using MQC is

$$\text{Total Cost} \sim O((|V| + |E|)N) \tag{5}$$

For a sparse graph like the D-wave's Chimera, the complexity will simplify to $O(|V|N)$. However, as the graph approaches full connectivity (i.e. $|E| \rightarrow \binom{|V|}{2}$), the complexity will go up to $O(|V|^2 N)$. But it should be noted that MQC will have a harder time with denser graphs and become totally ineffective when the graphs become fully connected (explained in the next section).

4.2 MQC Is Ineffective for Fully Connected Graphs

The MQC technique relies upon two conditions for it to be effective:
Condition 1: *At least two tunnels need to be formed for a given pair of runs, run1 and run2*
Condition 2: *The configuration of qubits that contribute the lowest energy for the tunnels shouldn't be all from run1 or run2 exclusively.*

Violating either of these conditions would lead to the complete selection of either run1 or run2 (i.e. it will not allow for the creation of a third 'new' run).

Theorem 1. *If the graph of the Ising Problem in question is fully connected. Then the MQC algorithm will not be able to optimize on the set of runs R it receives from the Ising solver.*

Proof. A fully connected graph will have every qubit (or vertex) be connected with every other qubit in the graph. Thus even when we have a set of qubits D that differ across $run1$ and $run2$, we won't be able to find multiple tunnels since there will be a single connected component in the subgraph. This violates Condition 1, a necessary condition for MQC to produce 'unique' runs with lower energies than its best input run.

4.3   The Result of MQC Can Depend on How the Runs Are Paired

In the general case of the Ising problem, the way runs are paired together can affect the final result of the MQC algorithm. In other words, the result of MQC is not independent of the initial pair configuration of the runs retrieve from the Ising solver.

Given a set of tunnels $T = \{T^1_{(1,2)}, T^2_{(1,2)}...T^k_{(1,2)}\}$ for two runs r_1 and r_2, it is important for us to understand that when we optimize for each tunnel (by selecting which energy is lower amongs r_1 and r_2 for that tunnel), we are essentially doing local optimization.

Argument: *In the general case, MQC can produce a different final result if the initial pairing is done differently, for a given set of runs R in the general case Ising problem.*

MQC can be compared to a greedy-descent technique [19], because it decides between two (mirror opposite configurations) for each tunnel that gets formed. The configuration that gets chosen is the one that contributes to a lower global energy (i.e the process takes the qubits outside the tunnel, which connect to it, into consideration). The same input runs in the set R paired differently may cause different tunnels to get formed, thus potentially yielding a different final result. Even if the same tunnels were formed as in a previous pairing arrangement, the algorithm may make a different decision based on which tunnels appeared first (as N runs are being reduced to 1).

It is important to note that this argument is solely based upon the working of the MQC technique. It does not take into consideration what optimizer is attached to it. There might still exist proofs for the pairing order of the input not affecting the result, when it comes to specific optimizers.

4.4   Discussion

MQC Relies on a lot of Unique Samples to Be Effective: Because the core of MQC essentially requires choosing between two configurations that are mirror opposites for each tunnel, it is safe to say that we miss out on a more nuanced approach for optimizing these tunnels. Thus, because of the simplicity of the technique and the fact that solutions don't get worse as they are processed

[4], more sampled runs would mean more opportunities for improvements of the result.

Sample Persistence and MQC: Both approaches work on two common principles: (i)Fixed variables/qubits based on which qubits have the same values across runs and (ii) the qubits that have differing values across runs form 'tunnels', that need to be optimized. The difference arises in how they treat the set of runs received from the quantum optimizer, and how they treat the tunnels. Where MQC is a purely classical technique, the Sample Persistence method believes in using the quantum annealer multiple times, in order to resolve the tunnels.

Thus, in theory one can expect a better solution in the case of Sample Persistence, since it does more than just compare between two configurations of a set of qubits. Maybe its even possible that it is more effective than MQC for a smaller number of samples. However, Sample Persistence is a highly parameterized technique [14], this brings about a different set of problems as different parameters need to be tested out in order for the technique to be effective. A thorough empirical comparison between MQC and Sample Persistence would be beneficial for us to assess which of these techniques is better. Unfortunately, this falls outside the scope of this paper but we would like to suggest it as a future work.

Even if Sample Persistence turns out to be more effective than MQC, a case can still be made for MQC because it is a polynomial time algorithm that requires classical resources. Sample Persistence requires additional calls to be made to the quantum optimizer. Thus, in the case where cost of classical resources is cheaper than the cost of accessing quantum resources (in terms of monetary value), it may be economical to use MQC over Sample persistence.

5   Experiment

Based on the analysis and discussion in the previous section, we want to empirically observe how pairing schemes might affect MQC's final result. By using the information of Sect. 4.3, we can choose to consciously pair the runs in a particular manner. For the purposes of our experiment, we will use two heuristics to pair the input runs:

1. On the basis of similar energy (Rank Ordering)
2. On the basis of difference in qubit values (Maximum Difference)

The inspiration for the first heuristic is the evolutionary computational approach [8], where the fitness of the individuals (or runs) inside the population (or the set of runs) is evaluated and the best-fit individuals are selected for reproduction (or form an input for MQC in our case).

The logic behind the second heuristic is based on the property of MQC that the output cannot be worse than both runs in the input pair. Hence, we pair runs in a way that are the most different from each other, based on the values of qubits. In this way, we hope to extract useful tunnels that may help improve the results of MQC. Another objective of this experiment is to compare MQC with the built-in post-processing technique that the D-wave API offers. This has not been done in any of the related works till date.

5.1 Experiment Setup

For this experiment, we create a set of 50 different problems based on the Ising objective function for the on-chip graph of a D-wave 2000Q machine. We used the OCEAN SDK with Python 2.7 for this task. Each one of our 50 problems utilizes all the 2038 available qubits of our D-wave solver: DW_2000Q_2_1. The coefficients are created by random uniform sampling (seeded to 316) in the range of $[-2, 2]$ for h coefficients and $[-1, 1]$ for Js. It should be noted that random chimera graph problems like these may not be considered as problems against which quantum speedup could be achieved [16]. However, these experiments are about studying the behavior of MQC and its variants on the results of quantum annealing.

The above problems are annealed in three modes: (a) without any post-processing, (b) sampling post-processing mode and (c) optimization post-processing mode. Although it may seem counter intuitive to use the sampling post-processing (which aims at a finite temperature) for a task that is optimization oriented (which aims at zero temperature), we get a more diverse range of solutions in terms of configuration and energy. This helps us see how the various versions of MQC perform on a set of runs that are not extremely similar to each other.

The results from (a) and (b) are then run using standard MQC, MQC with heuristic 1 (Rank Ordering) and MQC with heuristic 2 (Maximum Difference).

Each of the above 3 annealing operations is done for obtaining results for 1000 and 2000 runs of the machine with an anneal time of $20\,\mu s$/run.

5.2 Results and Discussion

Each value in the tables above is the number of instances or problems for which an energy comparison holds true (as indicated by its respective column).

In our results, there were no problem instances where the raw energies of the D-wave's results were better than the standard MQC's. During our tests, as Table 2 indicates, there were a total of only 6 instances where the (standard)

Table 1. Comparison between MQC done for raw and sampling (smpl) results

Runs	mqc on raw vs mqc on smpl		
	raw = smpl	raw < smpl	raw > smpl
1000	31	18	1
2000	40	8	2

Table 2. Comparison between MQC and built in optimization post-processing

Runs	Mode	mqc vs pp (built-in opt. pp)		
		mqc = pp	mqc < pp	mqc > pp
1000	raw	4	46	0
1000	sampling	5	42	3
2000	raw	9	41	0
2000	sampling	9	38	3

Table 3. Comparison between standard MQC and MQC with pairing heuristics

Runs	Mode	mqc vs rnk (Rank Order MQC)			mqc vs mdf-mqc (Max. Diff MQC)		
		mqc = rnk	mqc < rnk	mqc > rnk	mqc = mdf	mqc < mdf	mqc > mdf
1000	raw	48	1	1	48	1	1
1000	sampling	34	5	11	27	18	5
2000	raw	50	0	0	47	3	0
2000	sampling	41	5	4	34	13	3

MQC had worse energy than the built-in optimization post-processing. All of these 6 instances were when the sampling mode was used to generate the runs. While in the raw mode, there was no instance where a better solution was derived from built-in post processing over MQC. However, the amount of instances for which MQC has an advantage over the built-in technique drops as we move from 1000 to 2000 runs. This indicates that MQC is more effective when used for fewer runs, though further testing is required.

Table 1 shows the comparison between MQC done on raw runs and those obtained from the sampling mode. For the most part, the final results of MQC done on raw inputs is equivalent to the results of MQC done on the sampling mode. This number grows as we move from 1000 to 2000 runs. There are a very few cases where MQC done on the sampling mode got a better energy, which is good since operating MQC on the raw results would save computation time as well.

From our results in Table 3, we can see that neither of the two heuristics are conclusively better than standard MQC for general use. However, the experiment empirically shows that pairing order of the input can have an effect on the output of MQC. This would also indicate that there exists a pairing order that minimizes the end result the most, and it is not evident that the standard MQC is the best way to do so. The results from the sampling mode are more affected by permutation of inputs than the raw results of the D-wave. This means that the raw results of the D-wave are (a) robust against pairing order and (b) very close to each other. This is a good indication of the quality of solutions that D-wave provides. It will be interesting to see the behavior of MQC when it is used with optimizers other than the D-wave. The results with the sampling mode indicate that MQC would be more sensitive to the pairing order when it receives dissimilar outputs (in this case, approximating a Boltzmann distribution). However, this sensitivity to pairing order seems to diminish as the number of runs are increased. Further testing is recommended.

6   Concluding Remarks

In this paper, we theoretically analyzed and discussed the strengths and weaknesses of the Multi Qubit Correction (MQC) technique by Dorband. It was followed by an experiment where we show how the pairing order of the input could effect the final result of the MQC process. We also show that in most instances of our tests, MQC performs better or at par compared to D-wave's built-in post-processing technique for optimization.

Acknowledgments. We would like to thank John Dorband, Milton Halem and Samuel Lomonaco, Helmut Katzgraber and Nicholas Chancellor for their feedback. A special thanks to D-wave Systems for providing us access to their machines.

References

1. The d-wave post-processing documentation. https://docs.dwavesys.com/docs/latest
2. Adachi, S.H., Henderson, M.P.: Application of quantum annealing to training of deep neural networks. arXiv preprint arXiv:1510.06356 (2015)
3. Dorband, J.E.: Stochastic characteristics of qubits and qubit chains on the D-wave 2X. arXiv preprint arXiv:1606.05550 (2016)
4. Dorband, J.E.: A method of finding a lower energy solution to a qubo/ising objective function. arXiv preprint arXiv:1801.04849 (2018)
5. Farhi, E., Goldstone, J., Gutmann, S.: A quantum approximate optimization algorithm. arXiv preprint arXiv:1411.4028 (2014)
6. Farhi, E., Goldstone, J., Gutmann, S., Sipser, M.: Quantum computation by adiabatic evolution. arXiv preprint quant-ph/0001106 (2000)
7. Gallavotti, G.: Statistical Mechanics: A Short Treatise. Springer, Heidelberg (2013)
8. Greenwood, G.W.: Finding solutions to NP problems: philosophical differences between quantum and evolutionary search algorithms. In: Proceedings of the 2001 Congress on Evolutionary Computation, vol. 2, pp. 815–822. IEEE (2001)
9. Grover, L.K.: Quantum mechanics helps in searching for a needle in a haystack. Phys. Rev. Lett. **79**(2), 325 (1997)
10. Harris, R., et al.: Phase transitions in a programmable quantum spin glass simulator. Science **361**(6398), 162–165 (2018)
11. Houdayer, J.: A cluster Monte Carlo algorithm for 2-dimensional spin glasses. Eur. Phys. J. B-Condens. Matter Complex Syst. **22**(4), 479–484 (2001)
12. Jensen, F.V.: Bayesian updating in causal probabilistic networks by local computations. An introduction to Bayesian networks (1996)
13. Kadowaki, T., Nishimori, H.: Quantum annealing in the transverse ising model. Phys. Rev. E **58**(5), 5355 (1998)
14. Karimi, H., Rosenberg, G.: Boosting quantum annealer performance via sample persistence. Quantum Inf. Process. **16**(7), 166 (2017)

15. Karimi, H., Rosenberg, G., Katzgraber, H.G.: Effective optimization using sample persistence: a case study on quantum annealers and various monte carlo optimization methods. Phys. Rev. E **96**(4), 043312 (2017)
16. Katzgraber, H.G., Hamze, F., Andrist, R.S.: Glassy chimeras could be blind to quantum speedup: designing better benchmarks for quantum annealing machines. Phys. Rev. X **4**(2), 021008 (2014)
17. Markowitz, H.M.: The elimination form of the inverse and its application to linear programming. Manag. Sci. **3**(3), 255–269 (1957)
18. Neukart, F., Compostella, G., Seidel, C., von Dollen, D., Yarkoni, S., Parney, B.: Traffic flow optimization using a quantum annealer. Front. ICT **4**, 29 (2017)
19. Ochoa, A.J., Jacob, D.C., Mandrà, S., Katzgraber, H.G.: Feeding the multitude: a polynomial-time algorithm to improve sampling. Phys. Rev. E **99**(4), 043306 (2019)
20. O'Malley, D.: An approach to quantum-computational hydrologic inverse analysis. Sci. Rep. **8**(1), 6919 (2018)
21. O'Malley, D., Vesselinov, V.V., Alexandrov, B.S., Alexandrov, L.B.: Nonnegative/binary matrix factorization with a d-wave quantum annealer. PLoS One **13**(12), e0206653 (2018)
22. Peruzzo, A., et al.: A variational eigenvalue solver on a photonic quantum processor. Nat. Commun. **5**, 4213 (2014)
23. Preskill, J.: Quantum computing in the NISQ era and beyond. arXiv preprint arXiv:1801.00862 (2018)
24. Shor, P.W.: Algorithms for quantum computation: discrete logarithms and factoring. In: 1994 Proceedings of 35th Annual Symposium on Foundations of Computer Science, pp. 124–134. IEEE (1994)
25. Tanaka, S., Tamura, R., Chakrabarti, B.K.: Quantum Spin Glasses. Annealing and Computation. Cambridge University Press, Cambridge (2017)

Quantum Algorithms for the Most Frequently String Search, Intersection of Two String Sequences and Sorting of Strings Problems

Kamil Khadiev[1,2]([✉]) [iD] and Artem Ilikaev[2]

[1] Smart Quantum Technologies Ltd., Kazan, Russia
[2] Kazan Federal University, Kazan, Russia
kamil.hadiev@kpfu.ru, artemka.tema1998@gmail.com

Abstract. We study algorithms for solving three problems on strings. The first one is the Most Frequently String Search Problem. The problem is the following. Assume that we have a sequence of n strings of length k. The problem is finding the string that occurs in the sequence most often. We propose a quantum algorithm that has a query complexity $\tilde{O}(n\sqrt{k})$. This algorithm shows speed-up comparing with the deterministic algorithm that requires $\Omega(nk)$ queries.

The second one is searching intersection of two sequences of strings. All strings have the same length k. The size of the first set is n and the size of the second set is m. We propose a quantum algorithm that has a query complexity $\tilde{O}((n + m)\sqrt{k})$. This algorithm shows speed-up comparing with the deterministic algorithm that requires $\Omega((n + m)k)$ queries.

The third problem is sorting of n strings of length k. On the one hand, it is known that quantum algorithms cannot sort objects asymptotically faster than classical ones. On the other hand, we focus on sorting strings that are not arbitrary objects. We propose a quantum algorithm that has a query complexity $O(n(\log n)^2\sqrt{k})$. This algorithm shows speed-up comparing with the deterministic algorithm (radix sort) that requires $\Omega((n + d)k)$ queries, where d is a size of the alphabet.

Keywords: Quantum computation · Quantum models · Quantum algorithm · Query model · String search · Sorting

1 Introduction

Quantum computing [4,32] is one of the hot topics in computer science of last decades. There are many problems where quantum algorithms outperform the best known classical algorithms [16,21–23].

One of these problems are problems for strings. Researchers show the power of quantum algorithms for such problems in [8,30,35].

In this paper, we consider three problems:

© Springer Nature Switzerland AG 2019
C. Martín-Vide et al. (Eds.): TPNC 2019, LNCS 11934, pp. 234–245, 2019.
https://doi.org/10.1007/978-3-030-34500-6_17

* The Most Frequently String Search problem;
* Strings sorting problem;
* Intersection of Two String Sequences problem.

Our algorithms use some quantum algorithms as a subroutine, and the rest part is classical. We investigate the problems in terms of query complexity. The query model is one of the most popular in the case of quantum algorithms. Such algorithms can do a query to a black box that has access to the sequence of strings. As a running time of an algorithm, we mean a number of queries to the black box.

The first problem is the following. We have n strings of length k. We can assume that symbols of strings are letters from any finite alphabet, for example, binary, Latin alphabet or Unicode. The problem is finding the string that occurs in the sequence most often. The problem [14] is one of the most well-studied ones in the area of data streams [3,7,10,31]. Many applications in packet routing, telecommunication logging and tracking keyword queries in search machines are critically based upon such routines. The best known deterministic algorithms require $\Omega(nk)$ queries because an algorithm should at least test all symbols of all strings. The deterministic solution can use the Trie (prefix tree) [9,12,15,25] that allows to achieve the required complexity.

We propose a quantum algorithm that uses a self-balancing binary search tree for storing strings and a quantum algorithm for comparing strings. As a self-balancing binary search tree we can use the AVL tree [2,13] or the Red-Black tree [13,18]. As a string comparing algorithm, we propose an algorithm that is based on the first one search problem algorithm from [26–28]. This algorithm is a modification of Grover's search algorithm [11,17]. Another important algorithm for search is described in [29]. Our algorithm for the most frequently string search problem has query complexity $O(n(\log n)^2 \cdot \sqrt{k}) = \tilde{O}(n\sqrt{k})$, where $\tilde{O}$ does not consider a log factors. If $\log_2 n = o(k^{0.25})$, then our algorithm is better than deterministic one. Note, that this setup makes sense in practical cases.

The second problem is String Sorting problem. Assume that we have n strings of length k. It is known [19,20] that no quantum algorithm can sort arbitrary comparable objects faster than $O(n \log n)$. At the same time, several researchers tried to improve the hidden constant [33,34]. Other researchers investigated space bounded case [24]. We focus on sorting strings. In a classical case, we can use an algorithm that is better than arbitrary comparable objects sorting algorithms. It is radix sort that has $O((n+d)k)$ query complexity [13], where d is a size of the alphabet. Our quantum algorithm for the string sorting problem has query complexity $O(n(\log n)^2 \cdot \sqrt{k}) = \tilde{O}(n\sqrt{k})$. It is based on standard sorting algorithms like Merge sort [13] or Heapsort [13,36] and the quantum algorithm for comparing strings.

The third problem is the Intersection of Two String Sequences problem. Assume that we have two sequences of strings of length k. The size of the first set is n and the size of the second one is m. The first sequence is given and the second one is given in online fashion, one by one. After each requested string from the second sequence, we want to check weather this string belongs to the first sequence. We propose two quantum algorithms for the problem. Both algorithms has query complexity $O((n+m)\cdot\log n \cdot \log(n+m)\sqrt{k}) = \tilde{O}((n+m)\sqrt{k})$. The first algorithm uses a self-balancing binary search tree like the solution of the first problem. The second algorithm uses a quantum algorithm for sorting strings and has better big-O hidden constant. At the same time, the best known deterministic algorithm requires $O((n+m)k)$ queries.

The structure of the paper is the following. We present the quantum subroutine that compares two strings in Sect. 2. Then we discussed three problems: the Most Frequently String Search problem in Sect. 3, Strings Sorting problem in Sect. 4 and Intersection of Two String Sequences problem in Sect. 5.

2   The Quantum Algorithm for Two Strings Comparing

Firstly, we discuss a quantum subroutine that compares two strings of length k. Assume that this subroutine is COMPARE_STRINGS(s, t, k) and it compares s and t in lexicographical order. It returns:

★ -1 if $s < t$;
★ 0 if $s = t$;
★ 1 if $s > t$;

As a base for our algorithm, we will use the algorithm of finding the minimal argument with 1-result of a Boolean-value function. Formally, we have:

Lemma 1. *[26–28] Suppose, we have a function $f : \{1, \dots, N\} \to \{0, 1\}$ for some integer N. There is a quantum algorithm for finding $j_0 = \min\{j \in \{1, \dots, N\} : f(j) = 1\}$. The algorithm finds j_0 with expected query complexity $O(\sqrt{j_0})$ and error probability that is at most $\frac{1}{2}$.*

Let us choose the function $f(j) = (s_j \neq t_j)$. So, we search j_0 that is the index of the first unequal symbol of the strings. Then, we can claim that s precedes t in lexicographical order iff s_{j_0} precedes t_{j_0} in alphabet Σ. The claim is right by the definition of lexicographical order. If there are no unequal symbols, then the strings are equal.

We use the standard technique of boosting success probability. So, we repeat the algorithm $3 \log_2 n$ times and return the minimal answer, where n is a number of strings in the sequence s. In that case, the error probability is $O\left(\frac{1}{2^{3\log n}}\right) = \left(\frac{1}{n^3}\right)$, because if we have an error in whole algorithm it means no invocation finds minimal index of unequal symbol.

Let us present the algorithm. We use THE_FIRST_ONE_SEARCH(f, k) as a subroutine from Lemma 1, where $f(j) = (s_j \neq t_j)$. Assume that this subroutine returns $k + 1$ if it does not find any solution.

The next property follows from the previous discussion.

Lemma 2. *Algorithm 1 compares two strings of length k in lexicographical order with query complexity $O(\sqrt{k} \log n)$ and error probability $O\left(\frac{1}{n^3}\right)$.*

Algorithm 1. COMPARE_STRINGS(s, t, k). The Quantum Algorithm for Two Strings Comparing.

$j_0 \leftarrow$ THE_FIRST_ONE_SEARCH(f, k)   ▷ The initial value
for $i \in \{1, \ldots, 3 \log_2 n\}$ **do**
   $j_0 \leftarrow \min(j_0, $ THE_FIRST_ONE_SEARCH(f, k))
end for
if $j_0 = k + 1$ **then**
   $result \leftarrow 0$ ▷ The strings are equal.
end if
if $(j_0 \neq k + 1)\&(s_{j_0} < t_{j_0})$ **then**
   $result \leftarrow -1$ ▷ s precedes t.
end if
if $(j_0 \neq k + 1)\&(s_{j_0} > t_{j_0})$ **then**
   $result \leftarrow 1$ ▷ s succeeds t.
end if
return $result$

---

3 The Most Frequently String Search Problem

Let us formally present the problem.

Problem. For some positive integers n and k, we have the sequence of strings $s = (s^1, \ldots, s^n)$. Each $s^i = (s_1^i, \ldots, s_k^i) \in \Sigma^k$ for some finite size alphabet Σ. Let $\#(s) = |\{i \in \{1, \ldots, m\} : s^i = s\}|$ be a number of occurrences of string s. We search $s = argmax_{s^i \in S} \#(s^i)$.

3.1 The Quantum Algorithm

Firstly, we present an idea of the algorithm.

We use the well-known data structure a self-balancing binary search tree. As an implementation of the data structure, we can use the AVL tree [2, 13] or the Red-Black tree [13, 18]. Both data structures allow as to find and add elements in $O(\log N)$ running time, where N is a size of the tree.

The idea of the algorithm is the following. We store pairs (i, c) in vertexes of the tree, where i is an index of a string from s and c is a number of occurrences of the string s^i. We assume that a pair (i, c) is less than a pair (i', c') iff s^i precedes $s^{i'}$ in the lexicographical order. So, we use COMPARE_STRINGS($s^i, s^{i'}, k$) subroutine as the compactor of the vertexes. The tree represents a set of unique strings from $(s^1, \ldots, s^n)$ with a number of occurrences.

We consider all strings from s^1 to s^n and check the existence of a string in our tree. If a string exists, then we increase the number of occurrences. If the string does not exist in the tree, then we add it. At the same time, we store $(i_{max}, c_{max}) = argmax_{(i,c)}$ in the tree c and recalculate it in each step.

Let us present the algorithm formally. Let BST be a self-balancing binary search tree such that:

⋆ FIND(BST, s^i) finds vertex (i, c) or returns $NULL$ if such vertex does not exist;

* ADD(BST, s^i) adds vertex $(i, 0)$ to the tree and returns the vertex as a result;
* INIT(BST) initializes an empty tree;

Algorithm 2. The Quantum Algorithm for Most Frequently String Problem.

INIT(BST)	▷ The initialization of the tree.
$c_{max} \leftarrow 1$	▷ The maximal number of occurrences.
$i_{max} \leftarrow 1$	▷ The index of most requently string.
for $i \in \{1, \ldots, n\}$ **do**	
$\quad v = (i, c) \leftarrow$ FIND(BST, s^i)	▷ Searching s^i in the tree.
$\quad$ **if** $v = NULL$ **then**	
$\quad\quad v = (i, c) \leftarrow$ ADD(BST, s^i)	▷ If there is no s^i, then we add it.
$\quad$ **end if**	
$\quad c \leftarrow c + 1$ $\quad$ ▷ Updating the vertex by increasing the number of occurrences.	
$\quad$ **if** $c > c_{max}$ **then** $\quad\quad\quad\quad$ ▷ Updating the maximal value.	
$\quad\quad c_{max} \leftarrow c$	
$\quad\quad i_{max} \leftarrow i$	
$\quad$ **end if**	
end for	
return $s^{i_{max}}$	

Let us discuss the property of the algorithm.

Theorem 3. *Algorithm 2 finds the most frequently string from* $s = (s^1, \ldots, s^n)$ *with query complexity* $O(n(\log n)^2 \cdot \sqrt{k})$ *and error probability* $O\left(\frac{1}{n}\right)$.

Proof. The correctness of the algorithm follows from the description. Let us discuss the query complexity. Each operation FIND(BST, s^i) and ADD(BST, s^i) requires $O(\log n)$ comparing operations COMPARE_STRINGS($s^i, s^{i'}, k$). These operations are invoked n times. Therefore, we have $O(n \log n)$ comparing operations. Due to Lemma 2, each comparing operation requires $O(\sqrt{k} \log n)$ queries. The total query complexity is $O(n\sqrt{k}(\log n)^2)$.

Let us discuss the error probability. Events of error in the algorithm are independent. So, all events should be correct. Due to Lemma 2, the probability of correctness of one event is $1 - \left(1 - \frac{1}{n^3}\right)$. Hence, the probability of correctness of all $O(n \log n)$ events is at least $1 - \left(1 - \frac{1}{n^3}\right)^{\alpha \cdot n \log n}$ for some constant α.

Note that

$$\lim_{n \to \infty} \frac{1 - \left(1 - \frac{1}{n^3}\right)^{\alpha \cdot n \log n}}{1/n} < 1;$$

Hence, the total error probability is at most $O\left(\frac{1}{n}\right)$.

$\square$

The data structure that we use can be considered as a separated data structure. We call it *"Multi-set of strings with quantum comparator"*. Using this data structure, we can implement

⋆ *"Set of strings with quantum comparator"* if always $c = 1$ in pair (i, c) of a vertex;

⋆ *"Map with string key and quantum comparator"* if we replace c by any data $r \in \Gamma$ for any set Γ. In that case, the data structure implements mapping $\Sigma^k \to \Gamma$.

All of these data structures has $O((\log n)^2 \sqrt{k})$ complexity of basic operations (FIND, ADD, DELETE).

3.2   On the Classical Complexity of the Problem

The best known classical algorithm stores string to Trie (prefix tree) [9,15], [12,25] and do the similar operations. The running time of such algorithm is $O(nk)$. At the same time, we can show that if an algorithm testsso(nk) variables, then it can return a wrong answer.

Theorem 4. *Any deterministic algorithm for the Most Frequently String Search problem has $\Omega(nk)$ query complexity.*

Proof. Suppose, we have a deterministic algorithm A for the Most Frequently String Search problem that uses $o(nk)$ queries.

Let us consider an adversary that suggest an input. The adversary wants to construct an input such that the algorithm A obtains a wrong answer.

Without loss of generality, we can say that n is even. Suppose, a and b are different symbols from an input alphabet. If the algorithm requests an variable s_j^i for $i \leq n/2$, then the adversary returns a. If the algorithm requests an variable s_j^i for $i > n/2$, then the adversary returns b.

Because of the algorithm A uses $o(nk)$ queries, there are at least one $s_{j'}^{z'}$ and one $s_{j''}^{z''}$ that are not requested, where $z' \leq n/2$, $z'' > n/2$ and $j', j'' \in \{1, \dots, k\}$.

Let s' be a string such that $s'_j = a$ for all $j \in \{1, \dots, k\}$. Let s'' be a string such that $s''_j = b$ for all $j \in \{1, \dots, k\}$.

Assume that A returns s'. Then, the adversary assigns $s_{j'}^{z'} = b$ and assigns $s_j^i = b$ for each $i > n/2, j \in \{1, \dots, k\}$. Therefore, the right answer should be s''.

Assume that A returns a string $s \neq s'$. Then, the adversary assigns $s_{j''}^{z''} = a$ and assigns $s_j^i = a$ for each $i \leq n/2, j \in \{1, \dots, k\}$. Therefore, the right answer should be s'.

So, the adversary can construct the input such that A obtains a wrong answer. □

4   Strings Sorting Problem

Let us consider the following problem.

Problem. For some positive integers n and k, we have the sequence of strings $s = (s^1, \dots, s^n)$. Each $s^i = (s_1^i, \dots, s_k^i) \in \Sigma^k$ for some finite size alphabet Σ. We search order $ORDER = (i_1, \ldots, i_n)$ such that for any $j \in \{1, \ldots, n-1\}$ we have $s^{i_j} \leq s^{i_{j+1}}$ in lexicographical order.

We use Heap sort algorithm [13,36] as a base and Quantum algorithm for comparing string from Sect. 2. We can replace Heap sort algorithm by any other sorting algorithm, for example, Merge sort [13]. In a case of Merge sort, the big-O hidden constant in query complexity will be smaller. At the same time, we need more additional memory.

Let us present Heap sort for completeness of the explanation. We can use Binary Heap [36]. We store indexes of strings in vertexes. As in the previous section, if we compare vertexes v and v' with corresponding indexes i and i', then $v > v'$ iff $s^i > s^{i'}$ in lexicographical order. We use COMPARE_STRINGS($s^i, s^{i'}, k$) for comparing strings. Binary Heap BH has three operations:

* GET_MIN_AND_DELETE(BH) returns minimal s^i and removes it from the data structure.
* ADD(BH, s^i) adds vertex with value i to the heap;
* INIT(BH) initializes an empty heap;

The operations GET_MIN_AND_DELETE and ADD invoke COMPARE_STRINGS subroutine $\log_2 t$ times, where t is the size of the heap.

The algorithm is the following.

Algorithm 3. The Quantum Algorithm for Sorting Problem.

INIT(BH)   ▷ The initialization of the heap.
for $i \in \{1, \ldots, n\}$ **do**
    ADD(BH, s^i)   ▷ Adding s^i to the heap.
end for
for $i \in \{1, \ldots, n\}$ **do**
    $ORDER \leftarrow ORDER \cup$ GET_MIN_AND_DELETE(BH)   ▷ Getting minimal string.
end for
return $ORDER$

If we implement the sequence s as an array, then we can store the heap in the same array. In this case, we do not need additional memory.

We have the following property of the algorithm that can be proven by the same way as Theorem 3.

Theorem 5. *Algorithm 3 sorts* $s = (s^1, \ldots, s^n)$ *with query complexity* $O(n(\log n)^2 \cdot \sqrt{k})$ *and error probability* $O\left(\frac{1}{n}\right)$.

The lower bound for deterministic complexity can be proven by the same way as in Theorem 4.

Theorem 6. *Any deterministic algorithm for Sorting problem has* $\Omega(nk)$ *query complexity.*

The Radix sort [13] algorithm almost reaches this bound and has $O((n + |\Sigma|)k)$ complexity.

5 Intersection of Two Sequences of Strings Problem

Let us consider the following problem.

Problem. For some positive integers n, m and k, we have the sequence of strings $s = (s^1, \ldots, s^n)$. Each $s^i = (s_1^i, \ldots, s_k^i) \in \Sigma^k$ for some finite size alphabet Σ. Then, we get m requests $t = (t^1 \ldots t^m)$, where $t^i = (t_1^i, \ldots, t_k^i) \in \Sigma^k$. The answer to a request t^i is 1 iff there is $j \in \{1, \ldots, n\}$ such that $t^i = s^j$. We should answer 0 or 1 to each of m requests.

We have two algorithms. The first one is based on *"Set of strings with quantum comparator"* data structure from Sect. 3. We store all strings from s to a self-balancing binary search tree BST. Then, we answer each request using $\text{FIND}(BST, s^i)$ operation. Let us present the Algorithm 4.

Algorithm 4. The Quantum Algorithm for Intersection of Two Sequences of Strings Problem using *"Set of strings with quantum comparator"*.

$\text{INIT}(BST)$ ▷ The initialization of the tree.
  for $i \in \{1, \ldots, n\}$ **do**
    $\text{ADD}(BST, s^i)$ ▷ We add s^i to the set.
  end for
  for $i \in \{1, \ldots, m\}$ **do**
    $v \leftarrow \text{FIND}(BST, t^i)$ ▷ We search t^i in the set.
    if $v = NULL$ **then**
      return 0
    end if
    if $v \neq NULL$ **then**
      return 1
    end if
  end for

The second algorithm is based on Sorting algorithm from Sect. 4. We sort strings from s. Then, we answer to each request using binary search in the sorted sequence of strings [13] and COMPARE_STRINGS subroutine for comparing strings during the binary search. Let us present the Algorithm 5. Assume that the sorting Algorithm 3 is the subroutine $\text{SORT\_STRINGS}(s)$ and it returns the order $ORDER = (i_1, \ldots, i_n)$. The binary search algorithm with COMPARE_STRINGS subroutine as comparator is $\text{BINARY\_SEARCH\_FOR\_STRINGS}(t, s, OREDER)$ subroutine and it searches t in the ordered sequence $(s^{i_1}, \ldots, s^{i_n})$. Suppose that the subroutine $\text{BINARY\_SEARCH\_FOR\_STRINGS}$ returns 1 if it finds t and 0 otherwise.

The algorithms have the following query complexity.

Theorem 7. *Algorithms 4 and 5 solve Intersection of Two Sequences of Strings Problem with query complexity $O((n + m)\sqrt{k} \cdot \log n \cdot \log(n + m))$ and error probability $O\left(\frac{1}{n+m}\right)$.*

Algorithm 5. The Quantum Algorithm for Intersection of Two Sequences of Strings Problem using sorting algorithm.

$ORDER \leftarrow$ SORT_STRINGS(s)   ▷ We sort $s = (s^1, \ldots, s^n)$.
for $i \in \{1, \ldots, m\}$ **do**
    $ans \leftarrow$ BINARY_SEARCH_FOR_STRINGS($t, s, OREDER$)   ▷ We search t^i in the
ordered sequence.
    return ans
end for

Proof. The correctness of the algorithms follows from the description. Let us discuss the query complexity of the first algorithm. As in the proof of Theorem 3, we can show that constructing of the search tree requires $O(n \log n)$ comparing operations. Then, the searching of all strings t^i requires $O(m \log n)$ comparing operations. The total number of comparing operations is $O((m + n) \log n)$. We will use little bit modified version of the Algorithm 1 where we run it $3(\log(n + m))$ times. We can prove that comparing operation requires $O(\sqrt{k} \log(n + m))$ queries. The proof is similar to the proof of corresponding claim from the proof of Lemma 2. So, the total complexity is $O((n + m)\sqrt{k} \cdot \log n \cdot \log(n + m))$.

The second algorithm also has the same complexity because it uses $O(n \log n)$ comparing operations for sorting and $O(m \log n)$ comparing operations for all invocations of the binary search algorithm.

Let us discuss the error probability. Events of error in the algorithm are independent. So, all events should be correct. We can prove that the error probability for comparing operation is $O(1/(n + m)^3)$. The proof is like the proof of Lemma 2. So, the probability of correctness of one event is $1 - \left(1 - \frac{1}{(n+m)^3}\right)$. Hence, the probability of correctness of all $O((n + m) \log n)$ events is at least $1 - \left(1 - \frac{1}{(n+m)^3}\right)^{\alpha \cdot (n+m) \log n}$ for some constant α.

Note that
$$\lim_{n \to \infty} \frac{1 - \left(1 - \frac{1}{(n+m)^3}\right)^{\alpha \cdot (n+m) \log n}}{1/(n + m)} < 1;$$

Hence, the total error probability is at most $O\left(\frac{1}{n+m}\right)$.

□

Note that Algorithm 5 has a better big-O hidden constant than Algorithm 4, because the Red-Black tree or AVL tree has a height that greats $\log_2 n$ constant times. So, adding elements to the tree and checking existence has bigger big-O hidden constant than sorting and binary search algorithms.

The lower bound for deterministic complexity can be proven by the same way as in Theorem 4.

Theorem 8. *Any deterministic algorithm for Intersection of Two Sequences of Strings Problem has $\Omega((n + m)k)$ query complexity.*

This complexity can be reached if we implement the set of strings s using Trie (prefix tree) [9,12,15,25].

Note, that we can use the quantum algorithm for element distinctness [6], [5] for this problem. The algorithm solves a problem of finding two identical elements in the sequence. The query complexity of the algorithm is $O(D^{2/3})$, where D is a number of elements in the sequence. The complexity is tight because of [1]. The algorithm can be the following. On j-th request, we can add the string t^j to the sequence $s^1, \ldots, s^n$ and invoke the element distinctness algorithm that finds a collision of t^j with other strings. Such approach requires $\Omega(n^{2/3})$ query for each request and $\Omega(mn^{2/3})$ for processing all requests. Note, that the streaming nature of requests does not allow us to access to all $t^1, \ldots, t^m$ by Oracle. So, each request should be processed separately.

6   Conclusion

In the paper we propose a quantum algorithm for comparing strings. Using this algorithm we discussed four data structures: *"Multi-set of strings with quantum comparator"*, *"Set of strings with quantum comparator"*, *"Map with a string key and quantum comparator"* and *"Binary Heap of strings with quantum comparator"*. We show that the first two data structures work faster than the implementation of similar data structures using Trie (prefix tree) in a case of $\log_2 n = o(k^{0.25})$. The trie implementation is the best known classical implementation in terms of complexity of simple operations (add, delete or find). Additionally, we constructed a quantum strings sort algorithm that works faster than the radix sort algorithm that is the best known deterministic algorithm for sorting a sequence of strings.

Using these two groups of results, we propose quantum algorithms for two problems: the Most Frequently String Search and Intersection of Two String Sets. These quantum algorithms are more efficient than deterministic ones.

Acknowledgments. This work was supported by Russian Science Foundation Grant 19-71-00149. We thank Aliya Khadieva, Farid Ablayev and Kazan Federal University quantum group for useful discussions.

References

1. Aaronson, S., Shi, Y.: Quantum lower bounds for the collision and the element distinctness problems. J. ACM (JACM) **51**(4), 595–605 (2004)
2. Adel'son-Vel'skii, G.M., Landis, E.M.: An algorithm for organization of information. In: Doklady Akademii Nauk, vol. 146, pp. 263–266. Russian Academy of Sciences (1962)
3. Aggarwal, C.C.: Data Streams: Models and Algorithms, vol. 31. Springer, Berlin (2007). https://doi.org/10.1007/978-0-387-47534-9
4. Ambainis, A.: Understanding quantum algorithms via query complexity. arXiv:1712.06349 (2017)

5. Ambainis, A.: Quantum walk algorithm for element distinctness. In: Proceedings of the 45th Annual IEEE Symposium on Foundations of Computer Science, FOCS 2004, pp. 22–31 (2004)
6. Ambainis, A.: Quantum walk algorithm for element distinctness. SIAM J. Comput. 37(1), 210–239 (2007)
7. Becchetti, L., Chatzigiannakis, I., Giannakopoulos, Y.: Streaming techniques and data aggregation in networks of tiny artefacts. Comput. Sci. Rev. 5(1), 27–46 (2011)
8. Bennett, C.H., Bernstein, E., Brassard, G., Vazirani, U.: Strengths and weaknesses of quantum computing. SIAM J. Comput. 26(5), 1510–1523 (1997)
9. Black, P.E.: Dictionary of algorithms and data structures. Technical report, NIST (1998)
10. Boyar, J., Larsen, K.S., Maiti, A.: The frequent items problem in online streaming under various performance measures. Int. J. Found. Comput. Sci. 26(4), 413–439 (2015)
11. Boyer, M., Brassard, G., Høyer, P., Tapp, A.: Tight bounds on quantum searching. Fortschr. Phys. 46(4–5), 493–505 (1998)
12. Brass, P.: Advanced data structures, vol. 193. Cambridge University Press, Cambridge (2008)
13. Cormen, T.H., Leiserson, C.E., Rivest, R.L., Stein, C.: Introduction to Algorithms. McGraw-Hill, New York (2001)
14. Cormode, G., Hadjieleftheriou, M.: Finding frequent items in data streams. Proc. VLDB Endow. 1(2), 1530–1541 (2008)
15. De La Briandais, R.: File searching using variable length keys. In: Western Joint Computer Conference, 3–5 March 1959, pp. 295–298. ACM (1959)
16. De Wolf, R.: Quantum computing and communication complexity (2001)
17. Grover, L.K.: A fast quantum mechanical algorithm for database search. In: Proceedings of the Twenty-Eighth Annual ACM Symposium on Theory of Computing, pp. 212–219. ACM (1996)
18. Guibas, L.J., Sedgewick, R.: A dichromatic framework for balanced trees. In: Proceedings of SFCS 1978, pp. 8–21. IEEE (1978)
19. Høyer, P., Neerbek, J., Shi, Y.: Quantum complexities of ordered searching, sorting, and element distinctness. In: Orejas, F., Spirakis, P.G., van Leeuwen, J. (eds.) ICALP 2001. LNCS, vol. 2076, pp. 346–357. Springer, Heidelberg (2001). https://doi.org/10.1007/3-540-48224-5_29
20. Høyer, P., Neerbek, J., Shi, Y.: Quantum complexities of ordered searching, sorting, and element distinctness. Algorithmica 34(4), 429–448 (2002)
21. Jordan, S.: Bounded error quantum algorithms zoo. https://math.nist.gov/quantum/zoo
22. Kravchenko, D., Khadiev, K., Serov, D.: On the quantum and classical complexity of solving subtraction games. In: van Bevern, R., Kucherov, G. (eds.) CSR 2019. LNCS, vol. 11532, pp. 228–236. Springer, Cham (2019). https://doi.org/10.1007/978-3-030-19955-5_20
23. Khadiev, K., Safina, L.: Quantum algorithm for dynamic programming approach for DAGs. Applications for Zhegalkin polynomial evaluation and some problems on DAGs. In: McQuillan, I., Seki, S. (eds.) UCNC 2019. LNCS, vol. 11493, pp. 150–163. Springer, Cham (2019). https://doi.org/10.1007/978-3-030-19311-9_13
24. Klauck, H.: Quantum time-space tradeoffs for sorting. In: Proceedings of the Thirty-Fifth Annual ACM Symposium on Theory of Computing, pp. 69–76. ACM (2003)

25. Knuth, D.: Searching and Sorting, The Art of Computer Programming, vol. 3 (1973)
26. Kothari, R.: An optimal quantum algorithm for the oracle identification problem. In: 31st International Symposium on Theoretical Aspects of Computer Science, p. 482 (2014)
27. Lin, C.Y.Y., Lin, H.H.: Upper bounds on quantum query complexity inspired by the Elitzur-Vaidman bomb tester. In: 30th Conference on Computational Complexity (CCC 2015). Schloss Dagstuhl-Leibniz-Zentrum fuer Informatik (2015)
28. Lin, C.Y.Y., Lin, H.H.: Upper bounds on quantum query complexity inspired by the Elitzur-Vaidman bomb tester. Theory Comput. **12**(18), 1–35 (2016)
29. Long, G.L.: Grover algorithm with zero theoretical failure rate. Phys. Rev. A **64**(2), 022307 (2001)
30. Montanaro, A.: Quantum pattern matching fast on average. Algorithmica **77**(1), 16–39 (2017)
31. Muthukrishnan, S.: Data streams: algorithms and applications. Found. Trends Theor. Comput. Sci. **1**(2), 117–236 (2005)
32. Nielsen, M.A., Chuang, I.L.: Quantum Computation and Quantum Information. Cambridge University Press, Cambridge (2010)
33. Odeh, A., Abdelfattah, E.: Quantum sort algorithm based on entanglement qubits {00, 11}. In: 2016 IEEE Long Island Systems, Applications and Technology Conference (LISAT), pp. 1–5. IEEE (2016)
34. Odeh, A., Elleithy, K., Almasri, M., Alajlan, A.: Sorting N elements using quantum entanglement sets. In: Third International Conference on Innovative Computing Technology (INTECH 2013), pp. 213–216. IEEE (2013)
35. Ramesh, H., Vinay, V.: String matching in $o(\sqrt{n} + \sqrt{m})$ quantum time. J. Discrete Algorithms **1**(1), 103–110 (2003)
36. Williams, J.W.J.: Algorithm 232 - heapsort. Commun. ACM **7**(6), 347–349 (1964)

Author Index

Printed in the United States
By Bookmasters